T0327731

"WHERE ARE YOU FROM?"

Growing Up African-Canadian in Vancouver

Metro Vancouver is a diverse city where half the residents identify as people of colour, but only one per cent of the population is racialized as Black. In this context, African-Canadians are both hypervisible as Black, and invisible as distinct communities. Informed by feminist and critical race theories, and based on interviews with women and men who grew up in Vancouver, *"Where Are You From?"* recounts the unique experiences of growing up in a place where the second generation seldom sees other people who look like them, and yet are inundated with popular representations of Blackness from the United States.

This study explores how the second generation in Vancouver redefine their African identities to distinguish themselves from African-Americans, while continuing to experience considerable everyday racism that challenges belonging as Canadians. As a result, some members of the second generation reject, and others strongly assert, a Canadian identity.

GILLIAN CREESE is the associate dean of Arts, Faculty & Equity, and professor in the Department of Sociology and the Institute for Gender, Race, Sexuality and Social Justice at the University of British Columbia.

"Where Are You From?"

Growing Up African-Canadian in Vancouver

GILLIAN CREESE

UNIVERSITY OF TORONTO PRESS
Toronto Buffalo London

ISBN 978-1-4875-0679-7 (cloth)   ISBN 978-1-4875-3485-1 (EPUB)
ISBN 978-1-4875-2456-2 (paper)   ISBN 978-1-4875-3484-4 (PDF)

Library and Archives Canada Cataloguing in Publication

Title: "Where are you from?" : growing up African-Canadian in Vancouver /
    Gillian Creese.
Names: Creese, Gillian Laura, 1955– author.
Description: Includes bibliographical references and index.
Identifiers: Canadiana 20190169702 | ISBN 9781487506797 (hardcover)
Subjects: LCSH: Africans – British Columbia – Vancouver – Social conditions. |
    LCSH: Youth, Black – British Columbia – Vancouver – Social conditions. |
    LCSH: Students, Black – British Columbia – Vancouver – Social conditions. |
    LCSH: Children of immigrants – British Columbia – Vancouver – Social
    conditions. | LCSH: Black Canadians – British Columbia – Vancouver –
    Social conditions
Classification: LCC FC3847.9 .B6 C74 2019 | DDC 305.8960711/33—dc23

This book has been published with the help of a grant from the Federation
for the Humanities and Social Sciences, through the Awards to Scholarly
Publications Program, using funds provided by the Social Sciences and
Humanities Research Council of Canada.

University of Toronto Press acknowledges the financial assistance to its
publishing program of the Canada Council for the Arts and the Ontario Arts
Council, an agency of the Government of Ontario.

Canada Council   Conseil des Arts
for the Arts   du Canada

ONTARIO ARTS COUNCIL
CONSEIL DES ARTS DE L'ONTARIO
an Ontario government agency
un organisme du gouvernement de l'Ontario

Funded by the   Financé par le
Government   gouvernement
of Canada   du Canada

Contents

Acknowledgments

I am grateful for all the support I have received during the course of this project. I am especially indebted to the thirty-five women and men who agreed to be interviewed, and who shared their personal experiences, accomplishments, challenges and dreams. I remain humbled by their trust, and I hope I have managed to portray the strength, resilience and optimism that I heard in our discussions.

I thank friends and long-time collaborators in Vancouver's African community for encouraging me to pursue this project with members of the second-generation. I am grateful that friends at Umoja Operation Compassion Society, especially Edith Ngene Kambere, Amos Kambere, and Mambo Masinda, continue to believe that an 'outsider' can listen carefully and understand the issues facing the local African community.

I was fortunate to work with Veronica Fynn, Sanzida Habib, E.J. Shu and Jeannie Morgan as my research assistants during the course of this project. I thank each of them for their conscientious assistance and conversations along the way.

I am grateful for research funding from the Social Sciences and Humanities Research Council of Canada, through grant number 410–2011–0043. As everyone who undertakes a large research project knows, funding helps make the research possible.

I thank the 3 anonymous reviewers for the University of Toronto Press who provided careful reviews of the manuscript and made several useful suggestions that helped to strengthen the book. I am especially indebted to Jodi Lewchuk, my editor at the University of Toronto Press, for carefully shepherding the manuscript through the publication process. I am also grateful to freelancer Barry Norris for copy editing the manuscript and Gillian Watts for creating the index.

I also want to thank the anonymous reviewers who commented on parts of this manuscript that appear as journal articles. Parts of chapter four appeared in *Gender Issues* in 2015 ("Growing up where 'no one looked like me': Gender, race, hip hop and identity in Vancouver"), parts of chapter eight appear in *Racial and Ethnic Studies* in 2019 ("Where are you from? Racialization, belonging and identity among second-generation African-Canadians"), and parts of chapters five and seven are forthcoming in the *Canadian Journal of Sociology* ("Growing up African-Canadian in Vancouver: Racialization, gender and sexuality").

I am grateful to friends and colleagues who have engaged in conversations or commented on material related to this project, including Dawn Currie, Edith Kambere, Mambo Masinda, Arlene McLaren, Beatrice Okyere, Becki Ross, Nikki Strong-Boag, and Rima Wilkes.

Last but not least I thank my family, especially my daughter Jett-Lynn, for accepting my preoccupations, and providing important diversions along the way.

"WHERE ARE YOU FROM?"

Chapter One

Introduction

This book owes its genesis to an earlier study of adult migration and settlement in metro Vancouver. In *The New African Diaspora in Vancouver: Migration, Exclusion, and Belonging*, I examined ways that diverse migrants from countries in sub-Saharan Africa are carving out new spaces of belonging through community building and simultaneously experiencing systemic forms of marginalization. A key finding in that book is that, however hard migration to Canada has been for adults, it is considered worthwhile if it creates a better future for their children. *"Where Are You From?" Growing Up African-Canadian in Vancouver* explores how the adult children of migrants from Africa navigate their lives as members of a very small, yet hypervisible, minority, with a particular emphasis on the interplay of relations of racialization, gender, and sexuality.

For most adult migrants, resettlement in Vancouver has indeed been very challenging, coinciding with significant downward social and economic mobility, separation from extended family, clashes of cultural values, and persistent experiences of anti-Black racism, while at the same time building new African community networks that highlight resilience and mutual support. African immigrant parents express a common fear that they might "lose their children" to unfamiliar influences in Canada so that they no longer recognize themselves as African. At the same time, they seek equal opportunities for their Canadian-raised children who they hope will not experience the marginalization and racism that has marked their parents' lives. This raises the question: are first-generation immigrants' dreams of better opportunities and belonging for their offspring born out for the second generation? This book addresses this critical question by exploring what is it like to grow up African-Canadian in metro Vancouver.

"Where Are You From?" Growing Up African-Canadian in Vancouver is based on in-depth qualitative interviews with young adult men and women whose parents migrated from diverse countries in sub-Saharan Africa and who went to high school in metro Vancouver. The second generation must navigate their parents' expectations, embedded in their own cultural backgrounds, and the values that dominate Canadian schools, popular culture, and other local institutions. Unlike their parents, the children of immigrants have locally attained educational credentials, work experience, accents, and cultural knowledge that translate into advantages in the workplace and civil society. Yet it is also the case that the second generation shares their parents' physical appearance and African surnames, and are racialized as Black in an urban space in which they constitute a very small minority. Vancouver is a diverse metropolis, but only 1 per cent of residents are of African descent. The precariousness of their belonging in Vancouver is connected to racialization, as the local attributes embodied by the second generation are frequently rendered invisible to strangers who question their supposedly "foreign" origins by persistently asking where they are from.

This study draws on critical race theory, which recognizes racialization as historically located and shifting processes of power and subjectivity within which we are all embedded (Back and Solomos 2000; Essed and Goldberg 2002). Migration scholars point to the centrality of racialization for shaping settlement in Canada. The history of colonialism, preference for European settlers, and discriminatory laws and practices to limit or prevent migration of many groups of colour, including those from Africa, persisted in Canada until the late 1960s and produced a White "imagined community" that continues to shape racialization processes today (Bannerji 2000; Li 2003; Mackey 2002; Thobani 2007). Hence immigrants of colour – arguably, particularly those racialized as Black – face forms of racialization in the Canadian context that profoundly shape settlement. The master category of "Blacknesses," embedded in a specific Canadian history and refracted through US racial politics and popular culture, reshapes diasporic African identities in diverse ways (Abdel-Shehid 2005; Alexander and Glaze 1996; Ibrahim 1999, 2003; Kelly 1998, 2004; Matsuoka and Sorenson 2001; Walcott 2003; Wane, Deliovsky, and Lawson 2002). As Okeke-Iherjirika and Spitzer (2005, 221) note, before coming to Canada, most African immigrants "had little need to explore the larger African identity and never knew they were Black." In this context, immigrants from sub-Saharan Africa create new identities as they encounter marginalization in the labour market, policing, media representations, and other facets of everyday life in Canada (Brathwaite and James 1996; Creese and Wiebe 2012; Elabor-Idemudia 2000; Laryea and Hayfron 2005; Maynard 2017; Mensah 2002; Puplampu and Tettey 2005; Yesufu 2005). Schools are central for shaping the experiences of immigrant children, and those of African descent encounter a school system with a long and well-documented history of anti-Black discrimination (Dei 2005; Dei et al. 1997; Ibrahim and Abdi 2016a).

This study also draws on feminist theories of intersectional analysis to highlight ways that migration processes and racialization are mediated through other power relations – in particular, relations of gender, sexuality, class, and age that intersect in complex ways (Curran et al. 2006; Donato et al. 2006; Mahler and Pessar 2006). Scholars have examined how gender, sexuality, class, class of immigration, and language abilities have significant effects on settlement and integration in Canada (Agnew 2003; Boyd 2001; Boyd and Yiu 2009; Dossa 2004; Thobani 2007). For example, research on migration from Africa shows how definitions of femininity and masculinity are renegotiated in Canada, linked to uneven downward economic mobility for women and men, the intensification of domestic labour, and unfamiliar discourses of women's and children's rights that provide pressures to redefine gender relations (Creese 2011; Manuh 2003; Matsuoka and Sorenson 2001; Mianda 2004). Language abilities and accents also shape settlement outcomes, so that those who have weaker command of English, or French in Quebec, face additional obstacles to integration. Even fluent English speakers from Commonwealth African countries routinely experience discrimination against African English accents that contributes to downward mobility in Canada (Creese 2010, 2011). In addition, refugees typically arrive after years of dislocation in refugee camps, and experience prolonged separation from family members that adds to post-migration trauma (Boyd 2001; Shakya et al. 2010; Wasik 2006).

Unlike earlier cohorts of immigrants, most newcomers to Canada over the past three decades are more highly educated than other Canadians but experience long-term downward social and economic mobility (Frenette and Morissette 2005; Galabuzi 2006; Picot and Sweetman 2005). Indeed, adult migrants often frame their own class dislocation and hardships as a trade-off between self-sacrifice and future opportunities for their children (Anisef et al. 2010; Creese 2011; Creese, Dyck, and McLaren 2008). Such sentiments make it particularly important to address how the children of immigrant parents fare in the longer term.

Assessing diverse migration outcomes for the second generation has resulted in two competing macro models of integration: proponents of segmented assimilation, developed to address the specific situation in the United States, identify conditions under which many in the second generation sink into the "underclass" with their parents (Halli and Vedanand 2007; Portes and Zhou 1993; Waters et al. 2010). Other scholars argue for an overall "optimism model" of overachieving second-generation upward mobility as children outpace the economic and educational attainment of their immigrant parents (Boyd 2009; Farley and Alba 2002; Reitz and Zhang 2011). A key element of the "optimism" model is linked to the higher educational attainment of children of immigrants compared to other Canadian youth. For example, a national study by Statistics Canada (Abada, Hou, and Ram 2008) found that children of African immigrants have higher rates of university attainment than do children of Canadian-born parents, though lower rates than some other immigrant groups, including Chinese and South Asian. Nearly half (49 per cent) of the sample of African immigrant children, however, were White, while another 37 per cent were "other visible minority"; only 14 per cent identified as Black. When the data are analysed according to broader racialized designations, children of Black immigrants were among the few groups who did not achieve higher educational levels than their parents (Abada, Hou, and Ram 2009; Abada and Tenkorang 2009b), and Black men had the lowest odds of attaining a university degree (Abada and Tenkorang 2009a).

We do not have comparable data on patterns of educational attainment among Black African immigrants in Vancouver, but dropout rates among African youth are a great concern in a community that places a high value on education and recognizes its importance for social mobility (Francis 2010; Shakya et al. 2010). Many African immigrant parents express fears that they might "lose" their children, particularly their sons, if they reject African identity and values, and might compromise future prospects by dropping out of school or, in worst-case scenarios, engaging in criminal behaviour (Adjei et al. 2017; Creese 2011; Creese, Kambere, and Masinda 2013; Matsuoka and Sorenson 2001; Mondain and Lardoux 2013).

Diverse outcomes for the second generation are shaped by many factors, including the age at which youngsters arrive in Canada (with younger arrivals faring better in educational and occupational attainment), country of origin (linked to racialization processes, ethnic community formation, and social capital), and class of migration (with refugees facing more challenges) (Abada, Hou, and Ram 2009; Corak 2012; Kanu 2008; Wilkinson 2008; Wilson-Forsberg 2012). Poverty rates among different immigrant groups have also been linked to higher proportions of "at risk" youth and patterns of high dropout rates and low educational attainment (Anisef et al. 2010; James 2012). Gender differences have also been noted in some studies, with females having higher educational attainment than males, but earning lower incomes (Abada and Tenkorang 2009a; Stepick and Stepick 2010).

Most of this scholarship is based on large-scale survey research. There is remarkably little qualitative research on the second generation, yet such research is essential to explain more fully bifurcated patterns of integration and inequality among different immigrant groups. This is particularly the case for smaller immigrant communities, such as the sub-Saharan African diaspora in Vancouver, which remain invisible in surveys and receive very little scholarly attention. The new African diaspora in Vancouver – a term that refers to those who have migrated directly from Africa – is a small but growing, heterogeneous, and hyper-visible population. Only 1.2 per cent of the metro Vancouver population (29,830) identified as Black in the 2016 census, while 1.3 per cent (32,100) were born in Africa and 1.7 per cent (40,665) claimed an African ethnic origin (Statistics Canada 2016a, 2016b, 2016c). The importance of place in shaping the nature of integration and inequality is clear when comparing Vancouver and Toronto, where, in the 2016 census, 7.5 per cent of the population (442,020) identified as Black (Statistics Canada 2016e). In 2011 two-thirds of all Canadians who identified as Black lived in Toronto (42 per cent) and Montreal (23 per cent), but only 2.5 per cent lived in metro Vancouver (Statistics Canada 2013, 16, 2016d).

Although there has been a Black community presence in British Columbia since the mid-nineteenth century (Compton 2010; Kilian 2008), it remains very small compared to other racialized communities. Hence the experience of sub-Saharan African immigrants racialized as Black in metro Vancouver is distinct from that in other major immigrant reception centres in Canada with much larger populations from Africa and of African descent. In this context of small numbers and hyper-visibility, many in the new African diaspora in Vancouver self-identify as part of a pan-African community – a community that experiences significant marginalization and racism while simultaneously building diverse new spaces of belonging (Creese 2011).

The 1.5 generation – born abroad and raised in Canada – and second generation (born in Canada) grow up between or across cultures, which means navigating paths distinct from, and sometimes in conflict with, those of their parents (Berry et al. 2006; Handa 2003; Rumbaut 2004, 2012). These generational divisions lead to different forms of identity, with the second generation developing situational hybrid identities as it negotiates belonging (Berry et al. 2006; Handa 2003; Hirji 2010; Kobayashi and Preston 2014; Nagra 2017; Pratt 2004; Pratt and the Philippine Women Centre of BC 2008; Wilson-Forsberg 2012).

For example, first-generation immigrants in Vancouver adopt national and pan-African forms of identification, most commonly using the term "African immigrant" even when they are also Canadian citizens (Creese 2011). In contrast, their children are more likely to embrace a hyphenated identity as African-Canadians, adopting Canadian cultural values of liberal individualism and autonomy that frequently collide with their parents' emphasis on authority, respect, and deference based on age, family status, and gender (Creese 2011, 2019; Matsuoka and Sorenson 2001).

Research on African immigrant youth in Canada has, to date, focused on racialization processes of "becoming Black" and "acting Black," mediated through African-American youth culture, including hip hop, music videos, films, styles of dress, ways of speaking, and the celebration of athletes (Abdel-Shehid 2005; Ibrahim 1999, 2003; Kelly 1998, 2004; Okeke-Iherjirika and Spitzer 2005). Kelly (2004) refers to this as "borrowed identities" because it is so heavily influenced by American popular culture as the only space where African-Canadian youth can see themselves reflected bodily. Youth who arrive in Canada in their teens experience a more difficult transition than those who come as young children; this is particularly the case for child refugees, many of whom experienced significant trauma and might have little prior formal education but are placed in age-based grades in Canada (Francis 2010; Francis and Yan 2016; Kanu 2008; Shakya et al. 2010). The gendered and sexualized nature of generational tensions and adaptation strategies is also evident. For example, scholars have pointed out that girls from sub-Saharan Africa face stricter parental controls than boys, tend to focus more on school, and struggle to find "a definition of a good girl agreeable to both parents and daughter" (Okeke-Iherjirika and Spitzer 2005, 216), while boys often replicate American-dominated images of Black masculinity through youth culture and sports (Abdel-Shehid 2005; Ibrahim 1999; James 2016). None of these studies of African immigrant youth, however, addresses transitions to adulthood, so we know surprisingly little about how 1.5- and second-generation African-Canadians reflect on growing up or negotiate life as young adults.

Research and Social Location

One of the most important insights of feminist approaches to research is that social location affects how and what knowledge is produced. Critiquing the socially unlocated subject of positivist science, or what Donna Haraway calls the "god trick" of an all-seeing researcher, feminist scholars recognize that "situated knowledges" are always multiple and partial because all research is located within complex relations of power and privilege (Haraway 1991). Dissimilar social locations produce different vantage points, often leading to new research questions or diverse answers to similar queries. Beginning research from the standpoint of a socially marginalized group, therefore, is a method for shifting the gaze away from dominant perspectives and unsettling conventional wisdoms (Collins 1990; Smith 1987). This study attempts to do that through a qualitative study based on in-depth interviews with a group of young adult children of African immigrants, putting the diverse experiences of second-generation African-Canadians in Vancouver at the centre of the research.

Social location is always multidimensional, and some key differences among research participants are also explored. These include the importance of gender differences between boys and girls and men and women, distinctions between the 1.5 generation born abroad and raised in Canada and the Canadian-born second generation, and between those who arrived as young children and those who were teenagers when they came to Canada.

The social location of the researchers also matters. As the principal researcher, I share a history of migration as part of the 1.5 generation, born elsewhere and raised mostly in Canada without extended family nearby. My family's experience of migration, however, coincides largely with privilege, as working-class White British immigrants during a period of economic expansion in the late 1950s and 1960s. As such, there are few parallels in my personal experience with the routine downward mobility that African immigrant families have endured since the 1980s or with the effect of processes of racialization and racism as African-Canadians "learn to become Black" in a context of White privilege. The collective insights of my research assistants – Veronica Fynn, Sanzida Habib, E.J. Shu, and Jeannie Morgan – bring other dimensions of social location to the research process. Although we are all "outsiders" to the local second generation in the African diaspora, all but one of the research assistants are first-generation adult migrants (from Liberia, Bangladesh, and Australia, respectively), and all but one have some experience of marginalization in relation to local hierarchies of racialization (as Black, South Asian, and Indigenous Canadian).

How a researcher's position as community "insider" or "outsider" affects the construction of knowledge has been debated extensively (see, for example, Naples 2003; Ramazanoglu 2002). As Patricia Hill Collins observes, dichotomous framing of a researcher's relationship to her subject matter is problematic for many, including Black women scholars who simultaneously occupy positions as "outsider within" that have contributed to the development of a distinctive Black feminist thought (Collins 1986, 1990). As a White woman academic who is an outsider to the local African-Canadian community, I draw on work by Black and other feminist and critical race scholars to frame and interpret this research, seeking to work as an ally and speak alongside, rather than for, African-Canadian research participants. In an effort to highlight the voices of research participants, quotations from interviews are used extensively throughout the text, and I follow an ethic of caring suggesting by Collins (1990) and Naples (2003) respecting the individuality of participants, paying attention to emotions, and employing empathy in making sense of participants' experiences.

As Potts and Brown (2015, 17) argue, "[a] commitment to anti-oppressive research means committing to social justice and taking an active role in that change." My commitment to working for social justice is animated by analysing persistent racialized, gender, and class inequalities in Canada. I developed a long-standing engagement and collaboration with some members of the new African diaspora that emerged out of broader research on immigration. My previous book, *The New African Diaspora in Vancouver*, was the product of many years of collaboration with Edith Ngene Kambere and Mambo Masinda and the sixty-one men and women who agreed to be interviewed. After exploring key issues affecting African immigrants, including challenges involved in parenting the second generation, we partnered to conduct research with teenage migrants, focusing on challenges and strategies of resilience (Creese, Kambere, and Masinda 2013). Twenty-one teen migrants and thirteen mothers took part in that project, which was conducted in collaboration with Umoja Operation Compassion Society, a local African-run settlement organization in Surrey, British Columbia. I have been involved with Umoja for well over a decade, serving as the volunteer chair of the board of directors during much of that time. Although I remain an "outsider" to the African-Canadian community, I also have strong connections that facilitate and guide this research. Deep familiarity with the challenges, resilience, and accomplishments of the first generation in the local African community is an invaluable starting point from which to explore what it is like to grow up as both African and Canadian as part of the second generation.

Thirty-five women and men took part in this research. They, or their parents, come from Democratic Republic of Congo (DRC), Ethiopia, Ghana, Kenya, Liberia, Nigeria, Sierra Leone, Somalia, South Africa, Sudan, Togo, and Uganda. For the most part, however, place of birth and national/ethnic origin are less important than being raised by African immigrant parents in a context where they are usually the only

Black and African children in their neighbourhood and school. Almost one-third of participants were born in Canada, nearly half migrated before the age of twelve, and the rest were teenage migrants. For stylistic reasons, I use "second generation" throughout the book to encompass both those born abroad and raised in Canada (the 1.5 generation) and the Canadian born (the second generation proper), except when distinctions between these two groups are the subject of discussion. Similarly, terms such as "African immigrant" and "African-Canadian" reflect common usage among research participants despite the heterogeneous makeup of the local African diaspora. At the same time, I also explore local processes of homogenization through discourses of Blackness and the precarious nature of belonging as Canadians. Gender and sexuality are also critical for shaping the experiences of adolescents and adults, so I take care to address gender differences as well as the context of heteronormative assumptions in the community. Class also matters, not so much in terms of differences among participants, as in terms of common experiences of being parented by well-educated parents who experience significant downward economic and status mobility in Canada, while retaining middle-class expectations about higher education.

The Organization of the Book

As noted, this study is based on interviews with thirty-five women and men, ranging in age from nineteen to thirty-six, whose parents migrated from countries in sub-Saharan Africa and who grew up in metro Vancouver. Research participants experienced the unique confluence of growing up in a place where "no one looked like me" and yet popular culture is awash in representations of Black masculinity and femininity, emanating largely from the United States. In this book I examine the following questions: Is the second generation doing better than its immigrant parents and fulfilling the first-generation's long-term aspirations for migration? How do second-generation youth negotiate multiple challenges and identities as Black, as African, and as Canadian as they grow up? What is their sense of belonging as Canadian? How, as Black youth and adults, are they affected by the dominance of African-American popular culture and representations of Blackness in Canada? In the chapters that follow, I explore how the intersections of race, gender, (hetero)sexuality, class, and place shape the lives of these adult children of African immigrants as they navigate childhood, adolescence, and early adulthood.

In the first part of the book, I examine the context of the study and experiences during childhood and adolescence. In Chapter 2, "Imagined

Communities, Discourses of Blackness, and the New African Diaspora in Vancouver," I discuss theoretical concepts that guide the study. I explore how Whiteness remains central to the "imagined community" of Canada and how the prevalence of gendered discourses of Blackness are associated with beliefs about the lesser social value of people of African descent, and the effect of these discourses in Canada. I also provide an overview of settlement experiences among first-generation immigrants in metro Vancouver and their dreams of a better future for their children. The first generation has faced considerable barriers to integration – the disparaging of African English accents, the systematic non-recognition of educational credentials and work experience, and their relegation to "survival jobs" – and worked hard to build a resilient community and carve out new spaces of belonging. Immigrant parents recognize that their children must be raised to fit into life in Canada, while they also strive to instil African values in their sons and daughters, and express fears about "losing" them to a different set of values. Chapter 2 ends with an overview of key characteristics of the research participants, including their age, ancestry, place of birth, age at the time of migration, class of immigration, parents' education and occupations, and research participants' own educational background and current employment.

In Chapter 3, "'No one looked like me': Remembering Migration and Early Childhood," I explore memories of adjusting to life in Canada, of being young children in Vancouver, and experiences in elementary school. I examine differences between the Canadian born and those who migrated to Canada (the 1.5 generation) when they were old enough to remember the transition and can compare their lives prior to migration. The level of diversity in the neighbourhoods they grew up in and the schools they attended shaped their experiences as young children. Gender differences were clearly marked at a young age, as boys and girls negotiated friendships with peers. In general, African-Canadian boys recalled making friends quite easily, often by playing sports together, while many girls were isolated for prolonged periods.

Chapter 4, "'Cool Black guys' and Girls 'trying to feel good in your own skin': Navigating Adolescence," explores the teenage years, when gender and sexuality form more critical distinctions in relations with parents and peers. A key issue in adolescence is the way representations of Blackness – particularly through the widespread popularity of commercial hip hop music and videos – present gendered and sexualized images that shape African-Canadian men's and women's lives in very different ways. As adolescents, teenage boys experienced great popularity as "the cool Black guy." In contrast, popular culture provides no route to popularity for Black teenage girls and, excluded from dominant images of heterosexual attractiveness, they struggle more to fit in with high school peers.

In the remainder of the book, I examine the adult lives of second-generation African-Canadians who grew up in metro Vancouver. Chapter 5, "'More of my friends are Black': Friendships and Romantic Relationships," addresses the development of personal relationships as part of the transition to adulthood. Most men and women expanded their friendship networks and included more members of the local African diaspora. Marked gender differences are evident, however, when it comes to heterosexual romantic relationships. Most of the men had partners, most often White women who grew up locally. In contrast, most women were single, and those with partners were mostly in relationships with African men who were adults when they came to Canada.

Chapter 6, "'I have so much more opportunities': Education and Career Goals," explores research participants' educational accomplishments and trajectories and their occupational goals as young adults. Everyone who participated in this research had pursued some post-secondary education, with the majority of women and men poised to complete a university degree; some of the older participants were already working in their desired fields of employment. I also look at gender differences in higher education prevalent in the broader African-Canadian community, to assess why men in general are less likely than women to pursue post-secondary education.

Chapter 7, "Living 'under a microscope': Navigating Public Spaces," explores the way processes of racialization shape everyday interactions for second-generation African-Canadians. Both men and women are subject to heightened surveillance as hypervisible Black bodies in everyday contexts, from interactions in workplaces to walking down the street. Discourses of Blackness are gendered, so men's and women's experiences vary, with men experiencing greater levels of surveillance in public spaces, particularly by the police. The chapter ends with a discussion of the strategies of resilience that research participants developed for "living under a microscope."

Chapter 8, "'People still ask me where I'm from': Belonging and Identities," examines the effect that frequent queries about origins has on belonging and identities. The second generation embodies local attributes of Canadian English accents and local cultural and social capital. Yet other Vancouver residents see racialized Black bodies as incompatible with the "imagined community" of Canadians, and persistently ask "where are you from?" Second-generation identities are negotiated partly as strategic responses to this question, leading some to reject and others to strongly assert a Canadian identity. In adulthood the majority embrace a national or pan-African identity, most often in combination with a Canadian identity, simultaneously distinguishing themselves from homogenizing discourses of Blackness as African-American, and embracing and redefining their African heritage.

Finally, in Chapter 9, "Growing Up African-Canadian in Vancouver: Race, Gender, Sexuality, and Place," I return to questions of whether the first-generation's hopes for its children are born out and whether the Canadianization of the second-generation means it has lost its African identities. I conclude that, by and large, men and women who participated in this research are faring better than their parents. They are optimistic about their future, and work hard to seize opportunities. In contrast to its parents, the second generation embodies the local, expressed through its accents, education, cultural capital, and networks of belonging. At the same time, the second generation continues to experience considerable everyday racism that also challenges belonging, and to develop strategies of resilience to "living under a microscope." Discourses of Black masculinity and femininity shape men's and women's lives differently, with gendered effects on educational trajectories and significant gender differences in the local heterosexual market. Discourses of Blackness, racial micro-aggressions, and structural racism affected the adult identities of participants in complex ways, with most identifying fluid hybrid identities as African and Canadian and deepening their attachment to their African heritage, while accentuating the barriers to belonging fully in Canada.

Chapter Two

Imagined Communities, Discourses of Blackness, and the New African Diaspora in Vancouver

Migration and Diversity

Metro Vancouver[1] is one of Canada's largest and most diverse cities. In 2016 the population was over 2.4 million (Statistic Canada 2016a). Forty-one per cent of residents are immigrants, from a diverse range of countries, and three-quarters of these immigrants identify as people of colour (Statistics Canada 2016b).[2] Of Vancouver's total population, 49 per cent identify as people of colour (Statistics Canada 2016a).[3] The largest racialized communities correspond with immigration trends over the past four decades, with Hong Kong, China, India, and the Philippines constituting the leading source countries of new Canadians. Together, those of Chinese, South Asian, and Filipino origin account for 75 per cent of all those who identify as visible minorities in Vancouver, and make up 37 per cent of the city's total population (Statistics Canada 2016a).

In this context of diversity, growing up as a child of immigrant parents, negotiating across different cultural norms, and engaging with racialized hierarchies that privilege Whiteness is a fairly common

---

1 Metro Vancouver consists of twenty-one municipalities combined in one census area. The largest of the municipalities are Vancouver, Surrey, Burnaby, Richmond, and Coquitlam. Unless otherwise specified, Vancouver is used to refer to the metro Vancouver region.

2 Statistics Canada uses the term "visible minority" to refer to people who identify as neither of European nor Indigenous origin. Feminist and anti-racist scholars more commonly use the terms "people of colour" or "racialized minorities."

3 Among people of colour, 67 per cent are immigrants, 29 per cent are Canadian born, and nearly 4 per cent are not permanent residents – for example, those with work permits, study permits, or refugee claimants whose cases have not been processed (Statistics Canada 2011a).

occurrence. At the same time, the situation is very different for those growing up within large local ethnic communities, such as Chinese, South Asian, or Filipino, compared to children of immigrants who do not have a substantial community presence. The children of immigrants from sub-Saharan Africa grow up in a diverse cultural and racial- ized environment in Vancouver, but in a milieu in which they seldom encounter people like themselves. Few local residents have origins in countries in Africa, and even fewer are racialized as Black. Thus, in Vancouver, the children of migrants from sub-Saharan Africa stand out as a highly visible, yet very small minority, in a population dominated by those of European or Asian origin.

British Columbia, however, has a long history of African-descent communities going back to the middle of the nineteenth century. Six hundred members of San Francisco's Black community migrated to the colony of Vancouver Island in 1858 after an invitation from Governor James Douglas, a man of mixed African and European descent (Kilian 2008; Mensah 2002). Many settled in Victoria and nearby Salt Spring Island, while others were drawn to the Fraser River gold rush. They formed the first communities of African descent on the west coast of the colony, bought land, started businesses, and played a key role in civic life in Victoria, though many returned to the United States after the Civil War (Kilian 2008). By 1881 the number of Black residents recorded in the census for British Columbia had declined to just under three hun- dred (Barman 1991, 100).

By the turn of the twentieth century, Black families began to settle in the growing city of Vancouver. Most of the small Black population settled in the east side neighbourhood of Strathcona – particularly in Hogan's Alley, which ran between Union and Prior streets and was close to the railway terminus, where many Black men worked as rail- way porters (Compton 2010). Members of the emerging Black commu- nity started businesses and established restaurants and music venues. In 1908 they created the first Black church in the area and in 1914 the Independent Coloured Political Association (Kilian 2008). It is esti- mated that, in the 1940s, the Black population in Strathcona was around eight hundred, mostly living in and around Hogan's Alley (Creative Cultural Collaboration Society 2014). In 1958 the BC Association for the Advancement of Coloured People was founded, compiling a census that listed 950 Black people living in the province (Kilian 2008, 143).

The growth of the local African-Canadian community was hampered, however, by racist immigration policies intended to establish a White settler society on unceded Indigenous lands. White migrants were encouraged to come to Canada from the United Kingdom, northern

Europe, and the United States. By the early twentieth century, desirable newcomers expanded to include people from southern and central Europe, while non-Europeans were restricted or excluded through various measures. During this time, legislation and international agreements were enacted to prevent further migration from India (1908), Japan (1908), and China (1923)[4] (Fleras 2015; Hawkins 1991; Li 2003; Simmons 2010). The Immigration Act of 1910 prohibited "immigrants belonging to any race deemed unsuited to the climate or requirements of Canada, or of immigrants of any specified class, occupation or character" (Hawkins 1991, 56). The rationale of being "unsuited to the climate" was used to exclude people of African descent from settling in Canada, although exceptions were sometimes made when workers from the Caribbean made convenient sources of much-needed labour, including steelworkers in Nova Scotia and domestic workers in Ontario and Quebec (Calliste 1993/94).

With limited growth through immigration, Vancouver's historic Black community remained very small. In the 1960s urban redevelopment and plans for a highway through Strathcona to the downtown core promised to cut the community in two and threatened to demolish Hogan's Alley, considered a slum area by local politicians. As Wayde Compton (2010) notes, the deterioration of Hogan's Alley was a direct result of the 1931 rezoning of the area as industrial rather than residential land, which made it impossible to attain mortgages or loans for home improvement. As a result, the Black community had begun to move out of the area some time in the late 1950s. Few Black families still resided there in 1971, when Hogan's Alley was destroyed during construction of the Georgia Viaduct, the first phase of a freeway that residents of Strathcona successfully mobilized to stop (Compton 2010; Creative Cultural Collaboration Society 2014). The razing of Hogan's Alley marked the end of an identifiable Black community space in Vancouver, and the small population remains dispersed throughout the region. The demolition of Hogan's Alley also helped to erase the presence of Vancouver's historic Black community from public memory.

Canadian immigration policies changed in the mid-1960s, abandoning a focus on race and country of origin as the chief criteria for immigration and moving to a points system that emphasizes post-secondary

---

4 Further migration from India was halted in 1908 by legislation that required a
continuous journey from the country of origin to Canada; in 1908 a Gentleman's
Agreement was signed with Japan that halted most further male migration from that
country; and the Chinese Immigration Act of 1923, following head taxes that began
in 1885, excluded further immigrants from China.

educational qualifications and occupational skills (Fleras 2015; Hawkins 1991; Li 2003; Simmons 2010). The change opened new possibilities of migration from countries in Africa, Asia, the Caribbean, and Latin America. As a result, since the 1970s, the Canadian population has become increasingly diverse.

Largely as a result of changes in immigration, Canada's Black population grew from just over 32,000 in 1961 to 1.2 million in 2016, increasing from less than two-tenths of 1 per cent (0.17 per cent) of the total Canadian population to 3.5 per cent (Mensah 2002, 53; Statistics Canada 2016d). During this period, the proportion of immigrants coming from countries in Africa slowly increased from only 1.9 per cent prior to 1971 to 7.3 per cent in the 1990s, 10.3 per cent from 2001 to 2006, and 12.5 per cent from 2006 to 2011 (Statistics Canada 2013, 8). As Puplampu and Tettey (2005) argue, however, practices that they identify as "neo-racist," such as the location and number of Canadian immigration offices, continue to constrain migration flows from sub-Saharan Africa.

The growth of the Canadian population of African descent is uneven across the country, producing much larger Black communities in Toronto and Montreal than in Vancouver. The majority of recent immigrants from sub-Saharan Africa reside in Toronto and Montreal, settling alongside large Black communities from the Caribbean as well as multigenerational African-Canadians. Two-thirds of all Canadians who identify as Black live in Toronto (42 per cent) and Montreal (23 per cent) (Statistics Canada 2013). In contrast, only 2.5 per cent of Canadians who identify as Black live in metro Vancouver (Statistics Canada 2016d). According to the 2016 census, 32,100 immigrants from Africa were living in metro Vancouver, making up 1.3 per cent of the population (Statistics Canada 2016b). The largest groups have migrated from South Africa (8,205), Kenya (4,065), Ethiopia (1,665), Nigeria (1,205), and Somalia (1,010).[5] A slightly larger number of residents – 40,665 people, or 1.7 per cent of the population – claim an African ethnic origin (Statistics Canada 2016c); fifty-four different African ethnicities are identified, with those rooted in southern and east Africa accounting for 42 per cent.[6]

Many people who migrate from Africa or claim African ethnicity are not racialized as Black. Just over 1 per cent of Vancouver residents, or

---

5 The only other African country with at least 1,000 local people is Egypt, with 2,110.

6 The 2016 census lists African ethnic origins in metro Vancouver in four main categories: southern and east Africa (42 per cent), other Africa (29 per cent), north Africa (18 per cent), and central and western Africa (12 per cent) (Statistics Canada 2016c).

29,830 people, identified as Black in 2016 (Statistics Canada 2016a); of this number, 55 per cent were immigrants and 45 per cent were born in Canada. The majority of Black immigrants in Vancouver have come from countries in sub-Saharan Africa, with smaller numbers from the Caribbean, the United States, and other countries (Statistics Canada 2011a).[7] The Canadian-born population of African descent includes the children of immigrants from Africa, the Caribbean, and the United States, alongside others whose Canadian lineage might span several generations. Although the numbers are still relatively small, the growth in immigration from sub-Saharan Africa has produced a "new" African diaspora that self-identifies as the African community. The adult children in this community form the subjects of this book. They grew up in metro Vancouver, where they were usually the only African and Black children in their neighbourhood and school and where their racialized bodies made them stand out as highly visible among their peers, who were primarily of Asian or European origin.

Imagined Communities and Discourses of Blackness

Discourses about strangers are central to defining who does and does not belong in a given space (Ahmed 2000). Bodies are read for signs of recognition as belonging here or as being out of place; "recognition of those who are out of place allows both the demarcation and enforcement of the boundaries of 'this place' as where 'we' dwell" (Ahmed 2000, 22). Depending on the context, signs of unbelonging can include language, accent, age, gender, clothing, religion, and skin colour. Those who are perceived to belong constitute the "imagined community" that underlies discourses of nationalism (Anderson 1991). Borders are delineated in material as well as psychic terms, reproducing social, cultural, and mental boundaries between "us" and "them" (Brah 1996, 198). The borders of the nation, then, are not only geopolitical and material, but also discursive and imaginary, constituted through recognizing some bodies as strange and out of place and others as belonging to the nation (Ahmed 2000, 98).

---

7 The composition of the Black population by immigrant status and country of origin is available only for 2011. The 2011 National Household Survey records around two thousand immigrants each from Jamaica and Trinidad and Tobago, fewer than one thousand from Guyana, and a few hundred from Haiti. It also records more than twenty-six thousand from the United States. No racial breakdowns are provided (Statistics Canada 2011b).

Distinctions between who does and does not belong are embedded in place-based historical processes. In the Canadian context, the history of settler colonialism, marginalization of Indigenous peoples, and centuries of preference for European immigrants has shaped who is and who is not perceived by others to be members of the imagined community of Canadians, and which bodies are read as strange and out of place. Immigration is an ongoing process in Canada, and recognition of this fact, and the diversity it engenders, has become part of its national identity. Yet in everyday usage the term immigrant is a racialized concept, with Canadians of colour presumed to be immigrants even if they are born in Canada (Bannerji 2000; Ng 1990; Thobani 2007). In contrast White residents typically are perceived as local, as bodies that belong, even if they are immigrants, unless specific markers (such as accent) suggest otherwise.

The celebration of multiculturalism as part of official state policy and national identity in Canada has not decentred Whiteness even while it gestures to a more complicated historical legacy (Abu-Laban and Gabriel 2002; Day 2000; Mackey 2002). As Rinaldo Walcott argues, inserting multiculturalism within a bilingual (French and English) framework linked to "founding peoples" displaces Indigenous peoples and ensures that "the colonizing English and French are left textually intact as 'real' Canadians" (Walcott 2003, 118). All "others" from "elsewhere" constitute Canada's multicultural character but remain "tangential to the nation-state" (117). In addition, multiculturalism elides differences between ethnicity and race, and thereby helps to make racism less visible (Bannerji 2000; Barrett 2015). The peripheral location of "others" in the imagined community is buttressed by historical amnesia, with racialized minorities perceived as recent immigrants even when their presence extends over centuries. The problem of historical amnesia has particular salience for African-Canadians. Walcott (2003, 136) describes the erasure of centuries of history – from slavery in the colonies and waves of Black migration from the Caribbean and the United States before and after Confederation to more recent migrations from the African continent – as "the absented presence of blackness in Canada." Historical amnesia shores up myths about White settler colonialism, and marks Black bodies as strange and new even though their Canadian lineage goes back centuries.

Whether new immigrants or multigenerational African-Canadians, people of African descent are immersed in discourses about Blackness that transcend local geographies and boundaries of nation-states (Walcott 2003). As George Sefa Dei argues, "through colonial and Eurocentric knowledge, Black bodies have been rendered homogenous" and become "the perpetual exotic 'other'" (Dei 2017, 12). Stripped of diverse ethnic, cultural, and linguistic heritages in the diaspora, discourses of Blackness are embedded in long-standing racist assumptions about inferiority, violence, and criminality (Dei 2013).

In *Black Skin, White Masks* Frantz Fanon ([1957] 2000) describes an encounter with a White child that leads him to reinterpret his identity; the colonial gaze that names his racialized body is interpolated into his own subjectivity. As Fanon states, "I discovered my blackness," recognizing that, for others, Blackness overdetermines everything else about him (259). As this example suggests, processes of racialization are complex, entailing legacies of colonial oppression, ongoing power relations, and discourses that involve both external assertions and transformations in subjectivity (Gans 2017).

Within the Canadian context, scholars have explored how diverse peoples of African descent undergo a process of "becoming Black" in Canada (Barrett 2015; Dei 2017; Ibrahim 1999, 2006; Ibrahim and Abdi 2016a, 2016b; Kelly 2004; Okeke-Iherjirika and Spitzer 2005; Walcott 2003). For example, Awad Ibrahim (1999, 354) explains that the characteristics he used to define his identity in Sudan were fundamentally transformed after migrating to Canada, "whereby the antecedent [Sudanese] signifiers became secondary to my Blackness, and I retranslated myself: I became Black," He argues that Blackness in Canada is a "discursive space where they [African immigrants] are already imagined, constructed and treated as 'Blacks' by hegemonic discourses and groups" (Ibrahim 2006, 44). The homogenizing category of Blackness renders the diversity of African heritages invisible. These discourses are rooted in ideas and practices that can be traced back to European colonialism and the African slave trade and that animate settler colonialism in Canada.

Ideas associated with Blackness might be socially constructed, discursive, and imagined, but the realities of anti-Black racism in societies structured by White privilege means "there is also a materiality to Blackness and Black identity" (Dei 2017, 16). Materiality is linked to the hypervisibility of Black skin colour (and the invisibility of White skin colour) and the unequal treatment to which those of African descent have long been subjected (Dei 2013). As Dei argues, "[w]e can agree race is socially constructed. It is not a fixed or bounded category. But race is also real and has a permanence for some in the endurance of Black skin colour and anti-Black racism" (Dei 2017, 15). Discourses of Blackness, like other processes of racialization, are embedded within historical and contemporary power relations. Beyond asserting power differences, racialized discourses also rationalize and justify inequities between groups. As a result, distinctions between those with Black and White skin colour are not just about difference; rather, "skin colour operates as a signifier of social value and moral worth" (Deliovsky and Kitossa 2013, 169). Thus African-Canadians have to negotiate discourses of Blackness infused with value judgments about the lesser social and moral worth of people of African descent compared to those of European origin.

The negative associations with Blackness are not just a product of distant historical events; these discourses remain pervasive in contemporary popular culture – particularly in the US popular culture that is central to the cultural milieu in Canada. Whether new immigrants or multigenerational Canadians of African descent, discourses of Blackness in popular culture shape perceptions about Black men and women that affect their treatment in public spaces, whether as youngsters' experiences in school (Brathwaite and James 1996; Dei et al. 1997; Ibrahim and Abdi 2016a, 2016b), employees in the workplace (Creese 2011), or in interactions with institutions of the state (Maynard 2017).

At a time when the blatant discrimination found in previous eras is no longer acceptable, contemporary anti-Black racism is often expressed through racial micro-aggressions. As Fleras (2016, 2) explains, "[r]acial micro-aggressions may represent 'a new face of racism' that eschews the overt language of bigotry in exchange for covert codes perceived by the micro-aggressed to communicate dislike or aversion." Racial micro-aggressions can be understood as forms of "everyday racism" that can seem trivial in isolation, but that make up a systemic pattern of inequities (Essed 1991). These verbal and non-verbal assaults are "used to keep those at the racial margins in their place" (Huber and Solorzano 2015, 298). The frequent query "where are you from?" that frames Black bodies as "foreign" rather than local and as not belonging to the "imagined community" of Canadians, is just one example of a common racial micro-aggression experienced by African-Canadians.

Questioning the competence of people who speak with different English accents is another form of racial micro-aggression. As Pierre Bourdieu (1986, 245) reminds us, linguistic capital is a form of embodied capital that is "[mis]recognized as legitimate competence"; the power of speech is linked to the power (or lack of power) of the person speaking (Bourdieu 1977). The legacies of colonialism in Canada result in privileging local Canadian English accents so that "foreign" accents that are not British are treated as if these are not competent versions of English (Amin and Dei 2006; Creese 2010, 2011; Derwing, Rossiter, and Munro 2002; Henry 1999; Lippi-Green 1997; Munro 2003; Willinsky 1998). As Dei argues, linguistic racism is powerful because "it works with unspoken, unrecognized assumptions about white domination" (Dei 2006, 26). African immigrants in Vancouver, for example, recall demeaning encounters with strangers who challenged their grammar and pronunciation, and potential employers who suggested their African English accents meant their command of English was insufficient for more highly skilled jobs (Creese 2010, 2011).

Routine employers' preference for Canadian education and experience constitutes another form of racial micro-aggression with significant systemic effects in the labour market. Although post-secondary educational credentials are central to migration through the immigration points system, employers routinely privilege degrees attained in Canada and discount post-secondary education from countries other than the United States and the United Kingdom (Frenette and Morissette 2005; Li 2003; Oreopoulos 2011; Reitz, Curtis, and Elrick 2014). Prior professional and skilled work experience is also rewarded in the immigration points system, but employers routinely make experience in Canada a hiring requirement (Aydemir and Skuterud 2004; Oreopoulos 2011; Picot and Hou 2003; Picot and Sweetman 2005). This is a systemic problem in the labour market, with dire consequences for immigrants from the global South. As a result, for example, three-quarters of African immigrants in Vancouver experience significant downward occupational mobility in Canada (Creese 2011; Creese and Wiebe 2012). As we can see in these examples, racial micro-aggressions are embedded within, and reproduce systemic forms of structural racism.

Counterhegemonic discourses in popular culture and scholarship attempt to reframe Africa and African-descent communities and identities as positive, agentic, complex, and multidimensional. The debate over the concept of "Afropolitan" is a useful recent contribution to this reframing. The term was coined by Taiye Selasi to highlight experiences of global cosmopolitanism as members of a post-1960s African diaspora move seamlessly between cities in Africa, Europe, and North America (Selasi 2005). Thus "Afropolitanism suggests a reading of the African postcolonial identity as necessarily transcultural, transnational, indeed cosmopolitan" (Eze 2014, 239). Some scholars critique its middle- and upper-class bias, emphasis on consumerism, and attempt to disassociate from "ghettoized African Americans, who are conceived with all the stereotypes attached to Blackness" (Sterling 2015, 127). For these critics, pan-Africanism is a more useful model of progressive African identity because it is not limited to the middle and upper classes, and it deepens connections between nations on the continent and across the diaspora (Dabiri 2016; Sterling 2015). On the other hand, Adjepong (2018) argues that the concept of Afropolitanism can be a useful way to recognize the diversity and heterogeneity of Black populations in the context of North America. She argues that second-generation Africans in the United States develop Afropolitan projects as part of understanding their own identities as distinct from the larger African American community. Hence Adjepong identifies Afropolitan as a "Black ethnicity" in the United States that challenges "dominant negative conceptions about blackness as well as articulating the diversity of their black experiences" (2018, 251). In the context of metro Vancouver, both the concepts of pan-Africanism and Afropolitanism are useful. Pan-Africanism is important for understanding the way the first generation organizes across national differences to identify as a pan-African community; while Afropolitanism captures the way many in the second generation rearticulate positive diasporic African identities that challenge discourses of Blackness rooted in African-American popular culture.

The New African Diaspora: Community Building in Vancouver

Diasporic communities form in contexts of migration as groups that identify a shared origin redefine themselves with reference to a common homeland and in relation to other groups coexisting in their new home (Brah 1996; Brubaker 2005; Clifford 1994). More than a collection of people from a particular place, diasporas develop out of collective practices, including "remembering, imagining and engaging with the original homeland" (Zeleza 2008, 16). Diasporic African communities typically form along national, ethnic, and linguistic lines. In some contexts, however, new pan-African identities emerge that cross multiple national, ethnic, and linguistic divisions (Fumanti and Werbner 2010; Grégoire 2010; Werbner 2010). The emergence of a self-defined African community in metro Vancouver is one example of this. New identities as African take shape in the context of very small numbers from any specific ethnic or national origin, notions of shared values in a common continental homeland, and, equally important, experiences of racialization and marginalization in Canada (Creese 2011, 2013).

Shared experiences of marginalization as Black, as immigrants, and as African have fostered the development of support networks that build community within and across diverse African origins. In an environment where daily interactions are overdetermined by processes of racialization and discourses of Blackness, points of commonality extend beyond ethnic and national identities (Creese 2011).

Building bonds of community involves practices oriented towards the "homeland" in Africa and "homemaking" in Canada. The homeland is understood as "a mythic place of desire in the diasporic imagination," in contrast to day-to-day homemaking as "the lived experience of the locality" (Brah 1996, 192). Settlement processes are always gendered, affecting women and men in different ways and challenging expectations around appropriate gender relations (Donato et al. 2006; Lutz 2010; Pessar 2003). Community activities associated with the homeland are most often undertaken by men, and usually receive more public recognition (Goldring 2001). Women predominate in homemaking activities that are often less visible aspects of community building (Creese 2011, 2013).[8]

Members of Vancouver's African community are involved in creating formal organizations oriented towards their homelands, activities that also help build community in the local context. Several nationally focused organizations have emerged among the larger components of the African community – including those linked to the DRC, Ethiopia, Ghana, Kenya, Nigeria, South Africa, and Uganda (Creese 2013) – that are intended to maintain ties to the homeland and preserve cultural traditions in Canada. National organizations hold periodic social functions and festivals that build community among co-nationals and the wider African diaspora in the local context. In addition, several non-profit organizations focus on development in various parts of Africa, supporting projects such as building and running schools and medical clinics and providing safe drinking water in home villages. These development organizations are typically run by men connected to these villages, and help to maintain their status as important members of those communities (Creese 2013).

Women are less likely to be centrally involved in organizations that focus on the homeland, but are engaged in a broad range of less formal networks of support for one another. Such support includes advice on parenting in Canada, how to navigate local schools, health care, and social services, gifts and food for new mothers, babysitting, support for bereaved families, and emotional support found in commiseration with others facing similar challenges (Creese 2011, 2013). More formal women's groups have also emerged to meet a range of needs, including

---

8 Both men and women maintain connections with family in the homeland, but men more often become involved in homeland organizations, and derive some status from these positions. Women tend to be less involved with the latter, and more focused on homemaking activities linked to raising children, activities that build community in ways that are less visible.

supporting AIDS orphans in Africa,[9] lending circles to pool limited resources, organizing community meetings for problem solving, and providing information to new immigrants. Some of these support networks are organized along national lines – for example, Vancouver has specific Nigerian, Congolese, and Sudanese women's groups – but most provide support to women across diverse origins in Africa (Creese 2011).

As the vast majority of African immigrants in Vancouver identify as Christian,[10] churches are an important locus of African community development. Many in the community attend multi-ethnic churches, but several African churches have also emerged. In 2010 we identified twelve churches led by African pastors with congregations that were predominantly from Africa. There were no stand-alone African churches; each found space to use in other churches or multipurpose buildings. Fund raising was underway, however, to build a church that various African denominations would be able to use. African churches have become an important source of support for new immigrants, providing information and referrals to settlement agencies, as well as a place to build critically important friendship networks (Creese 2011).

The African community also plays an important role in providing settlement services for newer immigrants and refugees from Africa. In our 2010 survey, we found more than thirty African settlement workers, mostly women, working in a broad range of non-profit multicultural settlement organizations and schools in metro Vancouver. In addition, two African-focused settlement organizations provided targeted programming to immigrants and refugees (Creese 2011). One of these organizations no longer provides services, the other now does to people from many parts of the world.[11]

---

9 This was the only example we found of a women's network that focused on addressing an issue in the homeland.

10 In 2010 we estimated that 90 per cent of African immigrants in Vancouver identified as Christian. At that time we were unable to identify any mosques with a significant population of sub-Saharan Africans (Creese 2011).

11 Changes in government funding – moving away from ethno-specific organizations and mandating new partnerships between settlement agencies – made some smaller operations financially unsustainable. The Centre of Integration for African Immigrants closed in 2011. Umoja Operation Compassion Society continues to provide settlement services, but no longer focuses on sub-Saharan Africans. Umoja also has a dual-homeland focus, engaging in development work in Uganda and Tanzania.

Creating businesses that cater to the local community or that profile African heritage is another facet of community development. Although no doubt an underestimation of entrepreneurialism in the community, in metro Vancouver in 2010 there were at least eleven African restaurants, seven salons for hair and beauty products, and two specialty super markets, in addition to a handful of other home-based businesses (Creese 2011, 229). The African community has also become more visible at the cultural level. African dance companies, theatre, and storytelling groups have been created, as well as a francophone African radio program. By the early twenty-first century, African-focused peace festivals, music festivals, film and arts festivals, and soccer tournaments had all become part of the local cultural landscape (Creese 2011). Some of the latter spaces also foster links beyond the self-defined African community to connect with the larger Black diaspora in metro Vancouver.

The African community in metro Vancouver, through the diverse practices discussed above, encompasses informal support and formal organizations, with some oriented towards the homeland and many others concerned with homemaking in Canada. These activities of community building, most of which cross national and ethnic lines, emerge as members navigate their new home and come together to create new spaces of belonging. Not surprisingly, emphasis has been on issues affecting the first generation. Coming together in these ways challenges everyday racism and marginalization, demonstrates the resilience, resourcefulness, and contributions of community members, and raises the African community's visibility in the wider society. Practices of community building are central to claiming spaces of belonging in the quest to be recognized as full members of the larger "imagined community" and not treated as perpetual strangers. Thus the first generation is actively creating a pan-African community in metro Vancouver, although belonging in Canada remains precarious and contested.

Parents look to the future hoping that their children will be accepted more fully as Canadians, face fewer challenges, but still maintain their African identity. Higher education is a critical part of these dreams for their offspring, yet the tensions involved in raising youngsters across, between, and within diverse African and Canadian cultures lead to significant challenges in maintaining their African heritage. I argue that the first generation's fear that their children will forget their African heritage has not materialized, but their dream that the next generation will be fully accepted and treated equally as Canadians has not been realized either.

Second-Generation African-Canadians

Previous research on 1.5- and second-generation African-Canadians has addressed three main issues: challenges to integration, educational attainment, and negotiating identities. African immigrant and refugee youth who arrive in Vancouver face a range of obstacles, including high rates of underemployment and unemployment, anti-Black racism, and, for some, mental health issues resulting from spending time in refugee camps (Francis and Yan 2016). Yet services designed to tackle such issues are lacking, while mainstream youth programming also fails to address them. As Francis and Yan (2016, 95) note, "[i]t is the intersection of racism, immigration status, poverty, membership in a small and marginalized community, and social isolation that makes this group particularly vulnerable." The challenges their parents face in the labour market produce high rates of poverty, even for highly educated migrants, that in turn limit access to resources. As Zaami (2015) documents in the context of Ghanaian youth in Toronto, poverty also limits access to housing, resulting in spatial exclusion that in turn contributes to social isolation, which makes it more difficult to find employment and access services. In addition, social isolation of parents affects the well-being and resilience of their children (Beiser et al. 2011).

The link between education and employment is well documented. Access to education is a particular concern for refugee youth, who often spend years in camps with little access to formal education. Once in Vancouver, they find few supports to address psychological trauma or education gaps, are placed in grades based on their age, rather than on their academic preparation, and must leave the public education system when they turn nineteen (Francis and Yan 2016; Kanu 2008; Shakya et al. 2010; Wilkinson et al. 2012). As a result, a recent national study shows, refugee youth are nearly five times more likely than other immigrant youth to leave school before graduating, with the highest non-completion rates among males, those who arrived as older children, and those without prior education in English or French (Wilkinson et al. 2012).

Educational attainment is also shaped by the way discourses of Blackness affect the treatment of African-Canadian students. Institutional racism "is a trademark of mainstream schools in North America" (Shizha 2016, 196; see also Codjoe 2001). For young children in particular, "experience of discrimination and marginalization exerts a significant impact on their perception of themselves" (Roberts-Fiati 1996, 69). Black students from English-speaking backgrounds, including Africa and the Caribbean, are often placed in English as a second language (ESL) or dialect classes they do not need (Amin 2006). Conroy's (2013) study of young Black men shows they are overrepresented in special education classes, believe their teachers think they are unintelligent and intimidating, and their misbehavior is more likely to end in suspension. As a result, young Black men are more likely to drop out of high school or have a "higher push-out rate" and, consequently, also a lower rate of university attendance (Conroy 2013, 177). An Ontario study of African-Canadians who did not graduate from high school argues, however, that leaving early might be a pragmatic solution to negative experiences in school: "[M]any of these drop-outs are, in fact, 'push-outs,' having been motivated to leave school prematurely by the structures of schooling which institutionalize racial inequality" (Dei et al. 1997, 243).

Creese, Kambere, and Masinda (2013) report that teenage African migrants in Vancouver complain about being placed in ESL programs, experiencing racism from peers, and being underestimated by teachers, and they identify gendered advocacy strategies that help them negotiate high school successfully. Boys focus largely on learning to "stand up" for themselves with their peers, while remaining "mellow" to avoid censure from those in authority and avoiding the "bad stuff" associated with partying. In contrast, girls focus more on standing up to their teachers' low expectations so they can pursue more challenging courses and attain academic success.

James (2012) argues that stereotypes about male Black youth construct African-Canadian males as "at-risk students" as a self-fulfilling prophecy. Stereotypes that such students are immigrants, fatherless, troublemakers, athletes, and academic underachievers marginalize Black male youth and "structure their learning process, social opportunities, life chances, and educational outcomes" (James 2012, 467). As a result, among 1.5- and second-generation African-Canadians, women are more likely than men to attend university (Okeke-Ihejirika and Spitzer 2005).

The educational trajectory of African-Canadian youth is also affected by media glorification of Black male athletes. "Media play a significant role in manufacturing, selling, and (in)forming the aspirations of young Canadian black male athletes" to the detriment of their academic potential (James 2016, 168, 2012). Black male high school athletes are encouraged to commit time to honing their athletic abilities in an effort to win athletic scholarships at American universities. The chances of succeeding are slim, and the cost is less attention to their academic performance, although more emphasis on school is actually much more likely to improve future opportunities. As James argues, this illusion persists even though African-Canadian youth have "a better chance of becoming a professor than a 'star athlete'" (2016, 165).

Education is highly valued by African immigrant parents, who see it as a "means of ensuring upward mobility" (Okeke-Ihejirika 2005, 212), and most strongly encourage their children to attend university (see also Adjei et al. 2017). The emphasis on education is double edged, however, because schools are central institutions for socializing young people into Canadian norms and values, and the latter sometimes conflict with African values promoted by their parents. Thus, parents also perceive the influence of schools, and peers their children meet at school, as a potential threat to their ability to raise their children properly as Africans (Creese 2011).

Research on how the second generation negotiates its identities suggests that African immigrant parents' concerns on this score are not misplaced. The second generation negotiates fluid and multiple identities at the same time, as African, as Canadian, and as Black; not surprisingly, their notion of an African identity is not the same as that of their parents (Okeke-Iherjirika and Spitzer 2005). African-Canadian youth often struggle with their identities, particularly during adolescence, and are strongly influenced by immersion in American hip hop culture as a dominant form of popular culture and representation of Blackness (Creese 2015; Forman 2001; Ibrahim 1999, 2003, 2006; Kelly 2004). As Richardson and Pough (2016, 129) argue, American "hip hop and Black popular culture are central to global youth culture." Although strongly influenced by discourses of Blackness in the United States, however, the second generation simultaneously negotiates its African identities as distinct from that of African Americans. As Ibrahim (2006, 56) notes, "African youth 'choose' Blackness through arduous, complex, and mostly subconscious processes of 'translation' and 'negotiation'; not in opposition to their African identities, but at the same time." For Ibrahim, this is a "third space" of cultural hybridity, wherein second-generation African-Canadians simultaneously perform African and Black identities. He notes that this third space is gendered, with female bodies subject to more rigid policing about how African and Black identities are performed (Ibrahim 2006). Parents' definition of proper African behaviour is also gendered, so that, for example, daughters are subject to more parental control as they carve out ways to be an "African good girl" in Canada (Okeke-Ihejirika and Spitzer 2005).

Most of the research on second-generation African-Canadians focuses on adolescents in high school. Surprisingly little examines the identities and experiences of second-generation adults. This study helps to fill that gap, drawing on qualitative interviews to explore what it is like to be a child of African immigrants growing up, and subsequently living as young adults, in metro Vancouver.

The Research Participants

This study is based on in-depth qualitative interviews with thirty-five young adults who went to high school in metro Vancouver and whose parents migrated from countries in sub-Saharan Africa. Participants were recruited through advertising in the *Afro News*, distributing flyers at churches, cultural organizations, dance clubs, and an African-focused settlement organization, posting notices on campus bulletin boards, and obtaining referrals from other research participants to create a diverse purposive sample. Interviews ranged from one and a half to three hours, with an average time of two hours. Participants were asked to reflect on their early childhood, high school years, and adulthood, as well as memories of arriving in Canada if they were born abroad. Participants were asked about education and employment, challenges and accomplishments, friendships, romantic relationships, relations with parents and siblings, personal goals, and how they negotiate their identities. Interviews were conducted between 2011 and 2013.[12] All names used to identify participants are pseudonyms chosen by the participant.

The parents of the research participants originate from twelve different countries: the DRC, Ethiopia, Ghana, Kenya, Liberia, Nigeria, Sierra Leone, Somalia, South Africa, Sudan, Togo, and Uganda (see Table 2.1). Almost half of participants' families (46 per cent) came through the government-assisted or sponsored refugee programs,[13] another 43 per cent applied to come to Canada through the immigration points system for skilled workers, 9 per cent (3) were born to Canadian mothers and African fathers,[14] and one participant came on her mother's graduate student visa and was waiting for permanent

---

12 I conducted two-thirds of the interviews, research assistant Veronica Fynn conducted the rest. As in all research projects, different levels of rapport developed with different interviewees, but I did not detect different patterns based on racialization of the interviewer. Candid conversations about racism, for example, occurred in almost all the interviews, whether with me, a White woman raised in Canada, or with Veronica, a Black woman and adult migrant from Liberia.

13 Like newcomers who are selected through the points system, government-assisted refugees are evaluated for their ability to integrate into Canada, with the result that many are also highly educated.

14 In two cases the parents met in Canada and in one case the parents met in Africa; all three were born in Canada.

Table 2.1. Characteristics of Research Participants

Participant	Age at Time of Interview	Ancestry	Canadian-Born or Age at Immigration
Women (pseudonym)			
Danielle	21	Kenya	born in Canada
Jane	24	Ghana	born in Canada
Ayad	23	Ethiopia	born in Canada
Jessica	22	Ghana	born in Canada
Claudia	36	South Africa	born in Canada
Ashley	21	Ghana	5 months
Shukre	24	Somalia	7 months
Sarah	22	Sudan	3
Denise	26	Uganda	5
Emily	33	Ethiopia	6
Betty	31	Ethiopia	7
Tina	20	Kenya	8
Joy	27	Kenya	11
Linda	19	Nigeria	12
Ali	29	Ghana	14
Markor	20	Ghana	16
Ayinke	19	Nigeria	16
Stella	28	Nigeria	16
Charlotte	23	DRC	17
Men (pseudonym)			
Hobbes	22	Togo	born in Canada
Rylan	23	Ghana	born in Canada
Kweku	19	Ghana	born in Canada
Bob	27	Ethiopia	born in Canada
Devon	28	Ethiopia	born in Canada
Luke	20	Uganda	5 months
Jay	23	Uganda	2
Lamar	24	Uganda	4
James	26	Uganda	6
Maxwell	28	Uganda	7
Michael	19	Nigeria	8
Terrence	26	Liberia	9
Peter	19	Liberia	10
Jack	21	Liberia	15
Forlan	24	Liberia	16
John	23	Sierra Leone	17

residency at the time of the interview[15] – that participant was also the only one among those not born in Canada to arrive without permanent

---

15 One research participant arrived in Vancouver when her mother was a graduate student at a local university. After graduation her mother got a job with a temporary

Table 2.2. Distribution of Research Participants by Canadian Birth or Age at Immigration

Born in Canada or Age at Immigration	Number of Participants	Percentage
Canadian-born	10	29
1 month–5 years	7	20
6–12	10	29
13–17	8	23

Table 2.3. Age Distribution of Research Participants

Age	Number of Participants	Percentage
19–24	23	66
25–29	9	26
30+	3	9

residency status in place. Eighty per cent of research participants (28) identified as Christian, 9 per cent (3) as Muslim, and 11 per cent (4) as agnostic or atheist.

The research participants were fairly evenly divided by gender: 54 per cent were women and 46 per cent men.[16] All but one identified as heterosexual.[17] Almost one-third (29 per cent) were born in Canada; half migrated before they reached adolescence (20 per cent were five years old or younger and another 29 per cent were between six and twelve years old); and one-quarter (23 per cent) were teenagers when they migrated (see Table 2.2). At the time of the interviews, two-thirds (66 per cent) of participants were under age twenty-five, 26 per cent were between twenty-five and twenty-nine, and 9 per cent were in their thirties (see Table 2.3). The oldest, three women in their thirties, attended high school in the mid- to late 1990s; the youngest graduated from high school in 2010.

The majority of the parents of the research participants had a high level of education, with the highest degree most often attained before migrating to Canada. Eighty-six per cent of participants' fathers had a university degree, including 26 per cent with a master's or doctorate (Table 2.4), while 74 per cent of mothers

---

work permit and applied for permanent residency for the family. At the time of the interview, the family expected permanent residency very soon.

16 None of the research participants identified as trans, non-binary gender identity, or gender fluid.

17 One participant identified as bisexual.

Table 2.4. Education and Occupation of Research Participants' Fathers

Participant	Father's Education	Father's Occupation
Women:		
1	master's degree	self-employed
2	some university courses	small business owner
3	master's degree	planner
4	master's degree	church pastor
5	master's degree	unemployed (consultant)
6	bachelor's degree	labourer (truck driver, taxi driver, janitor)
7	bachelor's degree	pharmacist (in Africa)
8	bachelor's degree	retired CEO
9	medical doctor	medical researcher
10	PhD	government professional
11	PhD	pastor and college instructor
12	bachelor's degree	high school teacher
13	bachelor's degree	small business owner
14	law degree	church pastor and lawyer
15	bachelor's degree	unknown (deceased)
16	bachelor's degree	engineer
17	master's degree	manager
18	bachelor's degree	factory worker
19	high school	TV technician
Men:		
1	bachelor's degree	bus driver
2	some university courses	artist (in Africa)
3	bachelor's degree	construction worker
4	bachelor's degree	care aide
5	bachelor's degree	seaman (deceased)
6	unknown	unknown (deceased)
7	unknown	unknown (no contact)
8	bachelor's degree	accounting (deceased)
9	bachelor's degree	office supervisor
10	bachelor's degree	office supervisor
11	bachelor's degree	office supervisor
12	PhD	church pastor
13	bachelor's degree	small business owner
14	bachelor's degree	office supervisor
15	bachelor's degree	engineer
16	bachelor's degree	small business owner

had a university or college degree,[18] including 23 per cent with a graduate degree (Table 2.5). This pattern of well-educated parents

18 This includes three mothers who were trained as licensed practical nurses. In the Canadian system of higher education, licensed practical nursing is usually a two-year college degree, compared with a four-year university degree for a registered nurse.

Table 2.5. Education and Occupation of Research Participants' Mother

Participant	Mother's Education	Mother's Occupation
Women:		
1	dentistry degree	licensed practical nurse
2	bachelor's degree	small business owner
3	master' degree	elementary school teacher
4	licensed practical nurse	licensed practical nurse (deceased)
5	master's degree; PhD student	teaching assistant
6	registered nurse	registered nurse
7	care aide certificate	care aide
8	law degree	lawyer
9	registered nurse	registered nurse
10	PhD	small business owner
11	registered nurse	registered nurse
12	care aide certificate	care aide
13	registered nurse	registered nurse
14	master's degree	cleaner
15	support worker certificate	support worker
16	licensed practical nurse	licensed practical nurse
17	licensed practical nurse	licensed practical nurse
18	high school	homemaker
19	some college courses	actress
Men:		
1	registered nurse	registered nurse
2	some university courses	artist
3	bachelor's degree	clerical worker
4	some high school	retail clerk
5	high school; nursing student	nursing student (licensed practical nurse)
6	nursing degree	nurse (in Africa)
7	home support worker certificate	home support worker
8	bachelor's degree; registered nurse	registered nurse
9	master's degree	social worker
10	master's degree	social worker
11	master's degree	social worker
12	registered nurse	registered nurse
13	registered nurse	registered nurse
14	master's degree	social worker
15	nursing degree	homemaker
16	registered nurse	registered nurse

reflects the overall high levels of post-secondary training among immigrants to Canada as a result of the immigration points system. It is worth noting that this pattern was the same for families that came through the refugee system. Of the sixteen participants whose

families arrived this way,[19] fourteen reported that their father had a
university degree, while the other two did not know their father's
history; thirteen (81 per cent) also reported that their mother held
a university or college degree. So, while those participants whose
families had to flee their countries of origin faced additional challenges, including the trauma associated with seeking refuge, they
also grew up in families that were middle or upper class and relatively affluent before migrating, and where post-secondary education is highly valued and encouraged.

In a pattern that replicates trends documented elsewhere (Creese
2011), this high level of post-secondary education often does not
translate into jobs that require such credentials, and when it does
it is almost always a result of further training within Canada or the
United States. Those who work as professionals – engineers, plan-
ners, teachers, lawyers, or nurses (and fully 40 per cent of mothers are
nurses) – attained more education locally, in some cases completely
redoing their training in order to attain professional accreditation in
Canada (see Tables 2.4 and 2.5).[20] Some parents became self-employed
or started small businesses rather than retrain, and some with university degrees became less-skilled bus drivers, construction, or factory
workers, or retrained as aides and home support workers. For most,
then, migration marked a downward class shift to a less-affluent lifestyle, with less-skilled and lower-status jobs than their families had
known in Africa.

This conjuncture of highly educated and professional/middle- or
upper-class parental backgrounds and reduced social status and occupational attainment in Canada makes it more challenging to think
about how class intersects with racialization for the second generation. On the one hand, downward mobility of the first generation is
a class outcome of racialization and migration processes in Canada.
Most research participants grew up, at least during their early years in

---

19   The sixteen participants whose parents came through the refugee system were
     Betty, Shukre, Charlotte, Emily, Terrence, Jack, Forlan, Lamar, Denise, Luke, Jay,
     Ayad, James, Bob, Maxwell, and Devon. In a few cases, parents were international
     students in Canada when conditions in their home country deteriorated, and they
     applied for refugee status from within Canada. In most cases, however, participants'
     families were forced into exile and attained refugee status through the United
     Nations High Commission for Refugees before coming to Canada.
20   In order to preserve the anonymity of the research participants, pseudonyms have
     been omitted from the tables providing information about parents' education and
     occupation.

Vancouver, with working-class parents who struggled financially, often performing "survival jobs" while retraining for something better in the future. A minority of research participants – those whose parents came with North American university education and hold higher-status professional jobs in Canada – grew up in a middle-class environment. At the same time, regardless of present class location, parents espoused the middle- or upper-class cultural capital linked to their pre-migration lives. Some second-generation participants also had memories of that affluence, enjoying impressive homes, servants, and other forms of privileged consumption before migration. Class dynamics, therefore, are complex and multidimensional, and should not be deduced just from limited financial resources.

One limitation of this research is the inability to recruit participants who had not completed high school and/or had not gone on to pursue any kind of post-secondary education. Some participants mentioned siblings or friends who had dropped (or been pushed) out of school before graduation; others mentioned siblings or friends who began working in low-skilled jobs right after high school and showed no interest in pursuing further education. Participants were asked to reach out to these potential interviewees, and many provided e-mail addresses that we could follow up. Unfortunately, however, we were unable to recruit any adults in the second generation who had not completed high school. Moreover, everyone interviewed had taken at least one post-secondary course.[21] This means that the voices of an important segment of the second generation are not reflected here, except as observed through friends and siblings who followed a path to post-secondary education.

In light of the age distribution of participants, it might not be surprising that at the time of the interviews most were enrolled in post-secondary programs. Fifty-seven per cent were post-secondary students, all but two in programs that would lead to a university degree.[22] Four

---

21 This study is not intended to be a representative sample of African-Canadian youth. As already noted, some members of the second generation do not complete high school and some high school graduates do not continue on to post-secondary education. Unfortunately, statistics on high school completion and higher education in British Columbia are not available by visible minority status or ethnicity.

22 Two students were enrolled in college certificates that are not transferable to a four-year university degree (resident care aid and early childhood education); three were enrolled in two-year college diploma programs that can be transferred to university programs, and fifteen were enrolled in university.

Table 2.6. Highest Level of Education Attained by Research Participants

Highest Level of Education	Number of Participants	Percentage
Enrolled in college/ university program	20	57
Some post-secondary courses (no credential attained and not a student)	1	3
College diploma/certificate	4	11
Bachelor's degree	8	23
Master's degree	2	6

participants (11 per cent) had attained a specialized diploma or technical certificate from a community college, 23 per cent had a bachelor's degree, and 6 per cent had a master's degree (see Table 2.6). More women (58 per cent) than men (56 per cent) were current students, and more women (36 per cent) than men (12 per cent) already had at least one university degree. In contrast, more men had completed a shorter, more technically focused college diploma (19 per cent versus 5 per cent) or had taken courses that had not resulted in a certificate or degree (3 per cent versus none). Some of these differences might be connected to the older mean age of women participants (24.6 years) than of men (22.1 years). It is also the case that a significant number of men had sports scholarships, which help to pay tuition but could result in their taking fewer courses and making slower progress through academic programs.[23]

The pattern of post-secondary education was fairly similar among those with and without a refugee background. Forty-four per cent of participants with a refugee background had already attained a university degree, so fewer were current students (38 per cent) (see Table 2.7). This includes five of the six women and two of the ten men whose families came through the refugee system; in addition, two men had technically focused college diplomas, and five men and one woman were post-secondary students. This level of post-secondary education is somewhat surprising, since the literature suggests that refugee youth – particularly refugee men from sub-Saharan Africa – face additional barriers to pursuing post-secondary education in Canada (Wilkinson et al. 2012).

---

23 In all, six men and one woman attained sports scholarships that helped pay their way through college or university (four for soccer and one each for basketball, track and field, and wrestling).

Table 2.7. Highest Level of Education Attained by Research Participants with a Refugee Background

Highest Level of Education	Number of Participants	Percentage
Enrolled in college/ university program	6	38
Some post-secondary courses (no credential attained and not a student)	1	6
College diploma/certificate	2	12
Bachelor's degree	6	38
Master's degree	1	6

Table 2.8. Current Employment of Research Participants

Current Employment	Number of Participants	Percentage
Not employed (students)	7	20
Low skilled	10	29
Semi skilled	12	34
Highly skilled/professional*	6	17

*Jobs for which university training is a requirement.

Two people who already had a master's degree were currently employed in professional fields (in planning and as a post-secondary instructor), as were four with a bachelor's degree (in nursing, social sciences, and business). Altogether, 17 per cent of participants were employed in professional fields related to their degree (Table 2.8). One-third of participants were working in semi-professional fields where specific six-month to two-year post-secondary credentials are required (for example, carpenter, technician, care aid, health care administrative assistant, and licensed practical nurse) or where post-secondary training provides access to entry-level jobs (research assistant, finance, youth worker, and clinical assistant). Nearly thirty per cent were in lower-skilled employment that did not require more than a high school education (including in retail stores, a gym, a warehouse, tutoring, music lessons, a dance troupe, and movie extra).[24] Almost all of the

---

24 The participant who worked in the movie industry explained that many film and TV shows shot in Vancouver are actually set in the United States, where one might expect Black men and women to be visible. He was in such demand that he sometimes had more work opportunities than he could combine with his course schedule.

latter were currently also enrolled in a post-secondary program. In addition, 20 per cent were not employed while they were full-time students. Many research participants, including some of those who had already earned a college diploma or bachelor's degree, had plans to continue their education in the quest for better career opportunities in the future.

In summary, these second-generation research participants were a highly motivated, well-educated group of young adults from diverse sub-Saharan African backgrounds. They all went to high school in metro Vancouver, and all had parents who were raised in Africa and migrated to Canada as adults. Hence, they negotiated multiple sets of expectations from their parents, school, and peers that were sometimes at odds. They grew up with parents who were well educated, although their African credentials were not recognized in Canada and, for most families, downward mobility meant a less-affluent lifestyle than they had in Africa. In addition, they shared the common experience of being racialized as Black[25] in a city where they form a very small and hyper-visible minority. In the next chapter I explore what it is like to grow up in a neighbourhood where "no one looked like me," and consider how experiences vary by gender and age of arrival in Canada.

---

25 The three participants of mixed heritage all had a White Canadian mother and Black/African father. As discussed in Chapter 8, all three were identified as Black by non-Africans, although not always by everyone in the African community.

Chapter Three

"No one looked like me": Remembering Migration and Early Childhood

It was a bit culture shock. Like, no one looked like me. I was surrounded by White people.

– Denise

The children of immigrant parents navigate a complex environment across different sets of cultural norms and expectations. Families are central agents of socialization for all youngsters, particularly so in contexts of migration where parents play an even more critical role in transmitting cultural knowledge and heritage to their offspring (Costigan and So 2018; Kebede 2017). Peers constitute another important influence on young people, especially during adolescence, as they strive to form friendships, find ways to "fit in," and develop a sense of belonging in the wider community (Wilson-Forsberg 2018). Schools are also critical sites of socialization, both as spaces where peers interact and friendships form and through a curriculum that reinforces norms and values of the dominant society, including an emphasis on "nurturing of individual uniqueness" (Nunes 2018, 152). Beyond the official curriculum, Canadian schools also inculcate children in the "hidden curriculum" that reinforces neo-liberalism, Eurocentrism, and White privilege, even while advocating for multiculturalism and equality (Henry and Tator 2009). As several scholars have documented, anti-Black discrimination in particular has long been a feature of Canadian schools (Brathwaite and James 1996; Codjoe 2001; Dei et al. 1997; Ibrahim and Abdi 2016a; James 2012, 2018).

In addition to navigating the multiple and often competing influences that all children of immigrant parents encounter, those in Vancouver's African community grow up in an environment where they are part of a very small yet hypervisible minority of people racialized as Black and of sub-Saharan African heritage. As such, they navigate neighbourhoods in which they are often the only Black children, where they seldom encounter people outside of family members who look like them. At the same time, they are immersed in ubiquitous representations of Blackness in popular culture, representations that have no meaningful reference to their families' cultural heritage. Whether Canadian born or arriving in Canada during childhood, learning to be African-Canadian in this context is bound up with these processes of racialization that generate both high visibility as Black and invisibility as Africans.

In this book I use the term second generation to include those who are born in the country of settlement and those who migrate as children, sometimes also called the 1.5-generation (Rumbaut 2004, 2012). Research participants who were born in or grew up in metro Vancouver from the time they were of preschool age – nearly half of the people in this study – had only ever really known Canada as their "homeland." For these members of the second generation, memories of migration were mostly embedded in family narratives, although these narratives might still have been powerful anchors for identity, but their experience of growing up was fully located in Vancouver. In contrast, those who arrived as school-age children usually had distinct memories of dislocation from their first homeland and of learning to navigate their new home. In this chapter, I consider differences between these two groups, bearing in mind that all the participants negotiated multiple and often competing expectations as they navigated their places as Canadians and as part of the local African diaspora. As we will see, there are more similarities than differences in their experiences.

I begin by exploring issues of migration and adaptation to life in Canada for the 1.5 generation – those born outside Canada and old enough to remember the transition – paying attention to differences based on age at arrival and the experiences of those who came through the refugee system. Research on the second generation often stresses tensions between parents and immigrant children in the context of migration – as we saw in Chapter 2, tensions over values and behaviour are central to parents' anxieties. From the vantage point of early adulthood, however, the participants in this study highlighted their family as a source of support and resilience as they navigated competing influences. I then explore participants' memories as young children growing up in Vancouver with African parents, including when they first noticed their "difference" from other children. Finally, I address their experiences in elementary school, including friendships with peers, and general issues involved in growing up as one of the few Black and African children in their neighbourhood. Whether Canadian born or migrating as children, all participants navigated their racialized difference from the majority of their peers in elementary school. Moreover, friendships with peers showed distinct gendered patterns from an early age, with boys usually finding it easy to make friends and many girls experiencing long periods of isolation. I address the complex gendered and racialized dynamics of adolescence in high school in Chapter 4.

Migration and Transitions

TERRENCE: It was cold. That was, it was cold, and the cultural difference. Obviously, I would say there weren't that many Black people, obviously that was different to me, seeing different skin colour people. But besides that adapting was really kind of easy. It was an easy transition. I mean the language barrier, [the] so-called "your accent." Everyone basically knows you are not born in Canada. But besides that, it wasn't really difficult I would say … Coming to Canada was obviously was just our family. So it was my mother, my father, my sister. And we knew no one else here so it was just us. Whereas, in Sierra Leone, even though it was not our country, we still had other family members with us in the refugee camp, lots of family and friends. So it was a bit different at first, yes.

TINA: It was such a shock financially as well because we went from a place where you know we were quite well situated, to a place where my mom couldn't work and my brother was already born, he was two months when we came to Canada, so she had to be a house mother and she's not a housewife at all. She hated that. The first two years were definitely dark for my mom and in a way a lot of things I internalized because of it, because my mom was having her own issues with coping. It was much harder for her. She came when she was thirty-two. I came when I was eight so it was very easy. Much easier for me. So financially it was a big shock. Socially it was a big shock as well because I went into a Catholic school for the first time when I first came in … Also I was definitely ostracized through, not bullying per se, but pure ignorance, I suppose, from children my age.

As Terrence and Tina suggested, research participants who migrated to Canada in early childhood and before adolescence (Terrence at nine and Tina at eight), experienced a keen sense of dislocation when they first arrived. Common narratives focused on various kinds of "shock," including climactic, cultural, social, and financial. Many participants, like Terrence, had vivid memories of their first winter, and not surprisingly it took time to learn how to dress appropriately for the cold and rain and to acclimatize bodies used to a warmer environment. This task was more difficult for families without a support network in place and for those with limited financial resources who had more difficulty acquiring appropriate winter clothing.

Culture shock takes many different forms, and often spending extended time in the new home is the only remedy. All participants who remembered arriving in Vancouver experienced the shock of transitioning from being invisible as part of a racialized majority, to suddenly looking different from everyone else. As Terrence noted, "there weren't that many Black people." He also identified language barriers, accents, and the absence of extended family and friends as key challenges during the transition to life in Canada. Tina added concerns about the financial shock of downward mobility and class dislocation, the social shock and "ostracism" at her new school, and living with the consequences of her mother's difficult adjustment. These are all themes about the transitions associated with migration that recur in other interviews. At the same time, both Terrence and Tina said it was "an easy transition." For Terrence, coming to Canada meant security after living in a refugee camp, while Tina reflected on her mother's more difficult adjustment, and observed that it is easier for a child to adapt than for an adult.

In contrast to Terence and Tina, most research participants who came as pre-adolescent children remembered their move to Vancouver as a difficult transition. Peter arrived when he was ten years old and Betty came at age seven; both remembered the disorientation of not knowing how to do everyday things and not being able to communicate with others:

PETER: It's really hard. You know, for the first bit, it's hard. Because your English is bad and you don't know how things are, like in Canada how to move around. Like when we came here, we didn't know how [to take] SkyTrain or buses or anything. All we did was walk to a place, all walking. Just to stop and ask somebody, it's really tough, because if I'm talking in my African English, they are like "what are you talking about?" I'm like, "you don't understand me?" They are like, "no." They just look at you. OK, never mind. Just walk away.

BETTY: I think the hardest years were elementary, interestingly, which was understandable. Even expressing yourself by trying to figure out, do I speak now? What do I say? Is it appropriate? I was afraid. I was a quiet girl growing up, and most people were sort of surprised. I never talked at all, I don't even think, because I was shy. I just didn't know what to say. I was just observing, and I think that really helped me when I grew up ... when you start looking around and start talking, you kind of get some of the nuances, the cultural differences, and things like that.

Learning the "nuances, the cultural differences" (Betty) of her new home and modifying "my African English" (Peter) would take time. Over time, those who arrived prior to adolescence learned to speak English with a local Canadian accent and adopt other colloquial forms of expression that were largely indistinguishable from those of their peers. In the short term, however, several research participants recalled a period of isolation and relative silence when they first arrived as they all but gave up trying to communicate with anyone outside their family. As Denise commented, for example, the move to Canada as a five-year-old affected her so profoundly that it changed her personality:

DENISE: I went from being an outgoing, playing-with-everyone type of child to being a quiet, didn't-talk-to-anyone type of child. Not because I couldn't speak the language, I just didn't talk to anyone.

Michael arrived at age eight. He recalled a difficult adjustment to the downward class situation of his family. Having to share a house with another family was distressing, and he could not understand why his parents were unable to continue in their previous occupations. Indeed, his mother never returned to work after migrating to Canada. Like Denise, Michael reflected on how migration produced social isolation, and that made him a more introverted child:

MICHAEL: I honestly didn't know that there was such thing as a transition. I thought that my dad would just continue doing his [work for] Lufthansa here, my mother would continue being a nurse here, and we would just be fine. It was really confusing ... I had no idea how to do anything socially ... I just felt so out of it, like whatever I do people would look and just like "what are you" or [other] things. I would say I think that turned [me] into somewhat of an introvert.

Although Tina characterized her transition as "easy" in comparison to her mom, she also recalled significant social isolation for the first two years, a time when she did not talk to other people. After two years, she began making more of an effort to communicate as part of an attempt to become as Canadian as possible. In the process, she stopped identifying as Kenyan, and soon lost the ability to speak her first language:

> TINA: At the beginning I was definitely shell-shocked but eventually I just started, I knew where I was. I knew I wasn't being very exuberant so especially at the end of grade 5 and grade 6, I just started forcing myself to talk to people to engage in conversation of any type ... Another thing – unfortunately I'm very embarrassed about this – is not speaking Swahili or just not making myself known as a Kenyan, as an African, trying to get the Canadian accent.
> RESEARCHER: So, you were choosing not to speak Swahili?
> TINA: Yes. In fact, by the time I was ten I hardly knew any.

As we will see more later in this chapter, for many participants isolation led to withdrawing further from interpersonal contact, which had a significant effect on their adjusting to school and forming friendships with peers.

Those who arrived in their teenage years faced many of the same challenges as they adjusted to a new home in Vancouver. Acquiring a new language and/or a new English accent, learning local cultural capital, and in some cases making up for lost years of schooling while residing in refugee camps, all made transitions to a new home more complex for teenage migrants (Francis and Yan 2016; Kanu 2008). As noted in Chapter 2, all the participants in this research project were high school graduates who went on to pursue some form of post-secondary education, so the experiences of teen migrants who faced greater challenges and were less able to do well in the Canadian high school system are not reflected here.

Compared to younger children, older children have a more developed sense of their own identity, grounded in greater maturity and more years of socialization within their family and community prior to migration that can help them weather the challenges they face. On the other hand, adolescence is a time when the influence of peers and popular culture is strongest, so tensions between some African and Canadian cultural expectations might be heightened. Already internalizing expectations about how students ought to behave in their home countries, some research participants expressed culture shock about the behaviour of many of their peers. For example, Stella and Markor, both of whom came to Canada at age sixteen, reflected on the very different atmosphere in school that made it hard to relate to their peers:

> MARKOR: When I came here I got cultural shock, which lasted maybe one and a half years ... And [name of school] was not a good school for an immigrant – like someone who just came in – because it was a

lot of drugs, a lot of swearing, a lot of fighting and stuff like that which I wasn't used to because in Ghana it's just friendly with occasional fights ... And we usually address our teachers by their last name. So, when I heard a student called a teacher by her first name and he was kind of rude to her, I said "wow, that's new." It was really shocking.

STELLA: Sitting in class, sometimes you like to chat before the teacher comes, or when you want to ask questions some people even ignore you. They have cliques, the popular kids, the girls. It was really hard. No friends, no form of community. You're here in the house, nobody comes out of that house, which is completely different ... [At home] you can't get bored. All you need to do is just stand outside and definitely in ten minutes you're laughing or chatting [with someone].

INTERVIEWER: So what did you do to deal with it?

STELLA: I just put on a face, I can do it. Two more years, I can get through this. We'll get through this. I have no choice. I just focused on my studies, practically I just focused on my studies, study hard, got good grades.

Both Markor and Stella responded to this new environment by focusing on their academic performance and not trying to form friendships with their peers. In contrast Forlan, who also arrived when he was sixteen, remembered being "scared and lonely" for the first month or so, but soon found local students interested in him and "friendly":

FORLAN: When I came here, I don't know nobody and I'm not used to associate myself with other colour people, like White people, Brown people, so I was kind of scared and lonely for a while. But back home I had everybody, so that was a big difference when I came here. I was really sad at first, in the first month. But seriously, to be frank, people over here, like the students, were friendly, you know, they come up to you and ask you "where are you from?" Even though some people look at you strangely.

As I discuss in Chapter 4, there was a clear gender dynamic at play rooted in representations of Blackness in popular culture, with the result that African-Canadian teenage boys were befriended by their peers and treated as special, while girls were more likely to be ignored and isolated at school.

Participants who were teen migrants from refugee backgrounds were more likely to focus on new opportunities presented, rather than challenges experienced. Already once removed from their home country in traumatic circumstances, and often spending time in refugee camps before coming to Canada, these participants appreciated finding greater security in their new home. Charlotte, for example, compared the hard life her family experienced as refugees in Kenya to the greater comfort, access to food, and other resources more readily available in Canada:

> CHARLOTTE: I guess it was more comforting in Canada. I mean, you always say you miss home, sure you miss it, but life here is more comfortable. In Canada even when you are hungry you wouldn't, like, can't go to sleep not having food because there's food banks and all that stuff. Because when we came here we didn't know anything but the ISS [settlement agency] people helped show us things that we can do. So I think Canada is good. I mean you can go hungry in Kenya. If my mom couldn't find anything, there's nothing you can do. What you have to eat is just porridge with salt and that's it. So here in Canada it is much better.

Forlan concentrated on the personal opportunities he perceived in Canada: "the first thing I saw is opportunity." He appreciated access to career counsellors in high school and the availability of student loans to help him pursue post-secondary education as soon as he graduated from high school. Jack focused on greater safety in Canada compared to his time as a refugee in Ghana, asserting that, despite the challenges he faced, overall "it feels good growing up here":

> JACK: It's pretty good. It feels good growing up here because comparing the environment over here with the environment over there [in Ghana] it is very different … Here, the atmosphere is more safe.

Charlotte, Forlan, and Jack were between fifteen and seventeen years old when they arrived in Vancouver. Perhaps not surprisingly, their backgrounds as refugees generated a more mature frame of reference to reflect on the transition to their new home, with an emphasis on the expansion of safety and personal opportunities.

Research participants drew on a variety of strategies and resources to help them navigate their new environment. Some of these strategies included focusing on schoolwork and paying close attention to local ways of doing things in order to develop local cultural capital and a Canadian-English accent as quickly as possible. In addition, Denise kept a journal as a way to work through her experiences:

> DENISE: For a long time I kept a journal and everything that I was thinking or wanted to say to people but couldn't say, either because I didn't have the courage or it wasn't appropriate to say, I would write down in my journal.

Some drew on resources provided for integrating immigrant families, including programs for children and youth. For example, Jack attended a program twice a week where he got to know other teenagers from diverse immigrant backgrounds, and after a year he was asked to help as a volunteer to support other newcomers. Other participants mentioned meeting families who would become key support for their own parents. For example, Maxwell remembered a school friend he made early on whose parents befriended his own and helped them navigate the local school system, and later a tutor whose parents helped with legal advice.

Almost all participants discussed the strength they drew from their family during the transition to life in Vancouver. Both Shukre and Charlotte pointed to the advantages of having a large family with many siblings, something other Canadians were more likely to see as undesirable. As Shukre[1] noted, her family's isolation brought them closer together, particularly since her brothers and sisters were her only playmates in elementary school:

> SHUKRE: We were the only Black folks living in a community that was mostly entirely White. I think it forced my family to become much more insular than it had been previously … It was seen as kind of a negative thing that my mom had so many kids. But I don't think they realized, because we were already so isolated, we could be more insular because there were so many of us. We would go to a school and at any given point in time I had four siblings in school with me, you know? Which meant we could play together, we could hang out together.

Charlotte saw her family as a counterpoint to school. School might be alienating, but things were always better when she was with her mother and siblings. Like many other participants, Charlotte turned to her family for support whenever things got tough: "when you find something difficult, you know there will be someone there to like pull you up."

Almost all research participants discussed how important their parents' advice and support had been for helping them navigate

---

1 Shukre came to Canada at seven months old, but for the first four years she lived with her extended family in a largely Somali environment in Toronto. These reflections about the importance of a large insular family were in the context of her move to Vancouver at age five, now only with her mother and siblings, and of experiencing dislocation and isolation similar to those who first arrive in Canada.

their new lives in Canada, especially the potential pitfalls of adolescence.[2] This support ranged from advice about the significance of doing well in school to ensure a bright future to how to choose friends wisely, the importance of perseverance in the face of adversity, making do with what you have, and raising strong, independent children:

> PETER: That's what my parents told me, because when I came here they were like, "you got to study, you got to adapt to the kids here. Don't follow the bad friends. Take the good friends and follow them. And speak what they speak." And that's what I did. Followed my good friends, you see now I'm a grad and I'm in college because I followed the good friends but not the bad ones.
>
> JACK: Most of my life, my childhood life, I spent with my mom ... She was just trying her best to be a good mother. Working, if she's not working she's looking around to find something just to keep me alive and to keep me on track for my future.
>
> DENISE: I just remember my dad would say life is not going to be easy, life is never easy. You have to work hard for anything that you have and just because you are having a bad day it doesn't mean you let it get you down and stop you from moving ahead. You've just got to move forward.
>
> SHUKRE: My mother, a single mom raising six kids and was constantly working, was constantly, like just constantly. She did some amazing stuff. She was raising six kids, we never one day didn't have food ... She was like, "get it done." Do whatever you have to do to process it, but go. You got to do it. Who else? I think a big part of it is if you don't do it, who else is going to do it for you? And a big part of that was the independence piece.

From their vantage point as young adults, many participants expressed an ongoing appreciation of their current relationships with their

---

2 There were two exceptions. One participant migrated to Canada with his father and stepmother, and discussed at length how abusive his stepmother was towards him, especially after his father died. Another participant fled with his aunt to a refugee camp, and later to Canada, while his mother remained in his country of origin. He recognized that his aunt was an immense support in his life and for all intents and purposes had become his mother. Six participants had limited contact with fathers who, variously, died when they were very young, never came to Canada, or returned to Africa after a few years. These participants all focused on the support they received from their mothers or, in the case noted above, an aunt.

parents. For example, Markor continued to consult her parents about all major life decisions:

> MARKOR: Before I do anything I consult my dad because I think he's the wisest person I've ever known. He's really educated and he has a lot of knowledge about the world and he's experienced a lot of things. So I just like to see how he feels about something before I actually do it. And my mom, she's really supportive with everything. She's just, she does what a mom is supposed to do kind of thing. And she works so hard, so hard … I look up to her.

Linda similarly saw her parents as role models and as friends:

> LINDA: My dad, I admire him … Once you make up your mind, he'll support you all the way. When you haven't made up your mind, he will try to give you options, but once you've made up your mind to go to school … he's all the way for you no matter what … My mom, she's not my mom, she's like my friend, right?

Many participants had supportive relationships with siblings as well. In some cases, older brothers or sisters acted as parental figures. For example, Lamar had three older brothers who provided support, advice, and discipline, especially when he was younger. He noted that, in the absence of a father he had not seen since preschool, "growing up, definitely my brothers, they were like the father figure to me." Other participants were the older siblings in their families. Ashley, for example, observed that she "practically raised" her much younger sister with whom she maintained a close, almost mother-daughter, relationship.

Some participants commented on how their birth order brought with it some pressure to be good role models in their families. Charlotte identified herself as a role model and mentor for her younger siblings:

> CHARLOTTE: When you get grades, I want to look at them. Even my mom doesn't have time to. I want to look and will talk about it. And we'll do homework together. And we ask, what do you want to do with your life? We'll talk about it and research about [it] and see if that's realistic or not.

Similarly, Rylan felt pressure to "set an example" for his younger siblings:

> RYLAN: Because I'm the oldest one my mom wants me to set an example for them and go to school … It's not that I have to, you know, I want to as well, right? I want the best for them as well.

Rylan was committed to getting a good education leading to a successful career, and expected to help his siblings financially so they could
also pursue post-secondary education.

Many in the 1.5 generation acknowledged that, in what they saw as
a traditional "African way," their parents were quite strict compared
to parents of their non-African peers. Almost all said that, growing
up, they were not allowed to sleep over at a friend's house, something many of their peers did. Visiting the homes of friends was also
restricted, although exceptions were sometimes made for African
friends whose parents attend the same church. On the whole, however, their parents feared what might happen to their children in other
people's homes:

> DENISE: I remember always thinking I was never allowed to do
> anything because after school I had to come home while my friends
> used to be able to go hang out at their friends' house or have
> sleepovers. I wasn't allowed to have sleepovers. I later asked my mom
> and she said it was because we were the only ones in our community,
> we don't know what's going to happen to you or how they are going
> to treat you when you go spend the night at someone else's house.
> So that I can understand, because she was scared of what would
> happen when I was there overnight. There was so many times I came
> home crying [because] I didn't think she'd want me to stay over at
> somebody's house.

Girls typically led more controlled lives than their brothers, the latter having more latitude to hang out with friends after school or on
weekends. Almost all the women recalled being expected to be at home
when they were not in school:

> BETTY: For us as girls we are, culturally we are at home, we are never …
> They [brothers] would go out but we won't be able to. We just never
> asked because it is not a question that you ask. I was at home or I was
> doing sports. So, I was involved in school. It would be a form of school,
> an extension of school. There is no going to the mall. Going to the mall
> was this dream of mine that just never happened. And so my brother
> would be able to.

Some participants also remembered parents using strong forms of
discipline to instil cultural values of respect and proper behaviour, and
this too was largely viewed as positive. As Terrence noted, "we were
disciplined very well, so there was little room for nonsense." Similarly,

Ayinke argued that she had a strong cultural foundation as a result of her parents' discipline:

> AYINKE: I'm saying I'm happy for my upbringing, learning to respect and, you know, knowing the difference between good or bad. My parents really did a good job teaching us even though it was a very hard way.

At the same time, some participants found it difficult to conform to their parents' narrow notion of appropriate behaviour, especially since it conflicted with expectations of their peers. As we will see later in this chapter, many participants remembered a clear division between family and church friends, and relationships developed in school. For example, Michael's strict religious upbringing resulted in his adopting a "double life" in elementary school, behaving one way with his peers and differently at home:

> MICHAEL: So, it also led me to lead like a double life. At home I would be like, "Oh, Amen," but at school I would be like, "OK let's just do everything, guys. Let's just go crazy."

This was a much more common pattern among boys than girls, and for other participants it was associated with high school. As noted earlier, boys typically had more opportunities for freedom outside school and, as we will see in Chapter 4, the prevalence of hip hop as an important part of youth culture raised the popularity of African-Canadian boys in ways that it did not for their sisters.

Navigating the Early Years

Research participants who were born in Canada or arrived so young that their memories of childhood were all centred in Canada, did not face the same range of issues growing up with parents from countries in sub-Saharan Africa. For the most part, issues of language, local accent, and attaining local cultural capital were not a concern, as they grew up around English Canadian accents and local popular culture, alongside other languages and cultural influences at home. Fitting in rather than standing out as different was, however, a consistent theme. For example, Danielle, who was born in Canada, noted that "I was often the only Black child at school, in my church ... I just wanted so badly to be like everyone else." Danielle remembered intentionally singing off-key in her school choir in an effort not to stand out. She also recalled a "love/hate" relationship with her Kenyan heritage similar to that expressed by Tina, whose integration strategy included refusing to speak Swahili:

> DANIELLE: It was a love/hate thing. I loved the big family gatherings, the people that you'd see all the time, and the friends, and just everybody that was your Auntie and Uncle, and you'd come and say "Hi." I love that atmosphere. But sometimes I was ashamed of it in a way. Like bringing my ethnic food to school, and somebody would be like, "What's that? Ugh!" The kind of the reactions that kids have to something that's new and different. It would kind of hurt me. And as a result, I sometimes didn't invite people over because I was embarrassed of what they might see or the way my family is.

A common theme in narratives of the Canadian born was that they really did not notice that they were "different" in any way until they went to school, and then things changed. Rather than before and after migration as a turning point, therefore, second-generation narratives often focused on before and after entering the school system. For example, for Ashley, making friends was not a problem when she was very young:

> ASHLEY: The funny thing is that because the neighbourhood that I lived in there were lots of kids who were Indian [South Asian], or growing up a lot of the kids were Indian, fewer White. I didn't have a problem going at the playground and playing with them. They didn't see differences like that. But the moment I went to school, that's when I observed the differences.

At school Ashley found it very difficult to make any friends, and was singled out and ridiculed for all the ways that she was "different" from her peers.

Canadian-born participants were just as likely to recall their parents being much stricter than those of their peers, with a strong focus on African values of respect and deference to elders. They might have resented this authority when they were younger, particularly during adolescence, but almost all appreciated it once they became adults:

> KWEKU: I just didn't always understand what my dad was doing especially, and the extent to which he was doing it. But now that I understand things more now, I respect them a lot more.

Jane, whose father is African but her mother is not, also remembered challenging her father's rules when she was growing up, and she still resented expectations that she should clean his house when she came to visit:

JANE: Basically, he really put rules on us, like respect your elders. That was a huge thing with my Dad ... I [still] do his work for him, do you know what I mean? Before I do my own.

The tension related to expectations to behave in traditional African ways was even stronger between Jane's brother and father, leading to their estrangement for several years and an uneasy relationship in adulthood. Yet Jane intended to raise her own children similar to the way her dad raised her, and critiqued the more permissive Canadian style of child rearing that she experienced with her mother:

JANE: I think I'll parent like my Dad parented. Well, not [that] extreme.
I mean, five-year-olds doing math homework after school. But yeah, I believe in a lot of the values I think North American kids have lost. They have too much power in families. And I think that, at least the way my Dad does it, you have to respect. That's how it should be.

Jay also recalled resisting his parents' strict rules when he was a teenager, but expected to raise his children the same way because he now believed that "discipline is probably the biggest thing" to give children a good foundation in life.

Whether born in Canada, arriving too young to remember another homeland, or coming as older children who navigated challenging periods of transition that could last for months or years, the children of African immigrant parents all negotiated across, between, and through their parents' cultural expectations and other, sometimes conflicting, influences within Canadian society. Their family provided critical support and resources to help weather these challenges. At the same time, the influence of mainstream Canadian culture and institutions, especially schools, popular culture, and relationships with peers, provided alternative expectations that could be a source of tension.

As discussed in Chapter 2, parenting is unsettled by migration since appropriate parenting strategies often do not translate well across different social and cultural environments. Expectations around authority, deference, and respect for elders, particularly fathers, are considered core values across African cultures, but these expectations collide with the more individualistic orientation and permissive child rearing common in Canada. This can make it hard for children to live up to parents' expectations of what it is to be African. It is therefore common for parents to question the "Africanness" of their own children and to lament that they fear "losing" their offspring in Canada (Creese 2011; Creese, Kambere, and Masinda 2013). For example, Jane recalled that, when her Ghanaian father disapproved of her behaviour, he called her "whitewashed," a pejorative term that suggests she was not as African as she should be.

Lack of fluency in their parents' ancestral language, a common problem in small immigrant communities, widens the gap between immigrant parents and their offspring and can also prevent deeper forms of cultural understanding. Language fluency, along with other "tests of ethnic authenticity" (Awokoya 2012), are used as a barometer of how African different members of the second generation really are. This was a common problem for members of the second generation who never learned their ancestral language, but it also affected some participants who arrived as older children. For example, Joy migrated from Kenya to Canada at age eleven, but her adult inability to speak the language of her childhood affected her claims to a Kenyan identity:

> JOY: It bothered me before because people who had come as an adult, they'd be like, "Oh, oh you're from Kenya!" Then they'd talk to me. And I'd say, I don't understand. Like, I understand what you're saying, but I can't speak it. Then they'd be like, "Oh," and they'd use that to be better than me. Like, "Oh, you're half-Kenyan" or something.

Immersion in Canadian culture, especially through the school system and relationships with non-African peers, also fostered ambivalence about participants' own "Africanness." Danielle, who was born in metro Vancouver, explained that her inability to speak her parents' ancestral language often made her feel she did not belong to the local African community of her parents, while being "the only Black child at school, in my church" made her stand out as different from other Canadians. As a result, she said, "I sometimes felt a little like I wasn't part of either world, the Canadian or African." Others, like Michael, quoted earlier, described themselves as living a "double life," with one personality at home and another at school. In the next section, I address key influences outside of family that shaped growing up African-Canadian in Vancouver, with a focus on influences during elementary school. In Chapter 4, I look at the specific dynamics of popular culture and representations of Blackness as adolescents navigated high school in metro Vancouver

Negotiating Schools and Friendship

Growing up where "no one looked like me" was a common reality for participants in this research. Denise, who was five years old when she arrived in Canada, vividly remembered her culture shock:

DENISE: When we got here it was a bit of culture shock. No one looked like me. I was surrounded by White people.

Most participants lived in neighbourhoods where they saw very few people who looked like them. For some, like Denise, this was a largely White environment. Other participants grew up in diverse Vancouver neighbourhoods where there were many people of colour, although mostly from the larger Chinese, South Asian, and Filipino ethnic communities, but still very few racialized as Black. These scenarios of being "the only Black kid in my class" (Maxwell) and "the only Black child at school" (Danielle) were so common that going to school alongside other children of African parents, or indeed anyone racialized as Black, was unusual. For example, Luke remembered that, for a few years in middle school, one of his closest friends was a boy of Jamaican origin. When his family moved and he changed schools, he and his brothers were again the only Black children in his school. Hobbes remembered one school friend whose family was from Ghana, and Terrence recalled another family from Somalia. Rylan remembered some African friends in his local soccer league. Claudia remembered a few other Black children with African-American parents. These examples are exceptions to the more common narrative of standing out. As Jane put it, "I'd pretty much grown up my entire time being the only Black person in my class."

The small size of the African community in metro Vancouver and its spatial dispersal throughout the region meant that parents had to put significant effort into developing connections with other African families. Most occurred in church, in informal gatherings with family friends, or at occasional cultural events hosted by the growing number of national and pan-African associations, discussed in Chapter 2. Regional soccer teams were another venue where some men remember forming friendships with other boys of African descent. For participants whose parents were active in the larger diasporic community, separate childhood friendships formed that cut along cultural and racialized lines, dividing non-African school friends from African family and church friends. For many participants this led to a split between two parts of their lives that rarely crossed paths. In church and through family friends, some participants gravitated towards friendships with other children of African immigrants, and these relationships were separate from any friendships developed at school:

BETTY: I had my Ethiopian church. My parents were devoted Christians, so we took part in all those things. We were the older kids in that church. So it was like this is the responsibility you had to connect to that community. And so with that group of community I had this weekend life. And then I had my school life from Monday to Friday.

ASHLEY: I think that was important because I didn't realize, for a lot of Africans, – a lot of immigrants, period – if they can't find the community in where they're living, church provides that. So at church I made friends with a lot of people who were Black, Caribbean, or whatever – different, you know – and it was fine.

DANIELLE: We were the only Black family in my area. We did have a lot of other African friends and family, and we often socialized with them, but it was kind of very separate. So I had church, and then I had school, and then I had my African friends.

KWEKU: I always had this separation, like school friends and church friends. Church friends are mostly Africans. And then school friends were Asians, Whites, Filipinos. In Catholic school, there's a lot of Filipinos there. And it was always divided for me, like church and school friends, and there was always this difference. Church friends were Black.

For the most part, however, even for those whose families were well connected within the local African diaspora, contact with Africans who were not family members was episodic, related to church events on Sundays or less-frequent get-togethers.

Only three participants identified as Muslim. They remembered the mosque as a place where they formed friendships with diverse Muslims, although not especially others from Africa because they were so few in number. Sarah commented that she made "friends from all backgrounds ... I mean, you walk into a mosque and it's like walking into the UN." Sarah also attended a Muslim elementary school that she described as "multicultural," and where she made friends with other students from a wide range of cultural and ethnic backgrounds. As a result, although her cultural heritage was Sudanese, she did not grow up in "a Sudanese Muslim" environment; instead, "I grew up experiencing a Western Islamic culture."

Some families, like Bob's and Ayad's, were not religious, so religious institutions played no role in building friendship and community networks. Moreover, like those of a few other participants, Bob's family did not seek connections with others from their homeland other than extended family members they sponsored to come to Canada. Bob said his parents hoped to avoid the politics they left behind, and instead they urged their children to integrate into the wider Canadian society. For all research participants, daily life growing up was characterized by standing out as African and Black in their neighbourhood and school.

One result of the small size and spatial dispersal of the African diaspora is the way the diversity of cultural origins in the African community is largely overshadowed by dominant discourses about Blackness. In the context of very small numbers, participants came to see differences between those who were Somali, Ugandan, Ghanaian, or Ethiopian, for example, as less meaningful in many respects than the local processes of racialization that highlight Blackness as an important identity. Along with learning to become Canadian in public spaces such as schools, the media, and popular culture, and African – or, more specifically, Ethiopian, Somali, Ugandan, and so on – at home, participants learned to navigate the process of "becoming Black" in Canada. As Awad Ibrahim describes so eloquently, his migration process from Sudan to Canada involved retranslating himself from diverse identity markers that made him who he was in Sudan to being Black in Canada: "As a continental African, I was not considered Black in Africa; other terms served to patch together my identity, such as *tall*, *Sudanese*, and *basketball player*. However, as a refugee in North America, my perception of self was altered in direct response to the social processes of racism and the historical representation of Blackness whereby the antecedent signifiers became secondary to my Blackness, and I retranslated myself: I became Black" (Ibrahim 1999, 354, italics in original).

This process of "becoming Black" has different dimensions for men and women and for adult migrants and their children. As Kusow (2006, 536) argues, Blackness, like other racialized identities, is situational and "culturally mediated." African immigrants "are already constructed, imagined, and positioned" through discourses of Blackness *even before they enter Canada* (Ibrahim 1999, 353). As I discuss in more detail in Chapter 4, these representations are highly gendered and, from the perspective of parents, largely negative. Adult migrants have well-established ethnic and national African identities that counter these discourses. Some in the 1.5 generation also maintain strong identities tied to their first homeland. Others align more with the second generation, which is more fully immersed in North American popular culture and local institutions that often undermine parents' positive imaginings about their African homeland.

Children are socialized as much through local institutions as by parents, yet these institutional influences might be alien to, and even resisted by, immigrant parents. Public schools reinforce mainstream Canadian values about individualism, personal freedom, self-expression, and equality rights discourse. The values of Western liberal individualism are reinforced through other social institutions as well, from the media to more coercive sites such as social workers, police, and the family law system. Valorizing individualism, however, clashes with more extended-family-centred African values. Discourse about children's rights is even more controversial among the local African diaspora, as it conflicts with beliefs about the value of strong parental authority and discipline. As one youth worker suggested, the result of these tensions is that "the school criticizes everything that [African] parents do ... You find the children start thinking that what we're being taught at home is not right" (Creese, Kambere, and Masinda 2013, 171). Subtle and overt messages about the superiority of Canadian norms and, by corollary, the inadequacy of African ways of doing things are a source of tension between parents and offspring, and can undermine strong African identities among the second generation. Even more troubling, "institutional racism and whiteness that sometimes operate as colour-blind policies, roles, practices and politics" within social work can result in reinterpreting African parenting styles, intended to foster resilience in the context of systemic racism, as "poor parenting," and result in the apprehension of children (Adjei et al. 2017, 21).

It is at school that the children of African immigrants form friendships with non-African peers and engage with the powerful influences of North American youth culture (Abdel-Shehid 2005; Ibrahim 1999; Kelly 1998, 2004). Indeed, negotiating relations with Canadian peers and youth culture might be more formative for identities than anything in the official school curriculum. Although these influences and the desire to fit in with peers typically are strongest in adolescence, negotiating relationships with peers is also a large part of the elementary school experience for younger children.

Research on immigrant children in culturally diverse schools shows that children are "overwhelmingly more likely to choose friends from their own ethnic or racial group rather than others" (Scholtz and Gilligan 2017, 173). In Ireland, for example, girls from immigrant backgrounds made friends with other girls from diverse immigrant backgrounds, but hardly ever formed friendships with girls defined as Irish. Even though the latter displayed positive feelings about migrants, their friendship groups seldom expanded to include girls of diverse cultural or ethnic backgrounds (ibid). Other researchers document how young children negotiate social status through peer group inclusion and exclusion by engaging in name calling, stereotyping, and other forms of racial discrimination (Devine, Kenny, and Macneela 2008).

Friendship dynamics in diverse cultural contexts are also gendered. Devine and Kelly (2006) show that, in an elementary school in Dublin, friendships among boys became more inter-ethnically diverse over the course of a year, largely as a result of interactions through sports.

In contrast, girls' friendships became more polarized over time, and the small number of "minority ethnic girls" in the class formed a "distinct cluster, separate from their majority ethnic peers" (135). Devine and Kelly argue that bonding among girls is related more to "girl talk" about fashion, appearance, and boys that tends to exclude girls from other cultural backgrounds. Other studies also find that girls' friendships revolve around "talking with friends about problems," while boys focus on friends "for diversion and activities" (Morrow 2006, 95). Children construct gendered identities through interactions with their peers, and actively police one another from a very young age; by elementary school, most children gravitate towards same-gender friendships (ibid).

For most participants in this research, memories of elementary school were bound up with reminiscences about friendships with peers. Those who always found it easy to make friends in school were more positive about their elementary school experience. Those who were isolated and ostracized by peers, often most pronounced in the early primary grades, found elementary school quite distressing. Some also recounted negative and racist experiences with teachers. For the most part, however, it was treatment by peers that set the stage for whether or not participants felt accepted or struggled to fit in. Although most participants relayed some instances of sporadic racist behaviour among peers, overall narratives of easy friendships versus significant isolation were also gendered, with more men recounting the former and more women fitting into the latter group.

Four research participants attended private religious schools in metro Vancouver: three were in private Catholic schools and one attended a private Muslim school.[3] The rest attended schools in the public system. Seven were enrolled in French immersion for at least part of their elementary school education.[4] French immersion is popular among middle-class and well-educated parents seeking an enriched curriculum, and it does not cater to students with special learning requirements

---

3 Private religious schools in British Columbia normally charge nominal additional fees and are attended by students from a wide range of socio-economic backgrounds. Elite private schools, on the other hand, charge tens of thousands of dollars per year and are out of reach of most families, including those of the research participants. One participant won a scholarship to attend an elite private school for the final two years of high school.

4 Four of those were in French immersion from kindergarten through grade 12, two transferred out of French immersion to the regular public system while still in elementary school, and another joined French immersion only in grade 6.

or needing ESL instruction. Thus there tend to be far fewer children of immigrants in French immersion programs. The majority of participants attended the regular English stream in neighbourhood public schools, some in very diverse neighbourhoods with a high proportion of children of immigrants, and others in schools with few immigrants and a mostly White population.

Some participants remembered a diverse group of friends in elementary school, including other children of immigrants. This was a common scenario for second-generation men, most of whom found it easy to fit in with their peers. Hobbes, Bob, and Rylan were all born in Canada, made friends easily, and remembered being largely unaware of their racialized "difference" in elementary school. Although Bob lived in an overwhelmingly White, middle-class neighbourhood, and so most of his friends were White, Hobbes and Rylan grew up in more diverse, working-class neighbourhoods, and had friends from a wide variety of backgrounds:

> HOBBES: [Vancouver was a] great place to grow up ... I went to [name of] Elementary, I had a very diverse group of friends. I mean I didn't really see colour. Well, yeah. I remember wanting to have straight hair, I didn't even like, you know, some of the dyed hockey players, partly white, but I didn't really see it as a colour thing. I just saw it as, oh yeah, he's got cool hair. But there were very few Black-African, African-American role models at that time that I identified with. But yeah it was a great upbringing. I mean very multi-cultural, very diverse, and my group of friends was very diverse.
>
> BOB: I had a tight group of four [White] male friends, and we were super tight and that was great ... So growing up, I don't know, I think I was pretty naive. I was blissfully ignorant and I really enjoyed that. But every once in a while, things would come up. I don't think I understood a lot about racism or if there was any problem. I just didn't get it because I didn't really see myself as part of the Black or immigrant experience. I just saw myself as being Bob and my family is from Ethiopia and we eat Ethiopian food.
>
> RYLAN: I had some African friends at school. I had Chinese. I had Vietnamese. I had, you know, Caucasians, so it was pretty much like a mix ... A lot of my friends from elementary school played together in the same [soccer] league ... I think actually sport was a big thing, a big contributing factor to how we got closer.

Sports were identified as a venue to develop close friendships in many men's narratives. This was the case not only for the second generation, but also for some of the 1.5 generation who migrated to Canada while in elementary school. More than half the male participants who attended elementary school in Vancouver identified sports as a bridge to friendship, whether through organized teams or more informal games on the playground. As Rylan said, sports were an important way to bring people together from different backgrounds and to forge common bonds:

> RYLAN: It was a lot of different people, you came from different backgrounds. Sport kind of brought us all together, and we were all on the same team, had to work together, so it didn't matter how things were going on at school or how things are going, whether people were struggling. You know some people were getting As, some people were getting below average, we'd work together as a team.

James only realized that he was a good soccer player when other boys in his school kept asking if he wanted to be on their team. Playing informal soccer games together led to new friendships, self-confidence, and, eventually, popularity as an elementary school athlete:

> JAMES: That's when I started making friends ... when I started having confidence to make friends. Other friends introduced me to their friends, more so in grade 6 and 7. I had a best friend. He was popular. He helped me to become popular through sports and what not. So, yeah, grade 6, 7 was when James would be known as the popular guy.

Sports were a particularly important route to finding friends and fitting in for those who were already of school age when they came to Canada – as James said, "you join little sports teams to make friends." Peter and Terrence also remembered meeting their first friends on the soccer field, and those friends then introducing them to other friends. Lamar had the same experience on the basketball court after he moved to a new school. He made one friend playing basketball, and soon he had a whole network of friends: "I was embraced. I was one of the popular kids because of him."

Although the majority of men had little difficulty making friends and fitting in during elementary school, some also recounted instances of racism and differential treatment by peers. Peter, for example, resented being placed in ESL classes because, although he did not know how to speak English when he arrived at the age of ten, being singled out encouraged other students to "make fun of me because I didn't know how to speak English." As his English improved, he fairly quickly made friends on the soccer field. Rylan remembered that he developed a strong network of friends through soccer, but he also "used to get picked on a lot" by other kids who were not his friends "because of my skin colour and things like that." Similarly, Jay remembered the first time he felt "different" due to an incident in grade 2 or 3:

> JAY: One of my Chinese friends said to me, "we're trying to get an eraser to rub off your skin so you can be like everyone else." Yeah, that was the first time I felt different.

Similarly, Bob remembered being called a "chocolate éclair," which he understood as a pejorative term for someone who is Black on the outside and White on the inside. He also remembered one of his friends using the "N word" in reference to another friend (who was actually South Asian), without any sense that the term is racist and might upset Bob.

With one exception, male participants did not remember being isolated in elementary school. The exception was Michael, who migrated to Canada at age eight. For the first year, his family settled in Ontario, and Michael's experience there was distressing:

> MICHAEL: I would get little negative remarks in the bluntest way, like, "what are you doing?" like, "you're so weird!" kind of thing, over and over … And I kind of regret my choice there because I kind of started not caring what they thought, what anyone thought, because I was like, "yeah, I'm the African, whatever" … And honestly there was a ton of bullying now that I think about it. Yeah, I isolated myself because at one point I decided there was no point.

Michael's isolation during his first year in Ontario was linked to expectations about how local Black students, who were mostly of Caribbean origin, were expected to behave. It was expected that Black students should be "good at basketball" and "really into rap" music; in contrast, he defined himself at that point as "an academic nerd … who really loves reading." Michael did not fit other people's expectations, and the result was bullying and isolation. He took those lessons to heart, and when his family moved to Vancouver a year later, Michael decided the move provided an opportunity to redefine himself: "I'm going to be a hundred per cent totally different person." His route to popularity as a nine-year-old in a new school was linked to adopting the stereotypical mannerisms of Black masculinity from popular culture, focusing on athletics, adopting "typical Black English" and the cool pose associated with hip hop. This strategy led to a wide circle of friends, although Michael identified them as "the wrong kind of friends" who encouraged him to "do a lot of stupid things" and "act poorly to other people":

> MICHAEL: Honestly now that I think about it, they were the bullies of the school. But it's not that, they were like the cool kids, everyone loved these guys, they were the life of the school … They were all White. I was the only Black kid in school.

As we will see in Chapter 4, Michael's strategy of performing a particular type of Black masculinity in order to fit in with his peers in elementary school would become a common scenario for African-Canadian boys in high school. Although he succeeded in finding friends at school, he had to keep this part of his life separate and secret from his family, deepening Michael's sense of leading a "double life":

> MICHAEL: Our family is extremely religious, so a huge part of our parents is not immersing ourselves into other children that might lead us into the wrong [crowd] … So another part of isolation, I couldn't like, "oh, my friend wants me to come over, can I go?" They'd be like, "no, we need to meet this person, meet the parents, know how they are," et cetera, et cetera. So it also led me to lead a double life.

Michael referred to his "double life" as another kind of isolation because he was never able to really be himself in either context nor bring the two halves of his life together.

Women's narratives about elementary school were substantially different from men's. Sports did not figure centrally in any of the women's narratives about how friendships developed. Some, like Danielle and Betty, remembered making friends at school fairly easily, but also recalled forming much deeper friendships with their African and church friends. Most notably, almost half the women who went to elementary school in Vancouver recounted prolonged periods of isolation and difficulty forming friendships at school, periods that often spanned several years. This group included women in the second generation who had no memory of ever living anywhere other than Canada. This pattern is consistent with Wilson-Forsberg's (2012) research on immigrant youth in New Brunswick and Devine and Kelly's (2006) research in Dublin.

Ashley had lived in Canada since infancy. She contrasted her very "healthy environment growing up at home" with her negative experiences in elementary school, when she was picked on by other children and unable to make any friends:

ASHLEY: I just didn't realize I was different until going to school and that was the hardest thing for me. That haunted me in my childhood, maybe up to high school, like I didn't realize how different my home and environment was from other people's. My foods were not acceptable, my hair was unacceptable, so many things about me were just different than other children ... I was always picked on for different things, and I wondered, as a kid, I remember thinking, why, what is it about me that is so different, you know? For mom, "I need to stop packing these kinds of lunch for you and start packing this kind of lunch for you" because this is acceptable. So that people don't think, "what kind of food are you eating? why does it smell like that? what is the green stretchy stuff? like, what is that?"

In an effort to stop being bullied, Ashley began to take "salads and cheese" for lunch – food she did not care for but that other children would not ridicule. Her teachers were also "so ignorant of other cultures." She recalled one teacher in particular who frequently asked inappropriate questions that highlighted how "different" her hair was from that of others in the classroom: "How do you get your hair like that, and how do you wash it, and how do you keep it clean." Her parents moved her to a different school but that did little to help Ashley fit in. As she got older, physical education (PE) classes became a particular challenge:

ASHLEY: There were things, like, all of a sudden PE and gym became awkward issues because I'm thinking about my hair and all these things. So, yeah, thinking back, I've never actually sat down and thought [about] all this stuff, but thinking back, yeah, it did affect some parts of my education. I remember in PE class we had times when we would do dancing, square dancing, and things like that. And there were people who wouldn't want to be my partner because of my food or because of my hair.

Unable to build friendships at school, Ashley made strong friends at church and sought support from her family. As she got older, Ashley eventually made a small number of school friends, mostly of Filipino and South Asian background, but "I could count them on my hand."

Shukre also had been in Canada since she was an infant, living in a largely Somali environment in Toronto until her family moved to Vancouver when she was five years of age. Shukre's memories of elementary school were disturbing, as her mom's status as an immigrant single mother with six children, and the children themselves, were redefined in the French immersion school system as a "problem." Both teachers and other students ostracized Shukre and her siblings, so they did not develop any friendships outside the family:

> SHUKRE: People would throw banana peels at us. We weren't allowed to join activities, students would block us from activities, and we'd let our teachers know, and they'd be like, "Oh, you are taking it really personally just learn how to get along." And I remember my mom coming to the school almost constantly, and fighting. And counsellors pulling us out and being like, "you have a learning disability." And mom was like, "my child does not have a learning disability." First of all, and they would be like, "you are getting treated badly at home, right, right?" And we'd be like, "what?" It's bizarre ... She was a single mom. Her English wasn't very good. So we often translated for her, we communicated on her behalf. And so I guess that if your child communicates for you ... for the teachers at the time, it was a sign of incompetence of intelligence ... [The French immersion school] had no idea what to do with us, they had no idea. Like, we were being diagnosed with PTSD because we had come from a country with a civil war, even though half of my siblings were born in Canada. It was the most bizarre, they were just like, "you're problem kids," and we were like, "we don't get it, what are we doing wrong?" And I remember mom kind of being unable to formulate why it was so problematic, and just taking us out of the school and being like, enough is enough.

Once Shukre moved to a regular school in the English stream, things improved a bit. They were still the school's only African and Black family, but at least there were other children from large immigrant families, mostly South Asian. Still, she found it difficult to form friendships, and "up until grade 9 or 10 I was constantly only hanging out with my sisters."

Tina arrived in grade 3, and recalled being "ostracized" by other children and also getting little support from her teacher:

> TINA: I didn't understand a lot of the rules I don't know how, but I just didn't, so I didn't know there was homework. Or I remember once I had forgotten my math homework. I didn't know we had to do it, but it was just ... I felt everyone else knew this set of rules, I had not. I was not in on it, and I got a very long lecture from my teacher, and they were very much wanting to put me in a lower grade because I wasn't catching up, even though I knew the math that was being taught.

Tina was unable to form friendships with other students, and remembered becoming "introverted and "alienated." It was not until the last years of elementary school that "I made my first best friend in grade 6 … and in grade 7 I made another really good friend."

Denise had lived in metro Vancouver since she was five years old. Although she lived in a diverse neighbourhood and went to school with other children of immigrants, she found it very difficult to make any friends:

> DENISE: I remember having no friends for a very long time because there were immigrants there, like the Asian community, but they seemed to hang out with each other. And then there was the White community, and they hung out with each other. And then there was just me for a very long time.

She remembered being placed in ESL classes for two years, even though she already spoke English, and was told this was to help her "work on my communication." Denise was informed that people could not understand her African English accent, even though English was "what I had been speaking my whole life." Linda was also put in ESL classes when she arrived in grade 7, even though English was her first language:

> LINDA: When I got here, people thought I couldn't speak English. I was like, excuse me, I've been in English school since I was born. So you can't tell me I can't speak English. I had to go to ESL because I had an accent. But I'm from Africa, you know. I can speak English.

Denise was unable to make any friends in the first few years of elementary school, and remembered her first friendship developed in grade 3. After she moved to a new school in grade 5, she finally found a group of girls who became close friends, introduced by one friend to a larger network:

> DENISE: I don't know what it was about that year (grade 5), but I remember there was this one girl who was half-Black, half-White. I became friends with her, and she had friends who I guess I became friends with her friends. Her best friend was an Indian girl who became my best friend after she moved away. And she introduced me to so many people as well. I ended up having a lot of Indian friends with a few White friends here and there.

Although not all women participants experienced this degree of prolonged isolation from other students in elementary school, it is noteworthy that nearly half did. In contrast, the only male participant who experienced a period of isolation was Michael, and he was able to reinvent himself in a way that reflected popular stereotypes of Black masculinity when he moved to a new school. As we will see more in Chapter 4, there are no similar models of Black femininity for girls or young women to emulate, even if they wanted to. Most participants, both male and female, experienced other students' making fun of ways in which they were "different," be it through name calling or ridiculing their food, hair, skin colour, language, or accent. For the men and half of the women who shared their narratives, these incidents were episodic: frequent and hurtful enough to be remembered in adulthood, but not everyday events. Many men found sports to be a vehicle to build strong friendships, but even those who were not particularly athletic recalled no problems making friends in elementary school. In contrast, few women singled out sports as a site for building friendships, and nearly half faced prolonged bullying and ostracism from peers that formed a central feature of their elementary school experience. These patterns are rooted in the gender dynamics of childhood friendships. By elementary school, same-gender friendships predominate, and while boys tend to bond through activities such as sports, girls are more likely to bond through more intimate conversations that rely on shared cultural understandings (Devine and Kelly 2006; Morrow 2006).

Ashley reflected on these gender differences as she compared the experiences of the three children in her own family: her elder brother, herself, and her younger sister. Her brother was very popular, while her ten-year-old sister was going though many of the same struggles Ashley endured at the same age:

> ASHLEY: He said, "I'm blessed because I like sports. I'm into soccer, basketball, so that way I was popular. So people didn't really bother talking about my food or whatever because I was popular. So whatever I did, people liked, you know, my hair was cool and the fact that my hair was curly, different than theirs, they liked it." So he had quite a different experience than I did.

Ashley accepted her brother's explanation that he was popular because of his athleticism, and because he was popular he was not bullied about his "differences" in the way she was. At the same time, however, she understood that there were deeper gender differences linked to the racialization of Blackness at play on the school ground that affect her and her sister in ways her brother would never experience. Ashley worried about her younger sister's few friends and low self-esteem, and tried to help her navigate the world as a young Black girl in Vancouver:

> ASHLEY: So now she's going through some of the things that I went through when I was a kid, and that's the toughest thing for me to see her going through some of those things. And I try to really enforce to her that, you know what? You're beautiful just the way you are, you don't have to change your hair or your skin, you're beautiful! But as a kid you just want to fit in.

Ashley recognized all too well the profound impact that dominant beauty norms have on the self-esteem of Black girls and women and the desire to change one's body to eliminate "difference" and fit in with peers. As we will see in Chapter 4, these racialized gender differences, which begin to surface in elementary school, become much more pronounced during high school.

Chapter Four

"Cool Black guys" and Girls "trying to feel good in your own skin": Navigating Adolescence

"I was the cool Black guy"

– Jay

"It's hard to like just try to understand yourself and try to feel good in your own skin"

– Denise

In contrast to many of their experiences in elementary school, all research participants were acutely aware of their "difference" once they entered high school. Growing up in neighbourhoods where they were usually one of the few people racialized as Black and amid such small numbers from their parents' country of origin, their "difference" was mediated not primarily by cultural background, but by racialized discourses rooted in North American stereotypes about Blackness. The centrality of gender differences for those growing up African-Canadian in Vancouver also became more pronounced in high school as adolescents became more aware of their sexuality. The most common narrative among men was their great popularity in high school. Popularity among their peers was largely absent from women's narratives, however, which focused instead on the struggle to feel attractive and gain academic recognition. In this chapter I explore this paradox. Why is great popularity the dominant high school narrative among African-Canadian men growing up in Vancouver, and why is a similar discourse absent from women's narratives? The following discussion is in three parts. First I explore the broader meanings of racialized identities growing up as one of the very few African and Black people in school, while being immersed in African-American popular culture. I then examine how adolescent males negotiated Black masculinity through the filter of hip hop and racialized conceptions of heterosexual attractiveness. Finally, I compare these experiences to those of adolescent females as they negotiated Black femininity in high school.

Racialization, Masculinity, and Femininity

Gender should be understood as a social accomplishment: something we "do," rather than something we "are" (West and Zimmerman 1987). Gender is performed through everyday social interactions, discourses, gestures, dress, and other behaviours (Butler 1990). Dominant expressions of gender in North America typically, although problematically, are conceived as two opposites, male and female, and ignore the broader continuum of gender expression and identity. These dominant conceptions of male and female correspond with culturally and historically defined expressions of masculinity and femininity that are embedded implicitly within conventions around heterosexual sexuality (Butler 1990, 2004).

Intersectional feminist approaches highlight ways that bodies and subjectivities are constituted through the intersection of multiple relations of power and privilege, such that race, ethnicity, and class interact with gender and sexuality to produce multiple forms of masculinities and femininities that are hierarchically positioned within broader power relationships (Collins 2005; Connell 1995). In the North American context, more esteemed representations of femininity and masculinity are associated with White, heterosexual, cisgender, affluent, slim, able-bodied men and women, while devaluing and marginalizing racialized minorities, working-class, lesbian, gay, and trans people, and those with disabilities (Rice 2013). As scholars have pointed out, there are distinctive, and often pejorative, discourses about Black masculinity and femininity (Abdel-Shehid 2005; Collins 1990, 2005; Davis 1982; Henderson 2010). We need to recognize that gender identities are racialized and that racialized identities are gendered.

Although the active creation of masculine and feminine identities occurs throughout our lives, adolescence is arguably a particularly critical time. As Currie, Kelly, and Pomerantz (2009, 12) argue, how adolescents construct their gendered identities is important because "adolescence is a time when the explicitly sexualized nature of gender becomes apparent." The authors show that, as girls navigate adolescence, they actively mediate discourses of femininity and masculinity drawn from popular culture. For the most part these discourses also reinforce heteronormativity: the expectation that everyone is or ought to be heterosexual.[1] Similarly, young Black men and women of African origin growing up in Vancouver negotiated high school by navigating racialized notions of Black heterosexual masculinity and femininity, framed through American popular culture.

A long history of racialized conceptions of heterosexual attractiveness valorizes White standards of beauty. As Maxine Leeds Craig argues, "beauty is an historically specific evaluation of physical attractiveness that expresses prevailing racialized social hierarchies" (2003, 50). In the North American context, the Black male body symbolizes an object of strength and sexual desire, and is also associated with images of a dangerous predator. The Black female body, in contrast, is either considered unattractive and undesirable for failing to meet White norms of feminine beauty or is othered as sexually "exotic" (Craig 2003); as Kristen Myers (2012) argues, discourses of exotica reproduce sexual hierarchies of desirability.

Racialized notions of attractiveness and sexuality shape interactions differently for Black women and men in contexts of minority status, an issue of particular relevance to African-Canadians growing up in Vancouver. Research by Amy Wilkins (2012a, 2012b, 2012c) on identities and interracial relationships among Black American college students in predominantly White post-secondary institutions shows that Black women face "the combination of gender and racial disadvantages ... in the heterosexual market" in ways that increase their marginalization (Wilkins 2012a, 191). In contrast, Black men are objects of interracial heterosexual desire, and most interracial heterosexual relationships involve Black men and White women. Wilkins argues that Black men negotiate these spaces by learning to downplay racism, casting themselves as moderate and easygoing. Black women, on the other hand, experience more racial exclusion, and find themselves characterized as angry and political.

In the last decades of the twentieth century, the growing popularity of hip hop, a form of popular culture associated with African Americans, added new dimensions to cultural discourses about Blackness in North America. Hip hop originally encompassed four related art forms that emerged in the late 1970s in poor inner-city neighbourhoods. These expressions of break dancing, turntabling (or DJing), rapping, and graffiti emerged as oppositional expressions of creativity and commentary on the eroding conditions and opportunities facing young Black and

---

1 With one exception, participants in this research identified as heterosexual; one participant identified as bisexual.

Hispanic men and women in post–civil rights America (Petchauer 2009; Phillips, Reddick-Morgan, and Stephens 2005). Diverse expressions of inner-city life, ranging from glorification of street life to politically conscious invocation of social change, brought the potential for radical social commentary in a new form. By the 1990s, however, commercialization and consolidation in the music industry had turned hip hop into a genre of mass consumption while narrowing its range to profile particular forms of rap music. Gangsta rap, associated with inner-city and gangster lifestyles, performed largely by Black men, emerged as dominant, while more diverse artists, including many women, were marginalized (Rose 2008; Wingfield 2008).

The commercialization of hip hop coincided with consolidation of the music industry dominated by four global recording labels (Sony, EMI, Universal, and Warner) and the corporate conglomeration of US radio, with ten companies controlling two-thirds of the market (Jeffries 2011). According to Tricia Rose, the popularization of gangsta rap should be understood as "the result of marketing manipulation and the reflection not only of the specific realities of our poorest black urban communities but also of the exploitation of already imbedded racist fears about black people" (Rose 2008, 25). North American youth have become mass consumers of gangsta rap and the associated hip hop culture, which embraces styles of dress, speech, bodily performance, and attitudes linked to the glorification of street life, hyperheterosexual Black masculinity, and the ethos of "authenticity" and "keeping it real." Yet it is estimated that three-quarters of American hip hop consumers are young White men living in suburbs (Arthur 2006; Rose 2008). In Canada as well, hip hop has become an important element of youth culture among teens of all racialized backgrounds, forming part of the common repertoire of popular culture that informs how adolescents engage with the wider world.

Tricia Rose refers to the images that dominate commercially promoted rap as the "gangsta-pimp-hoe trilogy" (Rose 2008, 1). Images of Black masculinity are hyperheterosexual, homophobic, and violent (Collins 2005, 2006; Rose 2008). At the same time, however, the physical power, charismatic presence, displays of wealth, and chic "cool pose" epitomized by Black rappers garner wide appeal among fans (Arthur 2006; Jeffries 2011; Oware 2011). Dominant representations of Black femininity, in contrast, are more narrowly constructed. Although some women hip hop artists continue to contest narrow stereotypes, Black women in commercial rap are largely relegated to "heterosexual eye candy" (Emerson 2002; Phillips, Reddick-Morgan, and Stephens 2005; Trapp 2005). At the same time, Black women appear oddly

Whitened, with emphasis on light skin tones, thin body size, long straight hair, and fine facial features (Queeley 2003; Stephens and Few 2007a). Representations in commercial hip hop accentuate the objectification and hypersexualization of young women's bodies common in contemporary popular culture, including in advertising, film, and television (Reichert and Lambiase 2006), employing degrading representations of Black women as highly sexualized body parts (Stephens and Few 2007b).

These distorted images of Black masculinity and femininity reinforce conventional double standards that extol male dominance, male agency, and heteronormativity. They also reinscribe racist representations of Black men and women that date back to slavery and Reconstruction in the United States (Collins 1990, 2005), a lineage that enhances the marketability of hip hop today (Queeley 2003; Rose 2008). Indeed, Queeley argues that "[h]ip hop now lives in the ghetto of the white imagination ... the art form becomes a commodity, and is made to represent an essentialized Blackness: the Blackness of the white imagination" (2003, 14). In the context of the ubiquity of American popular culture – particularly the popularity of hip hop among youth – and the absence of a larger local Black population in Vancouver, hip hop culture constitutes a primary filter through which non-African youth engage with their African-Canadian peers and through which African-Canadian adolescents search for models of Black masculinity and femininity.

As noted in Chapter 3, growing up where "no one looked like me" had a significant effect on participants' identities, and this intensified during their teenage years. Most second-generation African-Canadians grew up in neighbourhoods where they saw very few people who look like them, and connections with others of African descent were episodic. As a result, the diversity of their cultural origins was largely erased in everyday interactions. At the same time, discourses about Blackness formed part of Vancouver's everyday social geography. In the context of very small numbers, participants came to see differences between Somalis, Ugandans, Ghanaians, or Ethiopians, for example, as less meaningful as local processes of racialization highlighted Blackness as a common identity.

As Awad Ibrahim (1999) has argued, migrating to Canada involves a process of "retranslation" as previous signifiers of identity become less salient in the context of local processes of racialization that emphasize being Black. Although growing up African-Canadian in Vancouver meant seldom encountering others who looked like them, participants nevertheless found themselves in a cultural milieu awash in representations of Blackness drawn especially from American popular culture.

Adult migrants have strong ethnic and national-African identities that counter these discourses, but the second generation is immersed in a sea of North American culture and social institutions, especially in school, that can undermine their parents' positive imaginings about African homelands. Importantly, representations of Blackness from popular culture also shaped the ways non-African youth interacted with their African-Canadian peers. Both men and women participants reflected on the tension between their African cultural heritage and their identity as Black. As Shukre commented, for example, although she understood herself as Somali, to everyone else she was Black:

> SHUKRE: I grew up Somali, and the entire world saw me as Black. And there's a huge cultural component that gets erased every time people look at me and I would get lumped in with everyone else, and it was very challenging because we grew up very culturally aware. And then to have people ignore that and just refer to us as Black consistently was very difficult.

The erasure of her Somali heritage was more hurtful because it undermined all the positive associations she had with being Somali. Instead, being redefined as Black was linked to negative assumptions about her character and her capabilities. Shukre was aware that other people's identification of her as Black "made them think of me as less":

> SHUKRE: Seeing myself as an African immigrant, I didn't feel less important. I didn't feel less because of that. But I know people's perception of me as Black made them think of me as less. Does that make sense? And I always knew that. I'm walking around, and I'm like, "I'm African and this is great!" But I also knew people didn't see me as Somali or African, they saw me as Black, and that wasn't great.

Given the close association between being Black and being African American in North American popular culture, as Terrence also noted, "people just obviously assume that you're from America," thus rendering his Liberian, African, and Canadian roots invisible.

Many participants remembered discourses of Blackness in popular culture as a point of tension in adolescence, being strongly influenced by them while recognizing that they did not align with their family's cultural heritage. Research in Alberta and Ontario has found that African immigrant youth growing up in Canada adopt "borrowed identities" drawn from so much exposure to African-American representations

(Forman 2001; Ibrahim 1999, 2003; Kelly 1998, 2004). To be sure, their parents perceived affinities with African Americans as "foreign," but for youth growing up in Vancouver, American popular culture was a fundamental element of local cultural geography. Local processes of racialization thus helped to emphasize the salience of Blackness among the second generation.

High schools are central sites where African-Canadian adolescents connect with non-African peers and with North American youth culture, even as they mediate practices and identities of femininity, masculinity, and heteronormativity. All participants in this research identified hip hop as a central influence during high school, although not always in the same way. The majority of men remembered great popularity if they behaved as the "cool Black guy" associated with hip hop, whereas women identified how hip hop shaped peers' unmet expectations while accentuating their own sense of inadequacy as young women. Below I explore how the images of Black masculinity and femininity in hip hop shaped the way these African-Canadian youth were positioned in Vancouver high schools, such that boys enjoyed great popularity while their sisters were found wanting.

"Cool Black guys"

> JAY: You know, I'm not going to lie, not going to exaggerate. I was the most popular kid in my high school, and my little brother when I was in grade 12 – he's in the next grade – he was really popular too. We're the only two Black kids in the school.

Jay's comments about his great popularity and recognition that this was linked to his racialized body illustrate the most common theme in men's recollections of high school. More than two-thirds of male participants, eleven of sixteen, identified their extreme popularity as the most defining element of high school, using terms like being "glamorized" (Jay), a "celebrity" (Maxwell), or, most commonly, noting it was just "cool to be Black" in high school (Hobbes, John, Lamar, Ryland, Luke, James, Kweku, Bob, Michael):

> KWEKU: In high school, I mean … it's cool to be Black people. It's rap music. Black people entertain a lot, right? So, a lot of entertainment that people listen to is Black people. So it's good, oh it's cool to be Black. Lots of expectations and a lot of the Black culture that people see here is the African-American culture.

These men's experiences in Vancouver high schools spanned the age range of participants[2] and included men in the second generation proper (four born in Canada and three who were preschool age when they arrived) and in the 1.5 generation (three were in elementary school and one was in high school when they migrated to Canada). The common feature among them was being male and Black in an environment where they stood out among non-African peers and where youth culture is saturated with African-American popular culture.

The minority of men, less than one-third, who did not emphasize extreme popularity as the defining aspect of high school, had a similar age range and generational attributes[3] and each recalled having a diverse range of friends. A key difference is that these men were often less athletic than the majority group and recalled being less drawn to hip hop culture, although they could not avoid how it influenced peers' expectations. For example, Devon recalled growing up as "awesome." Although he did not describe himself as among the most popular guys in high school, he noted that "every year I had a different nice girlfriend ... I had a wonderful high school experience. I had really close friends." He acknowledged that being Black and on the honour roll made him stand out in a good way: "I felt like I was a lucky guy, like I always felt quite special." At the same time, he kept his social circle limited to close friends and had little time for peers who expected him to act in a particular way just because he was Black. Although Canadian born, as a teenager Devon accentuated his Ethiopian heritage and its dissimilarity from that of African Americans:

> DEVON: I did have people who were like. "you don't look very like hip hop" or something like that. I'm like, "that's African-American, I'm from Ethiopia" ... I didn't want to be like a stereotypical Black kid who wasn't getting into school. I had no interest in that.

In contrast, most male research participants performed Black masculinity in ways that met peers' expectations, and this was central to

---

2 Men who identified their great popularity as the defining feature of high school ranged in age from nineteen to twenty-eight at the time of the interviews.

3 Men who did not characterize themselves as among the most popular in high school also ranged in age from nineteen to twenty-eight. One was Canadian born, two arrived in Canada while in elementary school, and two came in high school.

their elevated popularity in high school. The popularity of hip hop in youth culture, combined with reverence for Black athletes in professional sports and the scarcity of Black youth in Vancouver high schools, provided the context for the exaltation of the "cool Black guy." Being the "cool Black guy" had three dimensions: it was a form of enhanced cultural capital that corresponded with adolescence, in contrast to experiences as younger children or as mature men; it involved a wide range of peers who sought friendships with Black teenage boys so long as they performed Black masculinity in particular ways; and it involved considerable romantic attention from teenage girls, particularly White girls.

As we saw in Chapter 3, most of the men who grew up in Vancouver had little sense of racialized "difference" in elementary school apart from occasional racial micro-aggressions by peers. However, drawing comparisons with how they and their friends were treated makes it clear that, in high school, they were "different" in ways that enhanced their social standing. For example, Bob recalled that, unlike his closest friends, he could move among several popular social groups in high school:

> BOB: I mean, it was great. I was able to meet girls, and I was able to hang out with people. I think people wanted to be my friend and [be] friendly with me for different reasons. I think more White kids definitely knew about hip hop music than I did. I did a lot of smiling and nodding. It was a period of nodding and smiling and not knowing why things were – social relationships, people wanted my attention, people I didn't really know. And I didn't really understand why my friends didn't feel that same ease.

It did not take long for Bob to realize that being Black enhanced his popularity. At that point, he said, "I became more racially aware."

As Jay remembered, his friends first drew attention to how his new popularity in high school was linked to the colour of his skin:

> JAY: My friends would tell me, "they all like you because you're Black." And that was new to me, so I was trying to be more cautious of was it me or was it the Black guy?

Many of the men we interviewed heard similar remarks from peers. "Because you're Black" surfaced as an explanation for popularity and a reason to expect particular kinds of accomplishments, such as superior athletic performance or the ability to sing and dance. Several men indeed did excel at high school sports – in one case, later in professional sports – and one became an accomplished hip hop dancer. Framed through racialized representations of sports and entertainment in the United States (Abdel-Shehid 2005; Collins 2005), however, these accomplishments were seen less as personal achievements and more as innate characteristics of Black males. The overall outcome was both to expect and to diminish athletic or artistic accomplishments, as if they were easy or natural for Black men:

> BOB: People would say, "oh, you're good because you're Black." No, I'm good because I worked my ass off. In grade 8 I was in the gym every day lifting weights to get myself in good shape, that's what I did. It's not that I was born this way … So that was kind of frustrating. So, when I had my accomplishments being diminished by that, or when I went to a school dance and people were like, "oh, you dance because you're Black," and I'm like, "no, I dance because I freaking dealt with my insecurities and I got onto that dance floor." Don't diminish my accomplishments.

A wide range of peers sought friendships with Black adolescent boys because of how they were positioned through hip hop. The "cool Black guy" of hip hop culture entered Canadian homes through the streaming of endless rap music videos by Music Television (MTV) and Black Entertainment Television. As Bob noted, for example, "people saw a little bit of MTV and they thought I was cool." Bob referred to these representations of Black masculinity as an "MTV Black identity," an identity that a majority of male participants performed for some period of time. Embracing this type of Black masculinity was linked to expectations of peers and to the adolescent search for Black role models. With such a small African and Black population in Vancouver, it was not surprising that American popular culture played a key role in providing those role models for local Black youth:

> JAY: I did pay attention to the Black people in the media, African-American media. I guess, consciously or maybe subconsciously, I made an effort to dress like them and I just started to act like them … and hip hop culture, more in my early teenage years. And when people say music plays a big role in people, because I don't think I was the best teenager due to the music I listened to. I think I was just trying to find out who I'm going to be, right? So the different identity that I picked up, trying to be like my big brothers – they weren't the best models.

Most male research participants performed the "cool Black guy" in school by becoming athletes, listening to commercial rap music, and mimicking some of the dress, speech, and attitudes represented there:[4]

> JAMES: I was very popular in high school. Every sport, I got nominated for Athlete of the Year ... I listened to a lot of rap. I've danced the whole style.

In fact, in many respects it was easier to emulate hip hop culture than to challenge adolescent peers' expectations:

> KWEKU: I did initially, because that's what people expected of me. So, I was like, I'm going to give what people expect. I don't want to disappoint. So I kind of acted like that a little bit. And I think that most kids do.

Performing the "cool Black guy" brought significant social benefits to Black adolescent boys. Although their parents might have expressed disapproval of how their sons dressed and swaggered (Creese 2011), there were significant social rewards for meeting their peers' expectations. Beyond generally heightened popularity, most men also remembered getting a lot of attention from teenage girls. The "cool Black guy" was an object of heterosexual desire, and popularity typically included the ability to date attractive (usually White) teenage girls. Indeed, popularity also inscribed a gendered form of "exoticization," as some men recalled being aggressively pursued by White girls and women just because they were Black.[5] All this positive attention from peers was not easy to resist. Some research participants still looked back with considerable nostalgia. James, for example, summed up his experience by saying simply, "high school was awesome."

At the same time, some men we interviewed became acutely aware, even before the end of high school, that racialized stereotypes about adolescent Black masculinity were also harmful and demeaning. As Jay commented, "everybody wanted to be my friend because I was Black, and I was a commodity":

> JAY: And some of the things that I look back to were just extremely racist that I went through. Asking me, "can you dance for us, please?" "Let's

---

4 Performance of hip hop masculinity in high school was symbolically expressed through dress, music, and attitude; no one mentioned involvement in any type of street life.

5 In contrast to women, men did not use the term "exotic" with reference to themselves; however, their descriptions of girls and women pursuing them because they were Black signifies an exoticization of Black male bodies.

go play basketball, I want to watch you play basketball." "Jay, you're a good singer. I know Black people can sing." And I look back and I'm like, holy crap! I was so dumb. Because I was popular for the fact that I was entertainment, and it hurts thinking back.

For all the positive feedback friends might provide regarding the performance of the "cool Black guy," the range of acceptable behaviours was actually quite limited. Bob transferred to a different high school in grade 10 and experienced the same rapid popularity all over again. This heightened Bob's recognition that expectations linked to the "cool Black guy" undermined his real passions and accomplishments, and by senior high school he understood that playing that character had limitations:

> BOB: And then, with the benefits there are also traps and limitations. So you can be good at sports, good at dancing, you can be sociable, you can be loud and bombastic, but you can't be smart. You can't be serious. You can't be critical. You know you can be the guy they'll dance with or go to a party with, but never the guy they invite home for dinner.

When Bob decided to concentrate on academic pursuits, his circle of friends quickly diminished. He interpreted this as his peers saying, "this guy is not the right kind of Black. He is doing Black wrong." Jay and Luke also recognized the superficial nature of their popularity, and stopped performing the "cool Black guy" by the time they were high school seniors, detaching themselves from the popular crowd and redefining a small circle of friends.

Whether or not African-Canadian men recognized the drawbacks of their celebrity status while still in high school or not until later on, as we will see in Chapter 7, this exaltation among peers did not last much beyond high school graduation. Once removed from high school, where performing "MTV Black" was cool, these men found representations of Black masculinity in the broader society more negative. The gangsta rap imagery – the hyper-heterosexual, violent, and crime-prone Black man – fit with broader images of the Black male as sexually desirable but dangerous, playing out in the pervasive surveillance and harassment of young Black men in North America (Brunson and Miller 2006; Maynard 2017). Beginning in adolescence, Black men in Vancouver experienced greater scrutiny in public places, routine policing by authorities, learned to be "cautious" and "mellow," always to dress "respectably", and to avoid unwanted attention (Creese, Kambere, and Masinda 2013). As research on young Black men in predominantly

White colleges suggests, living in an environment where they constitute a highly visible minority requires Black men to exercise considerable emotional restraint and be more accountable for their behaviour
(Ray and Rosow 2012; Wilkins 2012b). For African-Canadian men
growing up in Vancouver, the positive cultural capital of Black masculinity among teens made it easier to negotiate a space of acceptance in
high school, but it was both superficial and short lived.

Trying "to feel good in your own skin"

Unlike their brothers, young African-Canadian women did not remember being "glamorized" in high school or sought out by those in the
popular crowds. They were not celebrated for their Blackness or
exalted for their prowess as performers or athletes, although some were
involved in high school sports (and one became a professional dancer),
and over time most developed a small network of female friends. Like
their brothers, the girls were expected to enjoy partying, hip hop music,
and African-American TV shows and movies, and to behave according
to representations of Black women in American popular culture. But
whether or not they actively engaged with these things, parallel images
of the "cool Black girl" did not emerge. Instead, two different themes
were central in women's narratives about high school: their inability to
measure up to dominant standards of female beauty, and the underestimating of their academic potential by teachers.

As a point of contrast, none of the men expressed insecurities about
their appearance in high school – in fact, as we have seen, attention
from teenage girls was part of the exalted status of the "cool Black
guy." Moreover, with a few exceptions, male participants rarely mentioned negative interactions with teachers in high school.[6] Those who
struggled academically linked their underachievement to lack of focus,
typically directed more to sports and socializing than to academic pursuits. At the same time, men recalled that being an athlete enhanced
their good relationships with teachers while motivating them to attain
grades sufficiently good to stay on school teams. Men who excelled
academically recognized that being an excellent student detracted, in

---

6 Only three men recalled any problematic encounters with teachers: a teacher who
   disliked immigrants (Jack), one who told a teenage girl she should not date him
   (Luke), and one who "talked down" to him (Rylan). Jack also remembered being
   unhappy about placement in ESL classes when he arrived, although he did not know
   how to speak English.

some cases quite intentionally, from the image of the "cool Black guy" while producing positive relations with teachers.

This pattern is in stark contrast to much of the literature on students of African descent in Canadian schools, which focuses more often on discrimination, alienation, and higher dropout (or pushout) rates among young Black men (Brathwaite and James 1996; Codjoe 2001; Dei 2005; Dei et al. 1997; Ibrahim and Abdi 2016a; James 2012, 2018). The different findings of this study might derive from the self-selection of the research participants, including the absence of any who failed to graduate from high school and had no plans to pursue post-secondary education, and whose experiences might have differed from those of the participants – as we will see in Chapter 6, the participants them-selves suggested that withdrawing from school was more common among men than women in the community. As well, male participants were often school athletes, and as such their popularity in high school seems to have embraced peers as well as teachers. Finally, their more restricted socialization with peers meant that African-Canadian teen-age girls generally focused more on academic achievement, and were sensitive to obstacles that affected their performance in school.

African-Canadian girls seldom enjoyed the same freedom of move-ment as their brothers, as their parents enacted gendered expectations around cultural norms (Okeke-Ihejirika and Spitzer 2005). Almost all women participants observed that socializing with classmates occurred at school or school-related events, not on weekends or in the evenings outside adult supervision. Hence, they had little scope to be part of the teenage social scene outside school; only one recalled engaging in "partying" with peers or dating during high school,[7] something par-ents consider culturally inappropriate for their daughters. For the most part, lack of interest in or ability to perform Black femininity in ways non-African peers expected made African-Canadian adolescent girls less interesting to their classmates – great high school popularity sim-ply was not part of these women's experiences. As we saw in Chapter 3, many of the women interviewed recalled difficulties forming and maintaining friendships during elementary school, and although some had a diverse group of girlfriends in high school, many more developed a small number of close girlfriends, almost always also from immigrant backgrounds. Some women were active in team sports during high school – one even won a sports scholarship to a prestigious American

---

7   The one woman who recalled engaging in these activities had a White Canadian mother and an African father.

university – but none recalled the kind of wide recognition and adulation as a school athlete that some of the men recounted.

Peers' expectations of how Black teenage girls should behave were also framed through African-American popular culture. As Betty and Tina commented, this made their Ethiopian and Kenyan heritages, respectively – along with their Canadianness – invisible:

> BETTY: I thought I was Ethiopian, and so that was my story. But what people had looking at me, you know, I think they related to me as this African-American identity, like the nuances of the Black girl who has these gestures, you know?
>
> TINA: There are a lot of assumptions made for me. For example, in high school, I would have people, I'm sure well meaning, who would, you know, [expect] the typical Black African-American accent, who would just assume I would talk like that. Who would be surprised I talked in a Canadian accent even though I'm in Canada ... Another thing was music. I love classical music, I love Indian music, I love folk music, I'm not big on rap. But a lot of people would send me [rap] songs and say this is exactly your kind of music.

Adolescent girls also had to contend with highly sexualized representations of Black femininity in hip hop, in the context of sexual double standards that lionize young men's sexuality while both promoting and censuring similar behaviour among young women. Sexualized representations of Black femininity in hip hop have little to offer most teenage girls by way of role models, and mainstream conceptions of beauty dominated by Whiteness cast young Black women as less desirable in the heterosexual market.

This is not to suggest that African-Canadian teenage girls growing up in Vancouver were unaffected by North American popular culture. On the contrary, as Black teenagers growing up "where no on looked like me," most were drawn to hip hop culture as the main representations they saw of Black women and men. Some women research participants identified strongly with forms of African-American identity during adolescence. For example, Sarah remembered experiencing a "hip hop phase" that involved searching for alternative forms of hip hop rather than listening to commercial gangsta rap on MTV:

> SARAH: Even as a Black Canadian, I mean unless you're a Black person living in Africa, African-American pop culture will follow you ... I think to some extent as a teen I did imitate or think of myself as a part of that culture, and to a certain extent today I feel part of that culture.

Few other women participants recalled seeking out less commercial forms of hip hop. Those over age thirty grew up in a time when more diverse and progressive forms of hip hop music were widely heard – before hip hop became so heavily commercialized. For example, Claudia, the oldest participant at thirty-six, argued that she still saw hip hop music as "very feminist" because she was influenced by feminist forms of hip hop in the 1990s:

> CLAUDIA: I grew up in a hip hop culture in the nineties when I was a
> teenager, which was very positive, and the music that we were listening
> to – you know, Queen Latifah, who was wearing all of her Afrocentric
> gear and everything and singing her song "U.N.I.T.Y."

Another older participant, Emily, age thirty-three, remembered being influenced as an adolescent by more political forms of hip hop:

> EMILY: We were into hip hop and all of that … I knew that I was Ethiopian
> and that I had a heritage and I know that, but at the same time I didn't
> know anything, any details of the culture. Or if I did, I didn't care
> as much. I was more into the Black culture here and learning about
> Malcolm X.

Although second-generation women might have listened to hip hop, emulating the models of Black femininity in hip hop culture had little appeal:

> DENISE: Because I was Black, I should be acting a particular way. And if I
> didn't want to go out and party or go out and get drunk, people thought
> I was odd … I think I grew up with the mentality of, because you think I
> should be this way, I am not going to be this way.

As girls negotiated Black femininity in Vancouver high schools, therefore, they did so without any popular models of Black femininity they could emulate and without any of the trappings of celebrity status attached to their brothers.

Women are judged more than men in terms of physical appearance, and beauty standards were a minefield for African-Canadian girls growing up in an environment where few people look like them. North American beauty standards are dominated by images of thin, tall, blond, White, cisgender women, and even with the inclusion of more women of colour in the beauty and entertainment industry in recent decades these images continue to marginalize Black women

(Craig 2003). Not surprisingly, the incongruity of both being Black and feeling beautiful was a feature of high school for almost all the women who participated in this research. The only ones who did not experience this level of dissonance migrated to Canada in their late teens and already had strong models of African femininity rooted in their country of origin.

For African-Canadian girls growing up in Vancouver, images of Black female beauty were few and far between, and those that existed typically were framed as hypersexualized and "exotic." Representations of Black women in hip hop, for example, as noted earlier, are often reduced to highly sexualized body parts (Stephens and Few 2007b). The notion of Black women as "exotic" objects of desire reduced them to their sexuality and devalued them in terms of dominant standards of attractiveness – reference to the "exotic," in fact, maintained racialized hierarchies in place (Myers 2012). Many of the women research participants encountered these stereotypes of Black women as "exotic" and "oversexualized" from an early age:

> SHUKRE: I think that there's this exoticization of Black women that's very problematic. Like, they're overly sexualized, they've got butts and hips. And they like having sex. There are these ideas that come up, that I knew growing up.

These images of Black women as highly sexual and "exotic" are as problematic as the White beauty standards that define most Black women as unattractive and undesirable. Both made it harder to develop a positive self-image among teenage girls who rarely saw women who looked like them.

Denise was most eloquent on this topic. Where, she wondered, were the women who looked like her? She noted that, when beautiful Black women came on TV or in music videos, they were often of mixed heritage, "where they got some White in them somewhere." Others have observed this phenomenon of the "Whitening" of Black women in hip hop and the entertainment industry more generally – see for example, Queeley (2003), and Stephens and Few (2007a). As a result, African-Canadian adolescent girls almost never saw themselves in the popular images of Black female beauty that do exist. Denise said, "I don't identify like with Beyoncé, I don't identify with Halle Berry or Naomi Campbell, but that's what you see on TV." In contrast, she pointed out, at least her brother regularly saw people in popular culture who looked like him. Denise provided a heartbreaking example of her mother's best friend's daughter, to illustrate why this absence of images of diverse

Black female beauty made it so hard for young African-Canadian girls and women "to feel good in your own skin":

> DENISE: She's just having a hard time with self-identity. She's Black, dark-skinned Black, but she has no one to look up to, so she's trying to emulate, like, Beyoncé. She doesn't feel beautiful because she doesn't look like Beyoncé, and I think that's what women have a hard time with. Not so much what other people perceive them as, what they perceive themselves as ... It's hard to just try to understand yourself and try to feel good in your own skin.

Internalizing doubts about their own attractiveness was a routine part of growing up for girls, linked not only to popular media images, or the lack thereof, but also to ways in which their own "difference" was materialized. Finding appropriate beauty products, for example, was more difficult than it would be in a city with a larger population of African descent. Items such as hair products, skin products, and makeup – "all those things identify racially" (Betty), and accentuated just how far African-Canadian girls and women were from the feminine ideal epitomized in the mass marketing of beauty products.

Hair has long been a particular concern linked to images of beauty in North America. "Good hair" historically referred to straight hair, rather than curly or kinky hair, since "Black people's hair has been historically devalued as the most visible stigma of Blackness, second only to skin" (Mercer 1987, 35). Hair styles are also political within the African-American community, with debates around the merits of straightening, afros, dreadlocks, and other styles (Mercer 1987). Women in our research remembered their hair was often a particular concern in high school, either constituting an unwelcome object of attention, such as when people made fun of it or touched it without permission, or something to be altered to fit in better with dominant notions of beauty. Some women adopted the strategy of chemically straightening their hair during high school, even though these beauty practices can be harmful. After years of straightening her hair throughout high school, Ayad shaved her head in first year university as "the only way to take out the chemicals in my hair."

Ideals of heterosexual attractiveness are also challenged by the stereotype of Black women as angry and aggressive. Some participants noted how this discourse also shaped their experiences in high school. Black women's greater marginalization in the heterosexual market and the preponderance of interracial romances between Black men and White women animated this discourse (Childs 2005;

Wilkins 2012a, 2012b). Being angry and aggressive is not considered an attractive quality in young women, and participants remembered trying not to be labelled angry lest it deter potential friendships in high school.

Teachers' underestimating their academic potential constituted the other central theme in women's experiences of high school. Under-estimation of the intellectual capabilities of Black youth is well documented in the Canadian literature, although most studies focus on African-Canadian boys and young men (Brathwaite and James 1996; Codjoe 2001; Dei 2005; Dei et al. 1997; Ibrahim and Abdi 2016a; James 2012, 2018). As noted, women participants typically remembered that their main focus was on academic achievement, not on their social life, so any obstacles to that achievement were important to them. In contrast, most of the men focused on their social life, athletic accomplishments, and great popularity.

A majority of the women (eleven out of nineteen) identified ways in which teachers underestimated their academic abilities and made it more difficult for them to succeed.[8] Two participants, Ayinke and Linda, came from English-speaking schools in Nigeria but were placed in ESL classes in high school. As a result, they fell behind in some required courses they had to make up later. Four participants (Joy, Charlotte, Ali, and Stella) were placed in the non-academic stream in senior high school, and advised to take lower-level math or English courses without understanding that these courses did not meet post-secondary admission standards. Each had to take additional makeup courses after graduation before being able to pursue post-secondary education. Three women (Emily, Sarah, and Stella) gave examples of "ignorant" racist remarks that teachers made in class, singling them out as "different" and creating an unwelcome learning environment. Stella, for example, recalled one teacher who frequently made derogatory comments about Africa, asking her questions such as "do they have houses?" or did she "hang out with giraffes?" As the only African and Black student in the class, Stella said, "I felt picked on – like, why do you ask me that every day?"

Three other participants (Betty, Shukre, and Denise) emphasized more subtle ways in which some teachers made it clear they were not expected to excel academically:

---

8 Three of these women are second generation (they came to Canada when they were pre-school age) and 8 are 1.5 generation (4 arriving in elementary school and 4 in high school). At the time of the interviews they range in age from 19 to 33.

> SHUKRE: It's like my intelligence was always questioned because of where I was from, because of the colour of my skin, because of my first language. Like, I was always questioned and told I wasn't good enough.

They provided examples of teachers' expressing surprise when they did well on a test, suggesting that they not consider pursuing science courses that were considered difficult, and trying to dissuade them from applying to top-ranked universities. Rather than discouraging them, however, such incidents motivated all three participants to work harder. As Denise noted, she had to work really hard for her good grades because "just being a Black person, ... like my father said, you have to work twice as hard to be treated the same." Even with hard work, she believed her strong academic performance "was a shocker to a lot of people." Betty also worked harder to gain respect for her capabilities:

> BETTY: You know what? I'm going to work even harder for you to respect me, to look at me as your peer, nothing less. So, that was just a huge part of my own coping with all those things.

Similarly, Shukre responded to academic obstacles by learning "to toe the line. Like, I knew exactly what I had to do and say." Her main motivation was to prove that her teachers' expectations about her were wrong:

> SHUKRE: I did well because people were so quick to tell me I couldn't do well. And I knew that, even as I was doing well, I was like, "I'll prove to you."

Thus, for many women we interviewed, racialized assumptions about intellectual capabilities and barriers to academic achievement motivated them to work harder in order to prove themselves.[9] Perhaps not surprisingly, women drew on their personal observations to suggest that the need to work hard and prove themselves contributed to much higher university attendance rates among women than men in the second generation, a topic that I explore in Chapter 6.

---

9 Some men, such as Bob and Hobbes, commented on stereotypes that Black men are not perceived as smart. These remarks, however, were raised in the context of stereotypes among peers and co-workers and in popular culture, not specifically in their interactions with teachers.

Concluding Thoughts: Navigating Race and Gender

African-Canadian youth growing up in Vancouver had little contact with anyone else of African descent outside family, and yet they inhabited an environment in which representations of Black masculinity and femininity, rooted largely in a specific national history in the United States, also formed part and parcel of their everyday cultural milieu. For teenage boys, hip hop was a site where they could see themselves reflected bodily and through which they could, at least for a time, attain social acceptance among peers and heterosexual capital by performing a particular brand of masculinity: the "cool Black guy." In contrast, their sisters neither saw women who looked like them in hip hop imagery nor found a space for social recognition among peers. As Bob noted, there is little in hip hop representations of Black women that might appeal to African-Canadian adolescent girls, and that also meant they did not run the same risk of being "trapped" by these representations:

> BOB: I think the female representation has too many negative connotations that there is no temptation among the Ethiopian women. It was less temptation among immigrant women to maybe fall into that stereotype. Women, I think, get treated like shit. They get treated like property. Why would you want that? There is no temptation to that. I just think that the MTV female-gendered position, this is not the Black, this is the MTV one, is one of denigration, disrespect. Why would you enter something that would treat you terribly? And I think because of that, there was a rejection of that, and so they don't get trapped.

No equivalent feminine performance of the "cool Black girl" is linked to hip hop or other genres of popular culture. Instead, "Whitened" forms of Black beauty and highly sexualized "exotic" representations in hip hop accentuated insecurities around the identities of these African-Canadian girls as they struggled "to feel good in your own skin."

Women who had brothers were keenly aware of how gender shaped their experiences as African-Canadian youth in high school and beyond. Several women participants pointed out that the easy acceptance of the "cool Black guy" among peers belied the greater stigma that young Black men felt in the wider community:

> TINA: Definitely, I find that I'm glad that I'm a female Black person because a lot of Black men get a lot of bad rap in Vancouver and in other parts of greater Vancouver. And there's a lot of violent assumptions put on them.

As Shukre observed, stereotypes about Black men meant that, from a fairly young age, her brother faced expectations that he would be aggressive, and these expectations increased as he matured. His physical appearance was enough to make people afraid:

> SHUKRE: If you were to be a tall – my brother is, like, six foot three, he's massive and he's wide. He's a big guy, and he walks down the street, and people are like, "what's he doing? He's up to no good." There are very few options available to young Black men. They either get so tired they fight back and get shoved into jail, or they get so tired they hide.

According to Shukre, her brother was not aggressive, but "a very soft guy" who grew up with several sisters and a single mom. He struggled academically, and although the "cool Black guy" provided acceptance in high school, his lack of attention to schooling closed off possibilities for post-secondary education and options for a more promising future. As Denise observed, too, the image of the uneducated Black man is another part of the stereotype of Black masculinity common in American popular culture:

> DENISE: I think males have it hard. I think even in regards to education, because when someone looks at a Black man, they think "gangster," they think "oh, he's going to rob me." They don't think he's an educated man right there. I don't think anyone ever sees a Black man and says, "I'm sure that guy went to university and has a master's in whatever." I don't think anyone thinks that, and that's why I think men have it harder because it's going to be a while before people's mentality changes that when they see a Black guy on the street that Black guy is not there to rob them.

Although the "cool Black guy" had some cachet among teenagers, the larger associations with Black masculinity are more negative: stereotypes that question intelligence while emphasizing physical prowess, and that suggest Black men are inherently aggressive, violent, and prone to criminality. Hip hop culture might have "glamorized" African-Canadian teenage boys and made it easier for them to attain acceptance in high school, but it also reinscribed stereotypes about Black masculinity that did little to help prepare them for adult life, where being Black men more likely would devalue their social standing (Abdel-Shehid 2005; Collins 2005). Their sisters, in contrast, had more difficulty negotiating the social side of high school, and were devalued by the White beauty industry and the heterosexual market, and therefore focused more on academic achievement, including working harder to attain academic recognition.

Place is a critical dimension of understanding the gendered experiences of African-Canadian adolescents in Vancouver high schools. In other large Canadian cities, where the density of recent immigrant communities from Africa is higher and larger populations of African descent reside, youth might engage with hip hop without routinely "glamorizing" Black teenage boys. Reflecting on his recently living in Toronto, where for the first time he was just one of hundreds of thousands of residents of African descent, Bob suggested "it was almost easier growing up where there were fewer Black people than if there were more." Indeed, the scarcity of young Black men in local Vancouver high schools helps to explain why non-African peers treated African-Canadian teenage boys like celebrities. Their rarity and the cultural currency of hip hop combined to raise them to an exalted social status among their peers. In contrast, girls had a more difficult time, and had fewer examples of women who looked like them to help disrupt the White normative gaze of the beauty industry or provide alternative models to the hypersexed party girl of hip hop. Brothers and sisters might have grown up in the same house and attended the same high school, but, as they navigated the spaces inhabited in adolescence and moved into adulthood, their experiences of growing up African-Canadian in Vancouver were shaped profoundly by discourses of Black femininity and masculinity.

Chapter Five

"More of my friends are Black": Adult Friendships and Romantic Relationships

"As I've grown older, more and more of my friends are Black"

– Jay

"A lot of Black men that I've met ... I see them prefer dating White girls"

– Tina

The transition to adulthood involves a series of milestones that might include graduation from high school, pursuing post-secondary education, finding employment that provides financial independence from parents and more autonomy over life decisions, and seeking long-term romantic relationships. Young adulthood is a time of considerable growth and change, and that includes transformations in personal relationships. Removed from the confines of high school and the heightened peer pressure associated with adolescence, young adults encounter more diverse contexts in which friendships and romantic relationships may develop. Beyond high school, research participants' personal relationships were not framed through hip hop culture in the same way as was the case during adolescence (see Chapter 4). Personal relationships among second-generation adults, however, were still affected profoundly by gendered representations of Blackness that persist in popular culture, and by their need to navigate Vancouver as members of a small and hypervisible racialized minority.

This chapter explores adult patterns of friendship and romantic relationships. Most men and women who participated in this study had an ethnically diverse friendship network. At the same time, almost all participants enlarged their circle of friends drawn from the local African diaspora; for some, these now became their central friendship network. When it came to heterosexual romantic relationships, however, clear gender differences emerged. The majority of men had current romantic partners and a history of dating women from other racialized groups, particularly White women. In contrast, the majority of women were single, and their dating history was overwhelmingly with Black men who were raised in Africa. As adults, dominant representations of Black men and women in popular culture might not have appeared to them as central to interactions with friends, but they continued to shape romantic relationships in gender-specific ways.

Diversifying Friendships

Most African-Canadians who participated in this research had a diverse group of friends, usually including some long-term friendships developed in high school and newer friends from college or university. Growing up in a multi-ethnic metropolis where people of African descent constituted only 1 per cent of the population, it is not surprising that friendships tended to reflect the diversity of the larger community.

Participants spoke positively about the ethnic and racialized diversity of their current friendship networks. For example, Danielle explained, "I have Caucasian friends, I have Filipino friends, I have Spanish friends, I have African friends." Similarly, Jessica identified her closest friends as coming from the Philippines, Trinidad, Hungary, and South Korea. Jane still maintained contact with some high school friends, who were "virtually all white," but her friends from university were much more diverse: "Latin, Indian, Malaysian, Filipino." Stella listed "White Canadian, Indian, Congolese, [and] Nigerian" friends. Men recounted similarly diverse friendship networks. For example, Terrence said, "my friends are mostly European, African, I have a lot of Filipino [and] other Chinese friends." James described a wide network of friends from many different backgrounds who were all interconnected:

> JAMES: I hang out with a lot of Africans, I hang out with a lot of White people. It's whoever calls who on the weekend, you know? And all my friends know each other. My whole soccer team is White, but there's me and one other [Black man], a Jamaican and me. And out in Surrey they are mainly Punjabi, and I hang out with them almost every weekend.

As we saw in Chapter 3, participants grew up in one of the few Black families in their neighbourhood and as one of the few Black children in their school, and most had few, if any, friends who were African-Canadian. Those who did form friendships with others of African descent did so largely through church, family friends, or community sports teams, rather than through school. Childhood friendship networks were navigated within the context of the ethnic composition of specific neighbourhood schools, some of which were predominantly White while others had large Asian communities – typically South Asian, Chinese, and/or Filipino. As we have seen, in elementary school most participants in mixed neighbourhoods tended to gravitate towards friendships with people who also had an immigrant background. As discussed in Chapter 4, these friendship networks expanded in high school for most African-Canadian boys, who were widely venerated by their peers, but similar experiences were not common among girls.

As adults, however, almost all participants developed a broader network of friendships with other young adults in the African diaspora – with other members of the second generation in the local African community and new adult migrants from Africa who had come to pursue post-secondary education in Canada. Fewer participants identified friendships within the broader Black community, whether from the Caribbean, the United States, or Canadian of many generations.

Some women, such as Markor, continued to identify their strongest friendships with other African-Canadians she had known since childhood, while others, such as Danielle, had lost touch with childhood African networks. As young adults, they followed different paths of work, career, and post-secondary education, and developed new friendships linked to their interests and spaces they came to inhabit. As Danielle explained, "the people I'm more close with are the people I [currently] go to school with."

A common pattern among research participants was forming new bonds with international students from Africa who were studying at local post-secondary institutions. Some women described gravitating to international African students in university and consciously building stronger connections in the local diaspora as they got older. For example, Ashley met her current partner at university when he was an international student. As a result, she said, "my closest friends right now are mostly African [from] Ghana, Nigeria, Zimbabwe, Kenya, Uganda." Denise had also extended her network in the African diaspora and, unlike in childhood, now routinely encountered "people who look like me":

DENISE: I needed to see the Black person, or see another Black person, or see people who look like me from time to time. Now as I'm older, I have Black friends, I have people from Africa, not necessarily Uganda, but a community where if I'm needing to relate I don't have to wait for that Independence Day.

Some men also stated that, in contrast to adolescence, their key adult friendship networks came largely from among the local African diaspora. Jay noted that, "as I've grown older, more and more of my friends are Black"; he still had several friends of South Asian background, but "not as many White friends" as he had in high school. Similarly Jack identified friends from the DRC, Sudan, Ethiopia, Somalia, South Africa, Nigeria, Jamaica, Afghanistan, Pakistan, and South Korea, and said he also kept in touch with some White friends from high school. Forlan listed friends from South Africa, Guinea, Ghana, Liberia, and Nigeria. In discussing his friends, Lamar said "most of them are Black, but I have one White friend," a man he identified as his best friend since elementary school.

This raises the question: why did so many research participants seek out new friends within the African diaspora? One part of the answer was an interest in learning more about African cultures. As Denise is quoted above, this interest need not be limited to an interest in her parents' ancestral culture – in her case, Uganda. In the context of very small local communities from any specific African country and the emergence of pan-African identities among the first generation (Creese 2011), Denise expressed interest in making connections with diverse African cultures. This could be accomplished locally, without the necessity of long-distance and expensive travel, by getting to know international students from Africa who were studying in Vancouver.

Friendships typically develop out of proximity and similar interests and experiences. For many research participants, processes of racialization were identified as a basis for shared experiences. As Kweku noted, being racialized as Black provided a point of commonality that fostered friendship:

KWEKU: I don't know what it is, but when you meet another Black person, it's just, for me, easier to [connect] because you already share something in common. So, it's almost like they meet and they immediately trust and accept you.

Lamar noted that all but one of his friends now came from the African diaspora. He explained this by saying, "when you go into a room you gravitate towards people who are like you." In a city dominated by people of European and Asian descent, the shared experience of being Black provided a point of mutual understanding.

Networks expanded to include more people in the African diaspora, but given Vancouver's demography, friendship networks also included people with diverse immigrant backgrounds. Just as racialization processes provided a basis for shared experiences, so too did recent family experience of migration cut across ethnic and racialized differences. For example, Michael noted that he had always been drawn to friendships with "second-generation immigrants." Given the neighbourhood he grew up in, Michael had many friends of South Asian descent. He argued that, despite cultural differences, their common immigrant background, family life, and personal struggles constituted a "bonding point." Betty made a similar observation about how she was always drawn to others who shared some experience of migration:

> BETTY: The majority of my good friends, the ones that are just constant and rooted, are of immigrant status ... who may have been born here, or born here and have a different culture, and relate to a different identity.

At university Betty said she sought out "different groups of friends, but it was always with students who [are] interested in international issues ... [and whose] parents are not from here." Some of these close friends shared Betty's Ethiopian and broader African heritage, but many others did not, although they all had a second-generation identity that transcended the mainstream Canadian.

As we can see, pursuing post-secondary degrees provided exposure to new experiences, and new friendships were forged with people who had similar educational backgrounds. As the second generation moved beyond post-secondary education and into careers, workplaces also became key sites to develop new friendships. Education and occupations correspond with class differences, and over time friendships tend to become more homologous in terms of class, although ethnic and racialized diversity likely persist.

As we saw in Chapter 3, sports can play an important role in the development of friendships among boys. This remained the case as adults for some men in this project, for whom engaging in sports or watching sports played a role in developing and maintaining friendships. James was quoted earlier explaining that his soccer team, which was almost all White, provided an important friendship network. In contrast, Jay observed that one reason he did not have many White friends anymore was because he shared little in common with his former high school friends, including their choice of sports:

> JAY: I think you try to be friends with people that are more like you. I'm not like my White friends at all. I really don't like hockey. I don't like drinking beer.

Hockey and beer are popular among White Canadian men, but Jay had a passion for soccer, which he still played. In his case, and unlike James's experience on a predominantly White soccer team, soccer was a shared interest among Jay's African-Canadian friends. Likewise, basketball facilitated friendship networks for Lamar, and many of the men he played with were Black. Whether sports teams are more or less ethnically and racially diverse, playing and watching sports are bonding experiences for many men, and as such, are spaces where friendship networks develop.[1]

One can conclude that social isolation was not a problem for the second-generation African-Canadians who participated in this research. Both women and men identified extensive friendship networks and, like most Canadians, their strongest connections were with friends of the same gender. At the same time, they lived "under a microscope" as people racialized as Black in Vancouver. That meant recognizing ways acquaintances might prejudge their character, and therefore being careful about whom they befriended. As we will see in Chapter 7, choosing friends carefully was an important strategy of resilience in the context of anti-Black racism in Vancouver. As research participants got older, friendship networks of both women and men tended to expand and included more connections in the local African diaspora as well as diverse friends from other ethnic and cultural backgrounds who shared recent immigrant experiences.

Finding Romance

The contrast between similar patterns of friendship for men and women and different trends in romantic relationships could not be sharper. Second-generation African-Canadian women and men occupied very different positions within the local heterosexual market. All participants identified potential romantic partners in a context of heterosexuality and family expectations that they marry opposite-sex partners and have children. Participants noted that heteronormativity was deeply ingrained in their cultural and religious upbringing, and there was little space for the expression of alternative sexualities.[2]

---

1   Women participants did not discuss playing on sports teams or watching sports in their narratives about friendship networks.
2   Almost everyone said their parents would find it difficult to accept an LGBTQ child, as would the larger African community. One participant identified as bisexual, but was not out, and expected a heterosexual marriage. A few had LGBTQ friends, but none was from the local African Diaspora.

Participants were asked what qualities they looked for in a partner. Both men and women indicated that they looked for romantic partners who shared similar interests, and the vast majority – 88 per cent of men and 74 per cent of women – indicated that ethnic or racial background was not relevant in their choice. They felt little pressure from parents about a potential partner's cultural or racial background, characterizing their parents as "open minded" on this issue. Three participants were themselves from mixed families, with a White mother and African father (Jane, Hobbes, and Claudia), and several others mentioned family members in Canada who were married to partners who were not of African descent. In this context, mixed relationships and marriages did not seem to raise any concerns.

On the other hand, parents with strong religious values made it clear that they expected their child's partner to have a similar religious background, a position with which most participants agreed. In addition, a few parents provided advice about people their children should not consider marrying, usually referring to other African communities with which there was some historical animosity. For example, Ashley's mother, from Ghana, had long advised her daughter never to date a man from Nigeria. Ashley's current boyfriend, however, was Nigerian, and she noted that, despite prior warnings, her mother got along well with him. On the whole, then, participants felt little parental pressure when it came to the attributes of potential romantic partners. The one exception was Michael, whose parents did not approve of dating and who expected him to marry someone from within their conservative African church. As a result, Michael could not introduce his long-term White girlfriend to his parents, and felt that, now an adult, he still continued to live "two different lives."

Descriptions of ideal romantic partners were similar for men and women participants. Desired attributes typically included being goal oriented, hard-working, well educated, family oriented, sharing a common religion, and having some connection to a recent experience of migration. The significance of faith for the majority of participants was evident from the importance placed on the religion of potential partners. Almost all of those who identified as Christian (80 per cent of participants) considered Christianity the most important criterion for a potential partner. Similarly, being Muslim was considered essential for two of the three participants who identified as Muslim; the third participant who was Muslim had a Muslim father and a Christian mother, and he said he would be happy with a partner from either religion.

Most participants also expressed a strong preference for a partner with an immigrant background. This was often referenced by the notion that a prospective partner must "have some kind of culture" that distinguished them from mainstream Anglo-Canadian culture.[3] Those who were perceived to have "some kind of culture" include those from many different heritages, including a number of different European backgrounds. For example, partners who were White and described as having "some cultural difference" included people described as of Italian, Ukrainian, Portuguese, Norwegian, Irish, and German heritage, with a common link in parents who were not raised in Canada. Multigenerational White Canadians, on the other hand, did not have a recent immigrant experience that might have provided a point of commonality.

Gender constituted a significant factor shaping romantic relationships among the second generation. As we saw in Chapter 4, discourses about Black masculinity and femininity positioned African-Canadian men and women differently in terms of heterosexual desirability. Both men and women contended with negative stereotypes about Blackness linked to sexual exoticization, but hip hop and other forms of popular culture also reinforced the desirability of Black men as potential partners, especially in contexts of scarcity. In contrast, White beauty norms and popular culture further marginalized African-Canadian women. As a result, the men who participated in this research appear to have had a much wider field of romantic opportunities than the women.

Overall, men were twice as likely as women to have a current partner (56 per cent versus 26 per cent), and women were nearly three times more likely never to have had a romantic partner (32 per cent versus 12 per cent), even though the women's mean age was older than the men's (24.6 years versus 22.1 years). One man was married with a child, one woman was married with a child, one woman was married and childless, and one woman was divorced with children; the rest were in a combination of short- and long-term dating relationships.

As Table 5.1 shows, at the time of the interviews, a majority of men (56 per cent) had partners. We can also see that men's partners had a diverse range of ethnic and racialized backgrounds: four current partners were White, three were described as African, one was Jamaican, and one was of Chinese descent. If we add single men who identified previous partners (another 31 per cent of men), all but one previous girlfriend was identified as White. Taken together, more than 70 per cent

---

3 During several interviews, participants suggested to me that White people who were not recent immigrants did not have a "culture." Sometimes this was followed by "no offence," to which I responded "no offence taken." The notion of culture at play here was clearly cultural difference from the dominant cultural forms in Canada.

Table 5.1. Romantic relationships among Research Participants, by Gender

Relationship	Men	Women
Current partner	9 (56%)	5 (26%)
African/Black	4	5
White	4	0
Asian	1	0
Currently single	7 (44%)	14 (74%)
No previous partner	2	6
Previous partner	5	8
African/Black	0	4
White	4	4
Diverse*	1	0

*One single man identified three former girlfriends: one Asian, one White, and one of Caribbean origin.

of men with current and former romantic partners developed relationships with women from other racialized groups, usually with White women.

Almost all men (88 per cent) stated that ethnicity and race did not matter in their choice of romantic partners. It is notable that less than one-third of participants (31 per cent) had ever been romantically involved with a woman from the African diaspora. One explanation is the small size of the local diaspora – several men said they did not know many Black women and that was why they had never dated one. Another reason might be, as Hobbes said, explaining the diverse backgrounds of women he had dated, "I think, in a relationship, people want something different." Of the four men with current girlfriends of African descent, three of their partners immigrated to Canada when they were children[4] and the fourth was in a long-distance relationship with a woman in his home country of Sierra Leone.

A few men expressed an interest in dating women from the African diaspora. For example, Devon, whose previous partners had all been White, expressed a desire to pursue a relationship with a woman from his parent's home country of Ethiopia. He had recently travelled to Ethiopia, and had discovered a large expatriate community of Western-educated Ethiopian men and women with whom he shared much in common, and he planned to return soon. Two other men also expressed

---

4 Two women came from Rwanda and Ethiopia, respectively, and a third came from Jamaica, all when they were children.

a preference for dating a woman of African descent. Lamar stated that race did not really matter to him, but although he had previously dated only White women, now, "I prefer Black." Similarly Luke explained that when he was younger, he dated White women of different backgrounds, but as he got older and was thinking about marriage and children, he wanted a Black partner:

> LUKE: Race and colour didn't really matter to me when I was younger, but now I would say it would start mattering to me because I want my children to look like me, you know? When I say look like, I want them to be Black like me.

Luke was one of four men whose current partner was from the African diaspora.

In contrast to the men, nearly three-quarters of the women participants (74 per cent) were single at the time of the interviews (Table 5.1), including three women in their thirties. Only 26 per cent of women had a partner, and all current partners were Black. Four of the five partners were of African heritage and one was of Haitian descent. If we add single women's former partners (another 42 per cent of women), four were identified as of African origin and four were described as White. Taken together, nearly 70 per cent of women with current or former romantic partners developed relationships with men of African descent, the inverse of the pattern among men.

Surprisingly, given the demography of metro Vancouver, only four women participants had ever dated men from other racialized backgrounds. Moreover, most of the women's romantic liaisons were with men who were raised in Africa and came to Canada as adults. Of five current partners, three grew up in Africa and two came to Canada when they were children – one from Kenya and another from Haiti. All of the four previous Black partners also grew up in Africa and migrated as adults. In most cases, African partners did not come from the same country as the participants' parents, and these relationships developed while men were international students at local universities and colleges. Of nine current or previous Black male partners, almost 80 per cent grew up in African countries and were adults when they came to Canada. Only one female participant (Joy) was partnered with another member of the second generation from the local African community.

The pattern of romantic relationships among second-generation African-Canadians raises questions about the degree to which women intentionally limited potential romantic partners to African men. As we saw above, three-quarters of women (74 per cent) said that ethnic or racial background did not matter in their choice of partner. At the same time, slightly more women than men (four women and three men) expressed a preference for romantic partners of African descent.[5] Women explained this preference in terms of the importance of "commonalities around culture" and "an analysis of race" (Shukre), the "mutual understanding" that comes from common African roots (Stella), desiring "a culture that compliments my culture" (Linda), and finding it "hard to relate" to those who are not African descent, so "I tend to look at Black guys" (Denise).

Some women who said that race and culture did not matter still explicitly ruled out potential partners raised in Africa. For example, Jane stated, "I would not marry an African" because the cultural expectations are too different. Likewise Tina said, "I wouldn't date an African from Africa" because she believed they have very traditional views about women. On the other hand, she also acknowledged that she was "definitely attracted to Black men," and would be interested in dating an African-Canadian. The only woman participant married to an African-Canadian (Joy) also believed that "I would not connect with someone who is from Kenya now." Similarly Sarah insisted that a potential partner "has to have a North American cultural background." Some women, like Emily, who previously had dated men raised in Africa, identified cultural clashes, especially around gender relations, and now sought a partner who was "open minded," "worldly," and not raised in Africa. Even Shukre, who wanted a partner of African descent, acknowledged that "navigating gender stuff" had been a source of conflict in previous relationships with African men. Likewise Claudia believed that being an independent woman with a successful career had contributed to breakups with two previous partners from different African countries.

As we have seen, only one woman and two men who participated in this research had ever been romantically involved with partners from Vancouver's second-generation African community. Two men and one woman had had partners from the larger local Black Caribbean diaspora. In addition, one man and eight women had current or former partners who were raised in Africa.

Tina, one of the women who would not consider dating "an African from Africa," was very interested in African-Canadian men. She said the lack of romantic connections among African-Canadians might be

---

5 One woman said that, as a result of previous experiences of sexual violence, she had no interest in a romantic partner and did not intend to marry. She loved children, however, and expected to adopt her own in the future.

because the population was so small that they did not meet each other often. She also suggested, however, that African-Canadian men were influenced by White beauty norms and chose not to date Black women:

> TINA: I'm definitely attracted to Black men. I don't know why it hasn't happened yet but there's also … I mean, a lot of Black men that I've met, I can't make generalizations at all, [but] I see them prefer dating White girls.

Markor made a similar observation: "African-[Canadian] men would rather date people outside of the African race or descent." These sentiments are in line with research in the United States that shows that relationships between Black men and White women are much more common than relationships between Black women and White (or other racialized) men (Childs 2005; Wilkins 2012a). This pattern is repeated in Canada, where 30 per cent of Black men are in interracial marriages compared with only 20 per cent of Black women (Livingstone and Weinfeld 2015; Milan, Maheux, and Chui 2010). The result is fewer romantic options for heterosexual Black women: "the odds that black women in Canada will find romantic partners are much lower in comparison to black men" (Livingstone and Weinfeld 2015, 9).

Several women participants observed that among their networks, most second-generation women in the community were single, while men in the community had little difficulty finding romantic partners, most often White women. Indeed, these patterns are born out in this research. African-Canadian men had diverse options for romantic partners. All but one had current or former partners who had been raised in Canada, the vast majority of European (White) heritage, usually with a fairly recent family history of migration. Betty, one of the older participants at age thirty-one, noted that out of the ten African-Canadian women she knew well, only two were married; eight were single and not in relationships. This led Betty and her friends to ask, "so where are the men?"

The very limited dating histories female research participants had with men from other racialized groups suggests that the prevalence of White beauty norms marginalized African-Canadian women and shaped their romantic prospects in the heterosexual market in Vancouver. The vast majority of women (74 per cent) indicated they were open to relationships with men of any ethnic or racial background. Yet for the participants, relationships with men who were not Black were relatively rare; even relationships with Black men raised in Canada seemed few and far between.

African-Canadian men faced the opposite problem. Several recounted being pursued by White women who fetishized Black men as an "exotic fantasy." For example, Bob currently had a "very nice" White girlfriend, but he was cautious never to date women he thought were only interested romantically in Black men:

> BOB: Nine times out of ten, you are going to meet somebody who wants a Black man, and that's just not going to end up too well … I don't date, period, women who want to date Black men. No, it's too much pressure.

Whether discourses about Black sexuality lead to exoticization or lack of romantic interest, neither provides a good basis for developing a long-term heterosexual relationship.

For the most part, the men African-Canada women were able to partner with were Black men raised in Africa, with Afrocentric cultural understandings of beauty and attractiveness. Emily recalled that she had been very attracted to international students from Africa because she was "eager to learn about the culture, and I found that attractive in my partner." Like some other participants, however, she experienced "a lot of clashes," especially around gender expectations, and now sought a partner who was more "open minded." Although men raised in Africa might be more likely to find second-generation African-Canadian women attractive as potential partners, compatibility across cultural expectations could be more difficult to bridge. This left heterosexual African-Canadian women with fewer potential romantic partners and a greater likelihood of remaining single.

Almost all research participants expressed interest in marriage and having children;[6] three currently were raising children. Both men and women expected their African heritage to influence their approach to parenting, with a strong emphasis on discipline, respect for adults, the importance of education and family, and pride in their heritage. At the same time, although most rejected the more permissive aspects of parenting common in Canada, several said they favoured local approaches to discipline that eschewed forms of physical punishment.

With few exceptions,[7] participants developed stronger connections to the African diaspora as they got older, and almost all intended to

---

6 There were two exceptions: as noted, one woman did not want a romantic partner but wanted to adopt children, and one wanted to get married but intended to remain childless.

7 For example, Jessica did not have much connection with the local African Diaspora, and felt little connection with her parents' homeland, so she did not feel the necessity

facilitate relationships for their children so that they "don't have identity issues" (Joy). Most intended to take their children on regular trips to Africa to get to know their extended families and see what life is like in Africa, experiences that financial constraints prevented many of their own parents providing when they were young. As Jane said, "I feel like I lost out a lot" because she did not go to Ghana until she was twenty years old. As a result, growing up, she had less knowledge to challenge the negative stereotypes of Africa she encountered in school and the media. Luke wanted his children to be born in Uganda – even though they would grow up in Canada – so they would "know where they are from." Markor would like her children to live in Ghana during their early years, "to give them a solid base." Tina would also like her children to live in Kenya for a period of time because "it is just such an awesome community place to raise a child," and "I think that it is important being surrounded by Africans." Shukre stated that, "if I ever did have children I wouldn't raise them in Canada, I would raise them in East Africa," where there is a large Somali diaspora:

> SHUKRE: I want my children to grow up around people who look like them, at the very least, so they can have a sense of normalcy about their place and their own bodies. So when they came here [Vancouver] they would have connection to something else.

Connections with the local African diaspora were also considered important, and developing more friendships with others of African descent was one way to help ensure children grow up around other Africans and acquire a strong sense of identity (Joy). Research participants expected to introduce their children to the food, music, and culture they grew up with, and some also hoped their children would learn their heritage language, even if they themselves (for example, Terrence, Bob, and Danielle) did not speak their parents' mother tongue. Several mentioned how important it would be to have their parents involved in raising their grandchildren. Joy, who also had African in-laws, extended that to the role she hoped her in-laws would play in raising her future children.

---

of facilitating links for her children beyond connections with her own family in Canada. Another exception was Michael, who could not tell his parents about his long-term White girlfriend. He thought his parents were "too rigid," and he expected to embrace a "Western" approach that allows children more freedom to make their own decisions and their own mistakes. At the same time, he expected to take his children to Nigeria to learn what it is like to live there.

The majority of participants recognized that they would need to be sensitive to their partner's cultural background as well. In light of the general openness to relationships across cultural and racial backgrounds, African-Canadian men's pattern of romantic relationships with women outside of the African diaspora, and African-Canadian women's relationships with men raised in Africa, it is very likely that many would raise the next generation of African-Canadian children while simultaneously navigating across two substantially different cultural heritages.

Chapter Six

"I have so much more opportunities": Education and Career Goals

"I have so much more opportunities, and that's why we came"

– Lamar

"I want to do something with my life. I don't want to be just an immigrant who came to Canada"

– Charlotte

Parents with university degrees are much more likely to have children who pursue post-secondary education (Krahn 2017; Turcotte 2011). Institutions of higher education are central to the reproduction and intergenerational transmission of cultural, social, and economic capital (Bourdieu 1984). In the context of Canada, immigration status also affects educational attainment, with the children of immigrant parents having higher attainment than people whose parents were born in Canada (Abada, Hou, and Ram 2008, 2009; Abada and Tenkorang 2009a, 2009b). Second-generation African-Canadians who participated in this research were no exception to this trend. As we saw in Chapter 2, the parents of participants were very highly educated: 86 per cent of fathers and 74 per cent of mothers held a university or college degree. Although education attained in their homelands was rarely recognized in Canada, and most parents experienced downward class mobility, they maintained middle-class expectations for their children.

Indeed, such expectations seem to have been born out. All of the research participants had some post-secondary education, and most (57 per cent) were enrolled in a post-secondary program at the time of the interviews. There was a general consensus among participants that post-secondary education was the norm for second-generation women in the community, but less true for men. Several participants had brothers who either had not completed high school or had not pursued any post-secondary education, and others compared themselves to male friends for whom this was also the case. As we saw in Chapter 4, and in contrast to much of the literature, women who participated in this research were more likely than men to encounter teachers who underestimate their capabilities, discouraged their academic ambitions, and otherwise placed roadblocks on their continuing their education beyond high school.

Well-educated immigrant parents might have imparted cultural capital that values higher education, and set clear expectations when it came to educational and career goals, but most families experienced downward class mobility after migration and were not able to provide much financial support for post-secondary schooling. A majority of research participants were self-supporting throughout their post-secondary education, combining part-time work and further study. Some participants pursued a short, career-specific college program first, such as care aides, medical receptionist, or technician, and used a job in that field to support themselves during the longer journey towards a university degree.

In this chapter I explore the strategies second-generation African-Canadians employed to do something meaningful with their life, and address the challenges and accomplishments as they pursued educational and career goals. I also examine reasons participants believed that second-generation women were more likely than their male counterparts to pursue post-secondary education. Both men and women were optimistic about their abilities and what they could accomplish in the future. Older participants expressed satisfaction with what they had already attained, although many had goals not yet met. Almost all expected their lives would be better than their parents' post-migration circumstances, except in the few cases where parents had high-status professional jobs in Canada. As I discuss in Chapter 7, however, this overall sense of optimism about opportunities was tempered by the recognition that being Black meant often having to work harder than others to reach goals.

Seizing Opportunities: Higher Education

Family circumstances shape young adults' strategies for the future. Within the local African community, downward class mobility associated with migration both reinforced the importance of higher education and made its attainment more complex. Participants were acutely aware of the challenges their parents overcame as they struggled to re-establish themselves in Canada, and how hard they had worked to provide a promising future for their children. Many witnessed first-hand the erasure of educational qualifications attained in their homelands and the consequent repercussions of limited employment opportunities. Terrence, for example, discussed the impact of his father's significant downward mobility after coming to Canada:

> TERRENCE: When he came here, he already had a degree in business administration, but when he came it's not credible. So, basically, his degree was just cancelled out. So, yeah obviously that struggle was there. Working, coming from working for the Ministry of Housing to being a security guard or a bus driver is obviously a lot different.

Others remembered the years of retraining their fathers and/or mothers underwent and the difficulty of "taking care of us, and taking night school, and working" at the same time (Emily).

Short-term financial demands limited long-term career options for their parents, sometimes preventing them from pursuing their own preferred career goals. As Shukre observed, her mother did what she needed to do, not what she wanted to do, in order to best provide for her family:

> SHUKRE: My mom never wanted to be a nurse. It was fuelled by what would do [to] make her the most amount of money. And I know it was because it would give. She went into nursing because it was into a medical profession, because it paid benefits to all of her children, it just did. And she knew it. And she knew it was based on seniority, and she knew that as long as she maintained a certain number of years she would continue having the same kind of access. She knew they had scholarship programs to get us into school. It would give her a steady pay cheque. She knew she would get off-time on sick days. She knew that.

Parents' sacrifices did not necessarily end when their children grew up, setting in place lifelong repercussions. For example, after retirement, Emily's parents sold their house in metro Vancouver, bought a house in Ethiopia, and now split their time between the two, at least partly in order to have a better of quality of life:

> EMILY: The thing is, working in Canada, their quality of life decreased. They were doing very well in Ethiopia, and so when they came here ... So, then they went back. Their quality of life is better now.

For half the year they were in Ethiopia and half the year they lived with their adult children in Vancouver. The cost of living was much cheaper in Ethiopia, so this strategy improved their standard of living. It also had the advantage of keeping them firmly connected to extended kin in Ethiopia, but it also meant that connections to their Canadian children and grandchildren were loosened for half the year.

Keen observers of their parents' struggles and hard work, research participants recognized that, "for the first generation, everyone had a difficult time" (Betty). As such, the second generation recognized ways in which they were more privileged and had a wider range of opportunities available to them. Advantages were linked to their local Canadian-English accents, which did not impede communication or signal immigrant status (linguistic cultural capital),[1] local educational credentials that employers easily recognized (educational cultural capital), extensive local networks derived from growing up in Vancouver (social capital), and locally acquired knowledge about how to negotiate local institutions effectively as they pursued their goals (institutional cultural capital).

Second-generation African-Canadian participants acknowledged that they had many opportunities, and believed it was up to them to take advantage of them, at least partly as a way to acknowledge the sacrifices made by their parents:

ASHLEY: I have huge opportunity and a huge head start in life that a lot of people don't.

LAMAR: I have so much more opportunities, and that's why we came, right? So, she [mom] brought us here so I can have a better life, and I think she has done that.

RYLAN: That was another thing that helped me growing up. It helped me kind of stay on the right path from my parents. You know, it's like you don't want to waste this opportunity because they didn't have that opportunity.

AYINKE: I have a better life than my mom because she gave me a better life, you know? That's the same way I want for my kids. Like she told us one time, "I'm giving you all the opportunities I never had as a young girl growing up. I want you to make use of all that opportunity. All what I'm doing is because of you guys, to make sure you guys succeed and have a better future."

---

1   As discussed more fully in Chapter 8, processes of racialization in Canada are such that an English accent that is not local is an important marker of immigrant status. However, other people still might have assumed that research participants were immigrants, even if they were not, based on skin colour, name, food preferences, and other cultural attributes.

Table 6.1. Research Participants' Highest Level of Education Attained, by Gender

Highest Level of Education Attained	Women		Men	
	(number)	(per cent)	(number)	(per cent)
Enrolled in college/university program	11	58	9	56
Some post-secondary courses (no credential attained and not a student)	0	0	1	6
College diploma/certificate	1	5	3	19
Bachelor's degree	6	31	2	12
Master's degree	1	5	1	6

MICHAEL: I don't want to waste it because I know how much hard work went into this, so I'm using that as a motivation. But it's the second generation I would say is guilt tripped. That's going to be it. The second generation is extremely guilt tripped because they're not advertising how much work it took them to get here, but they're not making it, they're not hiding it either.

Whether in response to what Michael called first-generation "guilt tripping" or Rylan saw as incentives "to stay on the right path," the downward mobility and lessons of hard work modelled by their immigrant parents served as motivation to seek out and seize available opportunities to build a better future for themselves.

For all the participants in this study, pursuing post-secondary education constituted a central strategy for building a better future. Long-term educational aspirations were high among both women and men, with, as noted, more than half enrolled as post-secondary students at the time of the interviews. As Table 6.1 shows, more women (seven) than men (three) already had a university degree, including one man and one woman each with a master's degree. The older mean age of women than men (24.6 years versus 22.1 years) partly accounts for this gender difference. In contrast, more men (three) than women (one) had an occupation-specific college certificate as their highest degree (as skilled construction, technician, care aide, and licensed practical nurse, respectively). Of the latter, the person in construction and the technician were the only two whose long-term career goals involved further training in blue-collar skills (furniture maker and electrician, respectively), and did not involve a university education.

When we compare the programs in which research participants were currently enrolled (Table 6.2), we see that the majority of women

Table 6.2. Type of Post-secondary Program Currently Pursued by Research
Participants, by Gender

Program	Women		Men	
	(number)	*(per cent)*	*(number)*	*(per cent)*
College certificate (not transferable to university)	2	18	0	0
College diploma (transferable to university)	0	0	3	33
Bachelor's degree	8	73	6	67
Graduate degree	1	9	0	0

(eight) were enrolled in a bachelor's degree program at a university and another was enrolled in a post-graduate degree program in dental school. Only two women were pursuing an occupation-specific college certificate, as resident care aid and early childhood educator, respectively, and they too had longer-term plans to attend university (one to complete a bachelor's degree in music and the other to become a registered nurse). Fewer men were currently in university (six), but another three were enrolled in college diploma programs that provide university transfer credit and a ladder into a bachelor's degree at provincial universities.[2] All three planned to transfer to university in their third year. At the time of the interviews, none of the men was enrolled in an occupation-specific college program. However, one man who had previously completed a few college courses and was not currently a student planned to register soon in a career-specific program to become a special education assistant. All the men who were current post-secondary students were either already in a university program or a college program that would count towards a university degree. College tuition is considerably lower than university tuition in British Columbia, so pursuing the first two years of university-transfer courses at a local college before transferring to a university is one strategy for containing the costs associated with post-secondary education.

As self-funded students, most research participants had developed long-term strategies to meet the financial costs of post-secondary training.

---

2 The post-secondary system in British Columbia includes a large number of community colleges that offer both short-term, career-specific, one- or two-year programs and university transfer programs. Many students complete the first two years of university-level courses at a community college, then transfer to a university for the last two years to complete a bachelor's degree.

For example, one woman took a nine-month program to become a clinical assistant. With that qualification, she obtained work in a medical clinic, where she continued to work while attending university. Part way through her degree, she got a better job as a clinical assistant in a large hospital. Since completing her bachelor's degree, she had been working in two different hospitals in the area while saving to pursue a master's in public health. Another woman trained as an eye technician and worked in that capacity while she pursued a bachelor's degree. Since graduating, she had continued to work in the same occupation while saving to pursue a master's degree in the field of health care.

Several participants held sports scholarships at various times for soccer, wrestling, basketball and track and field, which helped pay their post-secondary tuition. With the exception of one woman who held a sports scholarship at a major American university for two years, the men's scholarships were all at local post-secondary institutions. Many men had dreamed of going to the United States to play, but their scholastic aptitude test scores were not high enough or scouts did not recruit them for other reasons. As James (2016) argues, young Black men are encouraged to concentrate on sports in the hope of winning a scholarship to an American university, even though greater concentration on academic subjects is much more likely to provide a more prosperous future. Although the sports scholarships reduced the costs of postsecondary schooling, the commitment in terms of time to a school team also necessitates part-time studies, sometimes with little direction. In such circumstances, attending college to play sports might not provide the anticipated future opportunities. Maxwell offered a good example of this conundrum. He held sports scholarships at three different local institutions over a five-year period without ever declaring a major field of study. A few years after he finished playing on college teams, he decided to pursue a degree in business administration, a goal he was slowly pursuing at night while working full time to support himself.

Many research participants combined part-time work with part-time studies or, less often, full-time work with part-time studies. At the time of the interviews, only a small number of participants (four women and three men) were full-time students who were not employed at the same time. These participants were able to combine student loans, savings from previous employment, and/or family support without the need to hold down a part-time job. For most participants who were students, however, paid work was essential. For the majority, their part-time jobs – include jobs in retail, a warehouse, tutoring, music lessons, performing arts, movie extra, research assistant, office assistant, youth worker, and babysitting – were unrelated to their longer-term career goals.

The tensions between the demands of school and those of work were particularly acute for some male participants. Limited financial resources and the need to contribute to family income have been identified as barriers to pursuing post-secondary education for second-generation African-Canadians (Kanu 2008; Shakya et al. 2010). As Jay recalled, he found it hard to turn down opportunities to earn more money, but too much work could undermine his long-term education goals.

> JAY: So, I was working two part-time jobs while I was studying five courses. And the money I was getting was so good, I was making about three grand to thirty-five hundred a month. My marks suffered so much I failed two courses. So, I mean, I'm paying for it right now.

Failing even one or two courses can have long-term consequences for the ability to fulfil longer-term goals. In Jay's case, as we will see below, he wanted to go to law school, something that requires a very high grade point average to accomplish.

Some research participants felt pressure to complete their post-secondary education quickly in order to contribute more to family finances. For example, Rylan was almost finished his two-year diploma program at a local college. He wanted to transfer to university to complete his bachelor's degree, but knew that combining it with his part-time job would mean at least an additional three years or more to attain the degree. As the eldest child, already twenty-three, he was not sure he could commit that much time before needing to work full time and contribute more financially. Rylan said, "I feel pressure to finish and get school done with to help out" and support his mother and younger siblings. As we see in the cases of Jay and Rylan, parents had instilled the value of higher education, but the economic consequences of immigrant parents' downward class trajectory could be a barrier to attaining these educational aspirations.

Careers and Goals

The pursuit of post-secondary education is not usually a goal in itself – in most cases, higher education is connected to larger career aspirations. Many research participants identified career goals linked to finding socially meaningful work that would allow them to contribute in important ways to the larger community. For some, thinking about socially meaningful careers was directly connected to their own, or their parents', immigrant experiences. Several woman and men wanted to help immigrants and refugees navigate the often difficult process of settlement in Canada, their desire to help drawing on their own personal immigrant experiences as a way to contribute to the larger society:

> CHARLOTTE: I want to influence people in some way, I'm not sure how, but I want to make an influence. I want to do something, it's like you look and little girls can be like, "I want to be like her" … I want to be someone you can look up to. Because when they come here, they are discouraged completely.
>
> DENISE: My ultimate goal – I know it may be a long ways away, but I hope one day to attain it – is to work in an organization where I can help people coming from Africa … I do not know what that will be, but if you like, I would like to work with people and help people adapt to life in Canada.
>
> ALI: With a social work [degree], my area actually, I want to work with immigrants or refugees.
>
> TERRENCE: I want to work with troubled youth. I always felt the need to give back to Canada since I came here … And my dream is to hopefully one day to set up my own rec[reation] centre or something more focused on immigrant youth coming to Canada.

Participants identified a wide range of occupations they intended to pursue that address social issues, often but not always with a particular focus on immigrants and refugees. These included working in the fields of social work, youth worker, physical education teacher, coach, advocate for immigrants and refugees, and working in the criminal justice system as a customs officer or lawyer. The single most common career goal was to become a registered nurse (RN), a preference that might have been shaped by the fact that 40 per cent of participants' mothers worked in nursing.[3] One woman was already working as an RN and another as a licensed practical nurse with plans to upgrade to an RN.[4] A third woman who was pursuing a certificate in early childhood education had a longer-term plan to become an RN. In addition, one man working as a care aide hoped to become an RN in the future.

---

3 Nine mothers were RNs, four were licensed practical nurses (LPNs), and one was training to become an LPN.
4 An LPN is a two-year college diploma; an RN is a four-year university degree. Hospitals in British Columbia are staffed by RNs; LPNs typically work in residential care facilities.

Other research participants had a more global vision for their longer-term career goals, often linked to the desire to have an impact in their parents' homeland:

> MARKOR: As a family we do have a plan, mostly with my mom's research. She wants to do something with street kids in Ghana. So we work on that as a family and individually, based on what we do in school we will try to contribute in some way to Ghana.
>
> EMILY: I am planning to do my master's, probably in nutritional health.
>
> RESEARCHER: So, what is your broader career goal?
>
> EMILY: To work in development in public health or nutrition assessment, in my future, globally … I was thinking Cambodia, actually, before Ethiopia.
>
> LAMAR: One of my goals [is] I want to go back to Africa and start a [basketball] development league for Africans because I feel there's so much untapped potential out there. They've got the high athleticism, and if they just had the development programs in place, all over the NBA and they'd kill it … The thing is about basketball, what it did for me, was it taught me work ethic, discipline. And once you learn that, you can apply it to everything.
>
> KWEKU: I'm going to practise [law] and maybe go into politics. I've always had this dream that I'd go back to Ghana because you know how the political system is still a little corrupt. I always had this dream to go back and run for president or be in politics in Ghana.
>
> JAY: I plan to go to law school. If you asked me what I wanted for work, so I want to do human rights law and international law. My goal number one once I finish law school. I want to work with United Nations and then wherever that needs to be.

As we can see, whether it involved supporting street kids, public health, politics, or human rights law, some participants were very invested in the promise of making a difference well beyond the borders of Canada.[5] This desire to influence events in their parents' homeland speaks to the deep attachment many participants had to their African heritage.

Not all participants were motivated by an explicit desire to give something back to the larger society. Like other young adults, many were drawn to professional occupations that promised financial

---

5 It is noteworthy that those who planned to work abroad, largely in African countries, included both those in the second generation (Kweku was born in Canada and Jay and Lamar came at age two and four, respectively) and members of the 1.5 generation (Emily was six and Markor was sixteen when they came to Canada).

security, were interesting, or had more autonomy and scope for career development. Some participants were already working in professional fields, including as a nurse, chartered accountant, planner, designing programs for youth in crisis, and sessional instructor at a university. Several participants who already had a university degree planned to pursue a graduate degree or a professional degree in law, dentistry or medicine.

For the most part, participants who were working in a job related to their career goal or who had attained their career goal already were satisfied with their career so far. For example, not long after completing her degree as a registered nurse, Joy was hired at a local hospital in a job she described as "awesome." Devon enjoyed his work as a consultant, and observed that, as a chartered accountant, he had the freedom to find work anywhere in the world. Shukre was doing "exactly what I hoped to do," designing programs for youth, and her only concern was that "I'm only twenty-four and I'm like, what the hell is next? I think I've hit it." Bob was engaged in interesting work as a youth educator before the economic downturn eliminated those opportunities and sent him back to graduate school. At the time of the interview, he had just completed a graduate degree in planning and was enthusiastic about his new career. Although Maxwell had not finished his degree in business yet, he was already working in a financial institution and was confident his degree would enhance his opportunities for promotion. Maxwell said, "I'm ok with where I am now, starting off at the bottom and making my way up." Claudia drew on her master's in the performing arts, and considered herself fortunate to be able to make her living as a performing artist and sessional instructor at a local university. Thus, although the younger members of the second generation who participated in this research were still pursuing their educational goals in order to attain their desired career, some of those who were a little older were working in their chosen professional fields. As I discuss in Chapter 7, participants believed that because they were Black, they had to work harder to get recognition in their jobs, but they remained optimistic about the future and were determined to seize opportunities that came along.

Gender Differences

Everyone who participated in this research was optimistic about their own prospects, but they also suggested that, in the larger African-Canadian community, women were more likely than men to pursue post-secondary education and carve out a promising future. African immigrant parents typically place a very high value on education, and expect both sons and daughters to pursue higher education (Arthur 2010; Creese 2011). Nevertheless, gendered cultural expectations, and different treatment of Black men and women in the wider society, including in the school system, help to explain why fewer second-generation men than women pursue postsecondary education.

As discussed in Chapter 4, teenage boys in the community were allowed much greater freedom to engage with their peers, and experienced considerable pressure to emulate elements of hip hop culture and sports celebrities, pressure that might distract them from academic pursuits in high school. In contrast, teenage girls were expected to be either at school or at home and, lacking the interest from their peers that the boys received, tended to make academic achievement their primary focus. As Betty observed, these gender differences shaped her and her brother in ways that had long-term effects on their adult lives:

> BETTY: For us as girls, culturally, we are at home … [the boys] would go
> out but we won't be able to … So [my brother] hung out with his friends.
> This was his way of connecting and belonging. And we were like the
> girls who do what the parents want. And it was just accepted. I mean
> I never looked at it when I was growing up, I just thought, well, I have
> homework, I had to finish it. I had this mentality that was focused.

Betty was determined to pursue post-secondary education, and now had a bachelor's degree in hand and a relatively high-paying job in health care, and planned to pursue a master's degree to further enhance her career prospects. In contrast, her older brother, now in his mid-thirties, never performed well in high school, did not pursue any additional education, and continued to have precarious employment. She attributed this trajectory, at least in part, to the sharper identity crisis experienced by second-generation boys as they navigated peers' and parents' expectations:

> BETTY: My brother is the oldest and he is four years older than me … I
> think he was always bad with those things … just partying. You know,
> the typical person. And so it was just what he kind of had to go through
> in those times. I think there was a lot of pressure, too, for him as a
> Black man or boy. Was he African American? Was he Canadian? Was he
> Ethiopian?

Betty compared high school graduation and university attendance rates among second-generation boys and girls that she knew. "Out of the boys, one out of five graduated. There are tons of girls, ten out of ten."

Similarly Shukre said, "most young Black men that I know haven't finished high school. They're definitely not going on to university."

The stereotype of the "cool Black guy" that resulted in great popularity among peers in high school was connected with more negative associations in the broader society. As Ashley, Emily, and Shukre noted, common associations with crime and aggression devalue Black men in Canadian society, damaging, rather than enhancing, their self-esteem and discouraging many from striving for a better life through conventional routes such as higher education:

> EMILY: My brothers were seen, in a lot of cases, they were going to a store, they think they're thieves or they think that, you know, they don't go to school or anything. My brothers, I think they actually took that hard. And sometimes because of that perception, they're like, "well, they think of me this way, so why don't I just act this way."
>
> ASHLEY: I feel also like, in this society, men, they've been, I don't want to say, maybe devalued in the society a bit more than back home. Back home there's a respect for man and men are valued, women are too, which is very appreciable in Ghana. Women are valued, and men are valued. But here, men are often looked down upon and things like that, and so it doesn't push them to strive or to achieve anything.
>
> SHUKRE: My brother never did well in school. I think living as a young Black man in this society, people would set him up. They'd be like, "he's aggressive." He wasn't aggressive. He grew up with five sisters and a mom. He's a very soft guy, I think … And folks were like, "you are too aggressive." They wanted him to be aggressive because that's what young Black men are, right? They are aggressive. And so they were perpetuating that.

These women's descriptions of their brothers are resonant with much of the literature on African-Canadian youth and disengagement from schools in Canada. The school environment is alienating for African-Canadian students who do not see themselves reflected in the curriculum, or in the teaching staff, and who are subject to low expectations and other racialized stereotypes that result in heightened surveillance and harsher penalties for Black boys who misbehave (Codjoe 2001; Conroy 2013; Ibrahim and Abdi 2016a; James 2012). As Dei and colleagues (1997) argue, these are the very conditions that "push out" Black adolescents before graduating from high school and that sap any motivation to pursue higher education.

In addition to these patterns within schools, which can be particularly discouraging for young Black men, some research participants also pointed to the greater pressure on young men in the community to earn as much money as possible once they graduated. Cultural expectations that men should be economic providers, in a context where families had limited means to provide a lot of extras, helped steer men into full-time work as soon as possible:

> EMILY: I can only say, with my brothers and my cousins, like, their parents or my parents, it was very important that the man is the supporter or the man takes care of the kids or his wife ... Even though it was subtle it was distinct, and I think that's why education is not important even though education would probably get them more money in the long run. It's just the fast here and now.
>
> FORLAN: I think they [women] are doing great in education. I mean, the guys I know, after high school they just [found] work. And if the job pays a lot, that's it. No school.
>
> CHARLOTTE: I would say some kids, they finish high school and they start working, and they make a little money and they feel like it's OK, and they don't want to go back to school. So, I guess most boys do that. It's like, you make a little money and then you make enough to afford to buy some car, and you think it's OK to just stay there instead of actually doing something. Which is what my older brother [did] ... He got his high school diploma, but it's like he started working after that, and feels like he doesn't want to go back to school and do something. It's like I'm fine here getting fourteen dollars an hour and I don't want to do anything else.

This conflict between short-term and long-term earning power is common in low-income and working-class households. To see higher education as another viable option, young men have to conceive of the possibility of academic success – a tall order for those already disengaged in high school. As Lamar observed, as men get older, it becomes even more difficult to pursue post-secondary education, especially once they had their own family to support:

> LAMAR: The peers I grew up with ... They are reaching that age where they don't want to go back to school. They have families and stuff like that. So, they can't really pursue something like a law degree or something like that. They have to be content with, you know, working dead-end jobs.

Gendered cultural expectations around dating and marriage, as well as where second-generation African-Canadian women and men were located in the heterosexual market (see Chapter 5), also shaped women's greater likelihood of pursuing higher education. As Betty and Emily observed, the fact that teenage girls were not permitted to date in high school enhanced their focus on education. Women were more likely to put their energies into performing well at school, so it is not surprising that they were more likely to achieve the high grades, personal focus, and motivation to pursue post-secondary education. Over time, the focus on academic performance in high school shifted to pursuing longer-term educational and career goals:

> BETTY: I think a huge part of my high school, and that part in a young girl's life, was work. OK, this is what you do. You go to church. I think that also plays a huge part of the fact that you don't date. If you're going to date, then you're going to marry. There's no other thing going on there. And so, they don't leave you much of a choice. Then you work, go to school, and go to church. And those are the things that you need to do.
> EMILY: Whereas for me, because marriage was not an option, I think we were pushed to do school. School was very important, but we weren't pressured with marriage ... My parents were very "you need to be independent." So I think that's very key: "take as long as it takes to finish school and get the job that you need."

As other participants noted, for Black men, being objects of White heterosexual desire in high school and beyond was "such a big distraction" (Jay). This kind of distraction could impede academic performance and enhance the drive to make money as soon as possible. It was a situation that adolescent girls in the community usually did not encounter, and, as we saw in Chapter 5, most young women who participated in this study remained undistracted by romantic relationships. Without family pressure to marry young, and with limited ability to find romantic partners, women were encouraged even more to pursue long-term academic and career goals.

Chapter Seven

Living "under a microscope": Navigating Public Spaces

"I'm under a microscope being Black and being more visible because I'm not like everybody else"

– Jay

As outlined in Chapter 2, processes of racialization in Canada continue to privilege those who are identified as White.[1] White privilege is a product of centuries of colonization of Indigenous peoples, preference for European settlers, and discrimination against immigrants from other parts of the world, including Africa and Asia. The legacy of this history persists, despite the emergence of discourses of inclusion, multiculturalism, and reconciliation, so that White men and women remain at the centre of the 'imagined community' of Canada (Abu-Laban and Gabriel 2002; Bauder 2011; Day 2000; Li 2003; Mackey 2002).

Peggy McIntosh (1995) compares White privilege to an "invisible weightless knapsack" that provides useful tools, free passes, and other resources that can be used to help navigate daily life. Since it is invisible and weightless, McIntosh argues, most White people are unaware that they have any special privileges compared to other groups. The privileges associated with Whiteness are such that, in most situations, White people are judged by individual actions, rather than by preconceived expectations linked to group stereotypes. When group stereotypes do

---

1 Who is considered White changes over time. One example of this is the case of Irish immigrants, who were considered non-White in nineteenth-century England and North America. Indeed, Irish immigrants were sometimes depicted as Black. This example highlights racialization as a process linked to relations of power and inequality between groups, and not connected to any meaningful biological distinctions among humans (Jacobson 1999; Miles 1989).

come into play, it is typically to the benefit of White men and women. For example, Whiteness is central to perceptions about the type of person who makes a good political leader in Canada. A leader who is a member of a racialized minority is subject to a different level of scrutiny, and must work harder to prove themselves worthy. Racialization always intersects with other axes of power and privilege, including gender, class, sexuality, age, and (dis)ability. Continuing the example above, most political leaders in Canada are not just White; they are also overwhelmingly cisgender men, publicly heterosexual, able bodied, and from middle- to upper-class backgrounds.

Specific circumstances, like poor performance in a leadership position, a record of dishonesty, or being a woman, might bring into question the leadership capacity of a particular White individual. Questioning the qualifications of a specific White person, however, does not alter overall assumptions about White people as suitable leaders. Perceptions about leadership are shaped by historical patterns, which in turn influence normative assumptions about who belongs and who seems out of place, in different contexts. This analogy to leadership can be extended to the way Whiteness shapes positive perceptions about people in public spaces, be they co-workers, neighbours, or strangers. Whiteness operates as the unmarked (and unacknowledged) category of racialization, the norm against which all others are measured as different. For the most part, White men and women in Canada have the privilege of not thinking about how they are racialized as they move through public spaces and engage in their daily lives. The ability to remain unaware of how Whiteness aids most social interactions and navigation of public spaces in Canada is a critical dimension of White privilege.

In contrast, second-generation African-Canadians are acutely aware of how their racialized Black bodies, very small numbers, hypervisibility, and dominant discourses about Black women and men shape their social interactions and treatment in public spaces. African-Canadians cannot be invisible and "unmarked" in Vancouver. As noted previously, in the 2016 census, only 1.7 per cent of the metro Vancouver population identified as of African ethnic origin and only 1.2 per cent identified as Black (Statistics Canada 2016a, 2016c). Popular culture, meanwhile, is awash in representations of, and discourses about, Blackness, embedded in histories of British and French colonialism, the politics of race in the United States, and the history of anti-Black racism in Canada. In this chapter, I explore some of the ways processes of racialization shape everyday interactions in public spaces through the metaphor of living "under a microscope," including how gendered discourses about Blackness affect women and men differently. I then address what it means to live under a microscope at work, as research participants provided examples of racial micro-aggressions they had experienced in their workplaces. Finally, I examine strategies that research participants drew on to build resilience. In Chapter 8, I explore another dimension of racialization, as African-Canadians are presumed to be immigrants from somewhere else and are not recognized as being at home in Vancouver.

Living "under a microscope"

As adults, African-Canadian men in Vancouver did not enjoy the celebrity status most experienced in high school. As we saw in Chapter 4, female participants never enjoyed such adulation. Jay compared his transition from being "glamorized" as a teenager, when there was a positive association with being singled out by peers who sought his attention, to his being placed "under a microscope" as an adult:

> JAY: I feel like now I'm more under their microscope, especially at work, being Black. And as a teenager I don't know if I was under a microscope or if I was more glamorized ... So I'm under a microscope being Black and being more visible because I'm not like everybody else.

The analogy to living life under a microscope highlights the effect of heightened visibility for African-Canadian men and women in Vancouver, who were unable to melt into the background even if they wished to. Racialized Black bodies stand out, so their activities are magnified just as items placed under a microscope are enlarged for enhanced observation and evaluation. Rylan used a similar analogy – of feeling as if his activities were viewed through a magnifying glass: "it's almost like it's a target on me and everything I do is magnified as an African-Canadian."

In contrast to the ease with which White residents navigate most public spaces in metro Vancouver, African-Canadian men and women lived their daily lives under higher levels of scrutiny. Living "under a microscope" expresses the combined effects of hypervisibility as a very small minority and the prevalence of negative discourses about the supposed collective character of Black men and women. As a result, African-Canadians often found themselves prejudged by others' stereotypical expectations, and had to work harder to prove their individual capabilities.

Both men and women participants in this research observed that the behaviour of African-Canadian men was subject to an even higher level of magnification than was true for women, and this more intense scrutiny was directly related to popular discourses about Black masculinity. Shukre argued that "Black women are perceived to be safer than Black men," so women were less likely to be objects of fear in public spaces. She worried about the long-term mental health implications for Black men who live with a constant "feeling of being watched and stalked and surveilled." Jane noted that she sometimes argued with her brothers about the level of racism in Vancouver: "my brothers tell me that 'you just don't see it' or 'it doesn't happen to you because you're a girl, but there's still racism.'" As we will explore more later in this chapter, one significant difference is that almost all the men in this research recounted problematic interactions with police officers, while most women did not. Several women did, however, recount examples of their brothers' experiences with the police.

Intense scrutiny affects situations that range from the more mundane aspects of daily life, such as what to wear in different social situations, to those that can be life altering, such as interactions with the police. Many of these more mundane encounters seem trivial when considered in isolation, but make up what Philomena Essed (1991) calls the micro inequities of everyday racism. As isolated incidents, micro inequities can be hard to see until the overall pattern is brought into focus. Some scholars highlight the subtle yet aggressive nature of these interactions. Huber and Solorzano (2015, 298) define racial micro-aggressions as "a form of systemic, everyday racism used to keep those at the racial margins in their place." In a context where blatant racism is increasingly considered inappropriate, racial micro-aggressions can flourish because the interactions seem innocuous to those who are not targeted. Augie Fleras (2016, 2) suggests that racial micro-aggressions constitute "a new face of racism" in Canada. As we will see, second-generation African-Canadians in metro Vancouver encountered diverse forms of racial micro-aggressions as they navigated public spaces, micro-aggressions that are embedded within, and that reproduce, systemic forms of racism in Canada.

Living "under a microscope" required African-Canadians to be cognizant of how the way they dressed affected their treatment in public spaces. For African-Canadian women this meant modest dress to deflect from the discourses around hypersexuality. For men it meant being well dressed, rather than casual or unkempt, to send signals of respectability that countered discourses of the hip hop image of the gangster. For both men and women it meant presenting an image that differed from those that dominate popular culture, to distinguish themselves as reputable, to be taken seriously, and, for men especially, not to be feared.

Bob argued that he was always very conscious of the image he presented, and he had to modify his image depending on the part of town he was in, the specific location, and the time of day or night. He suggested that, in general, he needed to be "well dressed" to avoid uncomfortable situations. For example, if "I'm going out to a bar I have to dress up a little nicer"; but then again he could not be "too suave" either, or that could also send the wrong message. Bob noted that, occasionally, in the poorer part of town, being a Black man who dresses more casually could be an advantage because he was perceived as a "tough" guy who should not be trifled with:

> BOB: It also has other benefits of being a Black man, like going to the Downtown Eastside ... I could walk through the Eastside and no one would bat an eye. People thought I was Black, people also thought I was tough. Like I was also not a target.

On the other hand, contexts in which stereotypes about Black men can be advantageous are few compared to the range of situations in which outcomes can be problematic. In most situations, then, dressing well aided Bob's passage through public spaces. He observed that this also meant he "can't play" with different identities and fashion statements, unlike his White friends, who had more room to experiment without any negative ramifications.

Hobbes said he expected to be subjected to racial profiling because he anticipated other people would judge him according to stereotypes about Black men:

> HOBBES: If I really am honest with myself, I do kind of expect a certain level of racism. I do. I expect a certain level of racial profiling. I expect a certain level of preconceived ideas.

When asked what types of situations lead to racial profiling, Hobbes explained that it was most common in "unscreened interactions" or circumstances without a pre-existing personal relationship of some kind. Strangers, he reported, were most likely to profile him racially. Research participants were more likely to be judged on their individual capabilities by people they knew and with whom they had an ongoing connection. As we will see, sometimes co-workers, bosses, or clients also prejudged capabilities, but Hobbes said that random interactions with strangers had more potential to expose him to racism.

Other men also pointed out that dressing well was important to get respectful treatment in public spaces. Both Luke and Maxwell drew attention to the positive effect of wearing a business suit:

> LUKE: People judge you by the way you dress, you know, and I feel like some people, this is what I say ... If you want to survive as a Black in this society, you need to dress more formally. Because then people will look at you and be like, "yeah, this guy is proper, this guy probably has more money." You can be a poor guy wearing a business suit.
>
> MAXWELL: When you dress a certain way, people think, oh you're just a thug, right? You're a Black guy, you're a thug, yeah, that's what you should be wearing. Even now, when I go to work, I'm dressed up. So I go toward downtown and people are looking at me in a different way – oh, it's a very elegant-looking young man versus if I were walking downtown wearing baggy jeans halfway down my waist. They look at me like, "ugh." I'm still the same person but I'm just dressed differently.

A business suit is associated with a more esteemed class location, signalling greater affluence and a middle-class occupation. Hence wearing a suit or other attire associated with middle-class professional work eased African-Canadian men's and women's movement through public spaces by differentiating their class position and dissociating themselves from poverty and inner-city ghettoes in American popular culture.

When African-Canadian men were dressed more casually, the reverse was true. Looking unkempt suggests poverty and a disreputable character. Wearing track pants and hoodies is reminiscent of hip hop culture, although it is also typical attire for people involved in sports. Michael contrasted how he was treated when wearing a hoodie and sweat pants to his usual treatment in public spaces. Michael wears glasses, and he believes that made him look "brainy" and distanced him from less reputable images of Black men in popular culture, but he said he was not treated well when wearing athletic clothing:

> MICHAEL: I don't really care, but it's kind of funny, just having glasses and looking brainy and not fitting to that [stereotype]. I think it helps. It does the opposite. Like, I am actually treated well. It's just when I am lazy and don't like to do the work, or walking home in track pants and my volleyball hoodie that things start to get weird.

For example, Michael had been stopped by security guards and accused of shoplifting when he went grocery shopping dressed in his tracksuit after a volleyball game. As a result of such experiences, Michael no longer bought food on the way home from a game; he went all the way home, changed clothing, and went out again to buy groceries:

> MICHAEL: It's actually really annoying, like really. I can't go out in my volleyball hoodie, track pants. Because I'm tired, and don't feel like dressing and walk into a store and decide I want to buy anything, because it's just annoying.

The impact of clothing on the way African-Canadians were treated in public spaces was particularly marked for men, for whom differentiating themselves from images connected to hip hop culture was one strategy for appearing more respectable. At the same time, although apparently linked less to dress, women also had experiences of being followed in stores as potential shoplifters. For example, Tina recalled being followed by a security guard in the liquor store:

> TINA: Even in the BC liquor store. My mom and I were going shopping for wine or whatever, the security guard was following us, and it's like, "what?" My mom is very well dressed. I mean I'm not always well dressed, but you know even if we weren't, there's no reason other than the fact we are Black that I can think of. And it's happened a few times in the BC liquor store, but also in [other] stores. It's really funny. Even in just normal stores that aren't even family owned.

In Tina's experience, even being well dressed and with her mother, a much older adult, did not necessarily prevent this kind of surveillance. Ayinke pointed to another facet of racialized scrutiny in stores: assumptions that African-Canadians are poor and probably cannot afford to buy expensive items. She recalled one incident while shopping with an African-Canadian friend. A sales clerk promised to hold some dresses for her friend while she tried on more clothing, but instead the sales clerk put all the dresses back on the rack:

> AYINKE: The lady was like, "oh, I put them back in the rack because I thought you wouldn't be able to pay for it." And my friend, J.A. – I don't know if you know J.A. because she teaches about African immigration. So she was so angry and she said, "why are you being racist?" And the lady said, "oh, I'm not being racist, I just know you can't afford it."

Needless to say, neither Ayinke nor J.A. purchased anything in that store.

Hypersexuality is a popular discourse about Black women that can also shape treatment in public spaces. As Jane said, "guys always assume that Black girls are like crazy in bed." In most contexts, women typically dressed modestly, rather than in highly sexualized ways, so variations in women's dress were not necessarily linked to intensified public scrutiny. Stella, however, recalled an incident when she was walking down the street in the middle of the day and a police offer pulled over in his car for no apparent reason and asked if she was a prostitute:

> STELLA: The cop actually stopped, pulling over to the side, he come and they asked me if I was a prostitute. Yeah, like out of the blue. I wasn't wearing revealing clothes. I was wearing long pants with a t-shirt, covered t-shirt, and I just couldn't understand why the cop stopped and asked me that. And I was like, "why would you ask me if I'm a prostitute? What did I do? Did I stop any car? Did I stop anyone and ask them if they want anything? Why would you ask me that?" I felt dehumanized. I was upset, completely ruined my day.

Stella observed that this incident had no connection to how she was dressed or to anything else she could think of other than the mere fact of walking down the street as a Black woman. As Maynard (2017, 138) argues, the idea that "Black women in public are involved in the sex trade reproduces age-old associations between Black women and criminal sexuality." Indeed, this demeaning incident is inexplicable without reference to the prevalence of racialized discourses about Black women animating the police officer's behaviour.

A clear example of African-Canadian women's dress affecting treatment in public spaces is the response to Muslim women who wear a headscarf. Two women in this research identified as Muslim, and one wore a headscarf. As a result, Sarah said, "people don't see me as Black or African-Canadian, they see me primarily as Muslim." As such, Sarah was subjected to racialized stereotypes linked to rising Islamophobia in North America (Nagra 2017). She explained that "random people" came up to her in public spaces and asked her questions, often "with an intent to start an argument." She provided an example of a recent incident on the local rapid-transit system, SkyTrain:

> SARAH: The guy in the SkyTrain, he goes, "what do you think of the burqa? Because I don't think that that's right, and I think that if you're

going to wear the burqa you should just wear it at home." … The way
I dealt with that, I was very, very patient with him. Because that wasn't
the first time someone's come up to me and said something like that. You
know, the first time something like that happens, it's a shock because you
don't expect that. But after a while, a couple of SkyTrain encounters, I've
had someone ask me where I've got this costume from. So usually I try to
be as patient as possible and because I know they're not going to change
their minds about Islamic Muslims after a five-second conversation.

Although Sarah did not wear a burqa, the headscarf identifying her
visibly as Muslim was enough to engender this type of harassment in
public spaces. Sometimes stranger's comments were even more offen-
sive, and precluded any kind of conversation. One woman in a store
called her "al-Qaeda":

> SARAH: The first day of school I was at a shopping centre purchasing
> a phone, and an elderly Caucasian lady came up to me and said, "Al-
> Qaeda." And so ever since I would say, and I was dressed like this
> [casual clothes and a bright coloured headscarf], so it wasn't like I was
> covered up completely or dressed all in black or anything.

Sarah noted that this was the most abusive incident she had experienced, although her headscarf often elicited unwelcome exchanges
with strangers. Occasionally more positive interactions with strangers
also took place around her Muslim identity. On 1 July, Canada Day,
other people would smile at Sarah in appreciation when she wore "a
red scarf and a Canadian flag sticking out of my scarf." On another
occasion, a bystander who witnessed Sarah's being harassed on Sky-
Train offered her verbal support:

> SARAH: I remember at the end of the conversation with the man that
> asked me about the burqa, a woman, and of course everybody is
> listening because suddenly all conversation stops. I remember a woman
> as she walked out patting me on the back saying "I'm with you, girl." I
> was like, "thanks, OK."

Several men identified public spaces that required special care
because of the potential for violence. Scholars of masculinity note that
male violence towards other men is part of the way hierarchies of masculinity are established and patrolled by dominant men (Connell 1995;
Kaufman 1987). As Bob said, "there is a lot of violence and aggression
associated" with being a Black man in Vancouver. Claudia also said,

"I've always felt that the young men that we were with, were in much more danger" than women in the African-Canadian community. Bars and clubs were venues where fights might occur between men who had been consuming alcohol and where most African-Canadian men in this research said they were careful not to go to alone and never to get into a fight. Maxwell argued that the police always assumed the Black person started the fight. As a result, he said, he hardly ever saw African-Canadian men in a fight; "it's usually Caucasians that are fighting ... or an East Indian." Hypervigilance was required, however, to stay safe because other men sometimes tried to provoke a fight:

> MAXWELL: I usually play things in my mind like, OK, what's the scenario? What could happen out of this. If I'm in this situation what could happen? I'm going to get trouble for it. Do I want to be in that situation? Probably not. So I just totally avoid it ... for me, I just stay out of it.

Despite the popular discourse about Black men as aggressive and threatening, then, African-Canadian men in this research observed that they were more likely to be the objects of aggression by other men, and worked hard to avoid such encounters.

Threats of racialized violence can occur even in professional settings. One example occurred at a dance connected to a conference:

> BOB: I was at a conference ... I was half way through a dance [with a White woman], and this guy grabs my shirt and just yells at me. And he was pretty shy, he was off in a corner, and he yells "you fucking n*****, you big dick n*****." It made me laugh. I'm embarrassed to say it now. But he grabbed me by the collar – it's important that I mention that because the whole thing. Anyways so he grabs me by the collar, and he tries to swing a punch, and his friends grab him.

Bob was not hurt in this incident, though he might have been had the aggressor's friends not intervened. He expressed shock that this could even happen in a professional setting. The racist slurs made by the White assailant employed long-standing discourses about Black men as hyperheterosexual, and suggested that Bob's dancing with a White woman was enough to threaten some White men's sense of their own masculinity.

In some contexts African-Canadian men were perceived as threatening in general, especially to women and particularly at night. Several men participants discussed what it was like to have women routinely cross to the other side of the street when they were walking home at night. For example, Michael recalled women crossing the street as he walked home from volleyball practice:

> MICHAEL: I'm not very intimidating. I'm the friendliest African you'll ever meet. But I thought it was funny and shocking at the same time.

As Bob observed, all women are nervous about being followed by a man late at night. "I also think that applies to all men, but more so" to Black men. Stereotypes in popular culture so often depict the quintessential mugger or rapist as a Black man that it is little wonder that this affected African-Canadian men's navigation of public spaces after dark. Denise recalled similar situations experienced by her brother, and worried about the emotional toll this took on him:

> DENISE: He'll say things like, "I was walking home from wherever and I got close to someone and she crossed the street." And I know that affects him because my brother's a good kid. He's a very good kid, he's so nice. But I'm sure the fact that person went across the street the moment she saw him doesn't make him feel good.

Denise reminded us of the emotional costs of frequently being perceived as threatening to women for reasons over which African-Canadian men had no control, by virtue of the colour of their skin, rather than their individual behaviour.

Robyn Maynard (2017) observes that violence against African-Canadian women and men is part of a long pattern of brutality embedded in histories of slavery, colonization, and structured inequality in Canada. Research on violence against women suggests that socially marginalized women, especially Indigenous women, are disproportionately subject to gender-based and sexual violence, although there is little information available about immigrant women or various groups of women of colour (Benoit et al. 2015). As socially marginalized women, African-Canadian women were likely more vulnerable to sexual violence (Maynard 2017). One woman who participated in this research disclosed two incidents of sexual violence, one that had occurred before she came to Canada when she was a young child and another assault that had taken place recently in metro Vancouver. Research participants were not asked any questions about violence, so there is no way of knowing how many women had experienced gender-based violence; still, we should be careful not to interpret silence as indicating an absence of sexual violence in African-Canadian women's lives.

Policing in Canada is an important site of racialized treatment that perpetuates forms of violence against African-Canadians. There is a long history of racism in Canadian policing that in many ways mirrors patterns in the United States (Collins 2005; Henry and Tator 2009; Maynard 2017). Discourses of Black male aggression and criminality, and the subsequent overrepresentation of Black men in Canadian prisons,[2] animate police interactions with African-Canadian men in ways similar to patterns across the country. Maynard (2017, 102) argues that "Black communities live in a state of heightened anxiety surrounding the possibility of bodily harm in the name of law enforcement." Almost all the men in this research recalled situations in which they had been harassed and detained by the police for no reason other than being Black. As a result, the majority expressed distrust of the police. Two participants were pursuing criminology degrees and planned to work in the criminal justice system, although not as police officers. Stella was the only woman who mentioned a negative encounter with the police – as noted above, for no apparent reason a police officer assumed she was a prostitute. Although no other African-Canadian women who participated in this research recounted problematic encounters with the police, Maynard observes that there are many examples in Canada of police harassment of "Black women who fail to be subordinate and docile" (2017, 116).

African-Canadian men who participated in this study shared the belief that any time something happens, if a Black man is present the police automatically assume he is at fault. Terrence recalled one evening when he and five other African-Canadian men were downtown and witnessed a fight among another group of men. When the police arrived, they immediately assumed that Terrence and his friends were the troublemakers:

> TERRENCE: There was a fight with a group of, another party across the street. But they [police] came and they saw us, there were five or six of us. Six Black males across the street, and they came and just assume that we were causing trouble. And it was someone across the street that had to run to tell them that these guys had nothing to do with it.

Terrence recalled another time when he was charged with assault, even though it was his White friend who was responsible and the latter admitted his responsibility to the police. Nevertheless Terrence was charged and his White friend was not. The charges were dropped a few months later.

---

2 People of African descent make up 3 per cent of Canada's population, but 9 per cent of the federal prison population (Maynard 2017, 109).

Lamar described how he "got arrested at the fireworks" as he was trying to leave the crowded public event. He was handcuffed and detained as he tried to explain why he could not follow police instructions to turn down a particular street:

> LAMAR: The officer was like, "go the other way, right now, go home," right? And I said, "I'm looking for my friend, he's from Seattle and I have to be with him because I'm the only friend he has over here." And he won't listen to me, so he handcuffed me and embarrassed me in front of everyone. And the thing is, there are fights and people are drinking. I'm not doing none of that, and there's so much things going on downtown, and I was just arrested.

Rylan also recalled instances of police harassment for no reason other than "just walking on the street." For example, he was part of a group of five Black men walking down the street when two police cars stopped, and "a bunch of police officers jump out, you know, I get slammed against the wall and handcuffed." The police said they thought one of the men had a gun, but it turned out to be a flashlight.

Several men recall being stopped by police and questioned about their identity while walking home at night – most commonly among those who lived in middle-class neighbourhoods on the west side of town. Greater surveillance of new drivers also resulted in more frequent interactions with police. British Columbia has a graduated drivers' licensing system, whereby new drivers must display an "N" for the first two years. New drivers can lose their licence for almost any infraction, no matter how minor, and police have considerable discretion over enforcement. Several men in this research recalled losing their licences for very minor infractions. Claudia noted that this was also gendered: as a new driver, she was never stopped by the police, but her brother was stopped frequently:

> CLAUDIA: For instance, I got my driver's licence very late ... I was twenty-seven ... You know, I have never been stopped in my car ever by police. Whereas my younger brother – we got our N at the same time – rarely has his licence. It is always suspended.

Even once they passed the new driver designation, some men reported being careful to drive an inexpensive car so they would be less likely to be stopped routinely by the police.

Claudia observed that police harassment through enforcing traffic and parking fines was nothing new in her family. Since she was a child she had witnessed the way that small driving infractions could be transformed into major fines, and unpaid fines into time in jail:

> CLAUDIA: It angers me because I know there is a lot more police surveillance of Black males in this city, unnecessary police surveillance and harassment. And I know it because, well, because my family has dealt with it the entire time I grew up. I never really wanted to travel much in the car with my mom and my [African-American] stepfather. Throughout my entire childhood, we were constantly stopped by the police. Constantly, and they would harass him and gave him multiple parking tickets … They were very poor, and they would constantly rack up so many parking tickets that they could not pay, and they would eventually come with the paddy wagon and take him away and jail him. Then completely keep him for a long [time] just to harass him. Which obviously had a major imprint on my siblings and myself and made our childhood [difficult]. And my stepfather is not a criminal but just to make a point, and obviously it diminished our lives, made us upset, and it was terrible.

This kind of treatment could be intended only to humiliate poor Black families, since it served no useful purpose in relation to community safety. As Claudia recalled, these experiences taught her and her siblings to fear and resent the police.

As the controversy over "carding" of Black men in Toronto highlights (see Maynard 2017, 88–92), the heightened level of police surveillance of African-Canadian men is rooted in discourses that Black men are more likely to be involved in criminal activity. That this kind of routine surveillance persists in a city like Vancouver, where Black men are very small in number and definitely not a significant element in local crime, illustrates the powerful effect of racialized discourses that endure across very different policing contexts. Using information obtained from the Vancouver Police Department through an access-to-information request, the British Columbia Civil Liberties Association and the Union of British Columbia Indian Chiefs recently lodged a complaint about racial profiling and carding in Vancouver, arguing that carding disproportionately targets Black and Indigenous peoples in Vancouver (*Vancouver Sun* 2018).[3]

---

3 As noted, those who identify as Black make up just over 1 per cent of the population of Vancouver, but they are 4 per cent of those carded; Indigenous peoples are 2–3 per cent of the population, but 15 per cent of those carded (*Vancouver Sun* 2018).

As we have seen, there were some gender differences and class dimensions to living "under a microscope" for African-Canadian women and men. A few participants also observed that lighter and darker skin tones among African-Canadians were linked to more or less scrutiny in public spaces. Emily compared the experiences of her two brothers, and concluded that the brother with the darker skin tone had experienced more racism:

> EMILY: I think complexion [matters] as well. My younger brother is darker and my older brother is lighter. So my younger brother was picked on more than my older brother.

Linked to images in popular culture, dark-skinned Black men are imagined as criminals and a threat to public safety.

Similarly Claudia identified herself as "the lightest skinned" among her relatives.[4] As a result, her South African grandmother emphasized how wonderful Claudia's life should be, and found it strange that Claudia was so connected to her African heritage. As a light-skinned African-Canadian with a White mother, Claudia had more room to negotiate her identity. Nevertheless, she said her African heritage had always been central to her identity, and she understood from an early age that the White half of her heritage was not recognized by White people. At the same time, Claudia acknowledged the relative privilege that had come with both a lighter skin tone and a middle-class upbringing:

> CLAUDIA: I mean, I suppose, and I cannot lie, that me being a very light-skinned African-Canadian, growing up on the west side of Vancouver with middle-class parents, has been hugely helpful.

Claudia grew up in a middle-class neighbourhood, although her family was not well off, and, as noted above, her stepfather faced jail time when he could not pay parking fines. Her father lived with her grandparents in the same neighbourhood. Her parents might not have been that affluent, but she enjoyed the middle-class environment of her neighbourhood, local schools, and the cultural capital that came from parents who emphasized higher education. Claudia also recognized

---

4 The exception was Claudia's mother, who is White. Claudia noted that her father, stepfather, grandparents with whom she lived, her siblings, both partners/fathers to her children, and her children all had darker skin than she.

that being light skinned meant she had faced fewer barriers than had her darker-skinned siblings and her own sons.

The politics of skin tone might play out differently within the African-Canadian community, depending on parents' country of origin, although, as Claudia observed, legacies of slavery and colonialism across Africa continue to leave an imprint "about what it means to be what colour you are." Outside the African-Canadian community, there is little doubt that the more someone embodies darker skin tones associated with images of Blackness in popular culture, the more hypervisible or "under a microscope" they are in relation to the majority of Vancouver residents of European and Asian heritage.

Working under a Microscope

As we saw in Chapter 6, research participants were optimistic about diverse educational and career opportunities and foresaw promising futures. This optimism was tempered, however, by the realities of racism that play out in the workplace. Only one participant claimed that he had never experienced any kind of discrimination at work or anywhere else:

> JOHN: I don't know if some people are racist. I don't know, but I never experienced that. I'm not lying. Never experienced that in my life ... Our new generation, we need to inspire the youngest ones who we are raising now, to show them, look, this racism thing is over. We just got to learn how to move on with life, because we keep holding things back then, [with the excuse] "oh, because we are Black."

John's belief that "this racism thing is over" might be optimistic, but many participants agreed with his argument that it should not be an excuse for failing to seize available opportunities. With the exception of John, participants reflected on the diverse range of both subtle and blatant ways racism affected their lives in the workplace.

Sometimes being Black was considered an advantage at work. Hobbes said that his experiences and the added diversity he brought were an asset:

> HOBBES: Being Black, half-Black, whatever, is an asset because, I don't know, I feel a bit special I guess. I don't know if that's a good thing, but I do feel special. I feel like my experience is unique and valuable and that helps give me strength to do what I want to do and feel like I can do that ... I have encountered racism, and more than I ever would have

expected in Vancouver. But at the same time, now that I'm older and doing things, although again I come back to this thing about having to overachieve. And maybe because I'm an overachiever, now I'm feeling like I can do anything because I'm doing more than I need to. I don't know. I feel like it's an asset. I feel like people like having diversity, at least people in my generation like that, that's what I experience.

Echoing themes that emerged in other interviews, Hobbes believed that diversity was valued more among the younger generation than among older residents. Markor also said, "it is mostly the older generation who are still into that racist kind of mentality." Similarly Tina's negative experiences usually involved "straight-out racist reactions by older people." There might be a growing appreciation for diversity among younger people, but Hobbes still maintained he had to overachieve to be taken seriously. Indeed, his perception that being Black was an asset derived from the strength and confidence he developed from being an overachiever.

Expecting to work harder, to overachieve, to get the same treatment as other people whose performance at work was average was a central theme in the interviews of both men and women:

DENISE: All the time I feel like just being a Black person is just a daily thing. Like you kind of don't notice it anymore because like my father said, even when you're working you have to work twice as hard to be treated the same. I still have that mentality in my head. I need to do twice as much work as you for them to recognize that I am working. And I feel like I go through that every day.

MAXWELL: It just comes down to you just have to work twice as hard, this is what is going to happen. My parents told me that, being an African-Canadian, you need to work twice as hard as the next person because this is not your country. You're not expected to be on par with whoever is in front of you or whoever is in line with you. Right? You got to work twice as hard because they're not going to work as hard as you are, but they still get the advancement.

Being Black in a city where only a little over 1 per cent of the population identified as Black meant always being hypervisible at work, and hence always working "under a microscope." Many participants provided examples of what that meant. Jay explained how his appearance was closely scrutinized even when he dressed similar to his co-workers. Jay recalled two separate incidences when he was charged with being unprofessional for wearing clothing appropriate for the work he did with youth, and similar to that worn by his White boss and other staff. He recognized that, although his appearance actually had nothing to do with how he performed his job as a youth worker, nevertheless appearance could be used to discredit him at work:

> JAY: At work I can't dress like everybody else or people have a problem with it. I don't look professional because of how I carry myself in the morning, baggier sweat pants and baggier shirt even though my boss is also wearing baggy shirts and baggy pants.

> JAY: I had a co-worker complain that my shoelaces weren't tied, I was wearing runners. I was wearing them and this woman was saying she can't respect me in a leadership role because I don't dress professionally, my shoelaces aren't tied ... Why should the way I dress really affect how you respect me? It's the work I'm doing, not the way I dress. And I looked around and there's other staff, their shoelaces aren't tied. I mean people were wearing flip flops.

Narrow notions of what constitutes professional appearance could lead to pressure from other members of the African-Canadian community as well. For example, Ayad posted a picture of herself on a professional networking site – "it's a picture of myself with my afro." The picture elicited critical comments from other African-Canadians about her unprofessional appearance, particularly her hair:

> AYAD: "You need to have a more professional picture of yourself. You need to have a non-colourful shirt and your hair nicely put back." ... Why can't I just be natural and be myself, and my hair really should have nothing to do with it.

For Ayad this was an example of how, particularly as a woman, "I face discrimination from other Black people." It is also further evidence that, as one of the few Black women in the local business community, she confronted challenges at work unrelated to her skills and capabilities.

Betty explained that she always anticipated greater surveillance in her workplace. This led her to work even harder to try to dispel negative stereotypes about Black and African workers through her strong performance on the job:

> BETTY: If you're going to say something about me, then I'm going to actually show you something. So, much more positive because that fuels my passion to just show you different, to show you that's not what I represent or that's not exactly what I am. I think it does force you to work

a bit harder, for sure. To always be on your toes to make sure that you're not just this lazy person who is at fault. For example, I try not to be late, never late, because then you fall into the, you know, she's Black and she's African, and Africans are late.

Those working in the health care system, as nurses, medical technicians, and care aides, sometimes experienced abusive behaviour from patients. Emily recalled having some patients demand that someone else conduct a medical procedure. She had been told by patients to "go back to Africa, I have heard that many times." Forlan worked in a care home, and frequently encountered patients who "just don't like you for your colour." He expressed frustration that he was unable to respond effectively to blatant racism from patients because he did not want to lose his job, and he believed that complaining to management did not change anything:

> FORLAN: I really don't know how I deal with it because sometimes I feel like doing something like, you know, trying to fight or like just do something at that moment so that person will not say stuff like that again. But, at the same time, you don't want to lose the job because after that you don't have anything to do. And if you want to complain to [the boss], they'll pretend they're doing something about it, but at the end of it, it's just, just go like that.

Forlan had experienced racist interactions with customers and co-workers in other jobs as well. He worked in a fast food restaurant where a woman loudly queried whether he was wearing gloves, and refused to let him serve her. He also had a job in a laundry, where a co-worker, a "Spanish lady," kept complaining about his work, even though other co-workers said he was a good worker. The same co-worker also refused to acknowledge his presence at work:

> FORLAN: She never talked to me. I mean I'd pass by and, because I don't know how to avoid people, I'll pass by and say hi, but she won't say anything. She would just turn her face. Like, if she's sitting down at the lunchroom and I came in she would leave. I'm like, "why is this?" People like that, it's like they just hate you because of your colour.

Other participants related more subtle examples of racial micro-aggressions in the workplace. One woman, a nurse, recalled instances where she was mistaken for a cleaner and asked by family members to "call the nurse." The manager of a youth program was frequently mistaken for a secretary and ignored when people came to the office for assistance. A clinical assistant recalled the shock some patients and co-workers expressed when they discovered she had a degree from the University of British Columbia, as if they could not imagine that a Black woman was so capable:

> BETTY: "UBC? Oh my god. Wow, this is amazing" … But, yeah, those comments, even though they seem positive, they're somewhere like, "oh, it's just amazing that you are a university graduate." I'm like, it's really not that amazing.

Far from perceiving such comments as complimentary, Betty observed that they were embedded in racialized stereotypes about what Black women can accomplish. Ayad also noted that her accomplishments, including her business degree, were greeted with surprise and perhaps even disbelief. In Ayad's experience, overt racism was rare in Vancouver, but people still made it clear how perceptions about her racialized body limited their expectations of her abilities:

> AYAD: It's very confusing in Vancouver, though, because it's not overt, it's not like people are yelling things at you so much. It's more like, it's more just kind of people being surprised. Surprised by your presence, surprised by things about you, where you live, what you've accomplished. People are so very surprised when you're like, "oh, I've finished a business degree." They go "oh, that's very unlikely."

Research participants recognized that educational credentials sometimes could provide a buffer against racism in the workplace. For example, both Denise and Bob pursued specific university degrees and careers that required specialized knowledge so they would have credentials that confirmed their competence:

> DENISE: Part of the reason why I did my science degree [was] because my parents told me – well, my dad, more specifically – that arts is not the way to go. That as a Black woman you need to do something where you can go further because you are going to have to work twice as hard to be given the same treatment as everyone else. And so he told me [to take] sciences or engineering or something that could give you a solid job.
> BOB: I went into [graduate] school because I liked the options. It gave me the ability. I don't think I'll deal with structural racism the same way … I have that piece of paper, that credential which I think is a ticket in a sense where people don't have to judge me on my race. Regardless of my

ethnicity, where some people would have a hard time turning me down for a job, you know, both professionally and legally because I'm quite qualified.

Professional and technical jobs are by no means immune from everyday processes of racialization, as illustrated by the experiences of some of the participants who worked in the health care field, but they include some more objective means of certifying competence in specific occupations. Indeed, pursuing occupations that require higher education was a key strategy for navigating a social geography where African-Canadians were a hypervisible minority and where stereotypes about Black men and women shaped other people's assumptions about their character and capabilities.

Building Resilience

African-Canadian men and women developed strategies for living "under a microscope," learning to deal with the racial micro-aggressions and blatant racism that are part and parcel of everyday life without letting them define their lives. A key element of these strategies was building personal resilience. As we have seen, the members of the second generation who participated in this study were pursuing higher education and a wide range of careers. They addressed popular misconceptions about Black women and men by working harder than other people and thereby demonstrating their various capabilities and talents. At the same time, living "under a microscope" also involved many interactions in public spaces where there were no opportunities to demonstrate their competencies, so they also deployed a range of other strategies.

Michael observed that, as an African-Canadian man, he had much less ability to "mess up" than did his White counterparts. He had to be more disciplined so that he did not "contribute to that stigma" about Black men:

MICHAEL: The White kids are allowed to screw up like I can't because then they are just, "oh, he's Black." Like it's more damaging if I screw up because I don't want to contribute to that stigma. I would rather go against it. So I really don't have that much room to mess up.

Having little latitude to make mistakes was a common theme in interviews, especially among men. As a result, building a promising future depended on becoming highly focused and astute observers of social situations from a fairly young age. As we saw in Chapter 4, the relative social isolation of most African-Canadian women in high school might have helped them develop these qualities during adolescence. By early adulthood, honing the qualities of personal focus and social insight had become central to African-Canadian men's and women's navigation of life in metro Vancouver.

As Bob said, figuring out "who you are early" in life was important to send the messages one intended, messages that would ease interactions in public spaces and not make life more challenging:

> BOB: For me, I would describe being Black and growing up Black in the city [of Vancouver] as you need to figure out who you are early or you need to create enough space to figure that out. And to do that you need to put up, not barriers, but you need to put up specific symbols to get a message you want. And wherever you are, whatever the geography or time of day, you have to change those things constantly, and it's exhausting.

Paying attention to self-presentation and messages one wants to portray is a critical strategy for living "under a microscope." This includes some strategies that have already been discussed, such as the types of educational programs and careers one chooses to pursue, the way one dresses, and the places one frequents or avoids. It also includes decisions about the people one chooses to associate with or stay away from, and the way one interacts with strangers.

To a considerable extent the messages that second-generation African-Canadians sent were geared towards dispelling the myths associated with discourses about Black men and women in popular culture, while simultaneously building their own strengths, competencies, and self-esteem. For example, Hobbes described stereotypes of Black men as "prone to violence," "disorganized," "not quite as smart," – perceptions that he consciously fought against in order to prove himself:

> HOBBES: I probably still struggle with that, but the constant battle against what I feel is the perception of me, even if it might not be the perception of me, but what I feel is the perception of me. I feel like I always need to do better and I need to overachieve. You know, I want to go to McGill and study law. Do I really want to become a lawyer? Actually, I don't think I do. But I think I want to get that piece of paper and that would make me feel so at peace ... I know, it's a strange thing to want to prove, but I think it's also proving to myself that I can do it. But it is also, you

know, to kind of shift the perspective and to gain credibility in a world where I don't think Black men are perceived as the most intelligent or articulate or carrying responsibility.

Pursuing a law degree sent multiple messages at the same time: it was an external validation of Hobbes's competencies, a personal demonstration of his own determination and abilities, and a repudiation of the assumption that Black men cannot excel. As such, it reinforced his personal resilience even in interactions with strangers who would not see his law degree, because it affected Hobbes's self-esteem and thus his presentation of self.

Developing a strong sense of identity is important for staying mentally healthy while living "under a microscope." For example, Betty explained that her solid grounding helped her "push past" situations when she encountered racial micro-aggressions:

> BETTY: I think having a good grounding as a young person, I think that helped me because I pushed past a lot of those things."

Personal strength is a resource that is built in the context of family, friends, and community. As we saw in Chapter 3, most participants recalled that their parents were a particularly important support for building resilience. So, too, was choosing which people to associate with and whom to avoid. As Jane said, referring to people who were negative and criticized her, she chose "not to surround myself with people who are like that." For Charlotte, who was seventeen when she came to Canada, this included avoiding some members of the African-Canadian community who she believes too often discouraged rather than encouraged her family's goals:

> CHARLOTTE: Some other Black people, they will tell you that you can't do anything because you are Black ... It's like that's why we stay alone and away from other [Black] people ... They discourage you from doing anything that you really like, [that] you have set your heart on. They discourage you.

Surrounding oneself with people who are supportive and will encourage ambition is important to help people persevere, especially when challenges are encountered. For most participants, this included family as well as diverse friends drawn from within and outside the larger African-Canadian community. As Hobbes suggested, being careful about the people he associated with was also a strategy for limiting his exposure to racism: "I know that racism does exist but I don't need that and the people I have around me aren't like that."

Avoiding people and situations that had the potential to be difficult was a common strategy, but racial micro-aggressions and instances of blatant racism could not always be avoided. Therefore it was also critical to develop strategies to respond in ways that did not invest more power in negative encounters. Given the likelihood that racist incidents would occur from time to time, Maxwell, Rylan, and Hobbes argued that the most important thing was how they responded to such events:

> MAXWELL: There is discrimination and racism, it's always going to be there, it's going to be indirectly thrown at you. But it's just the way of how you respond to it.
>
> RYLAN: It's just something I'm going to have to deal with, so I'm used to it by now. I know how to kind of conduct myself and let things slide and, you know, just take the high road and don't think it's a big thing. And don't let it get to you, just stay on your path.
>
> HOBBES: There are shitty people out there, and you're going to encounter that, but I'm [not] going to be sad about it and internalize that. No, it just is what it is, you know?

They suggested that a low-key, measured response was always best. Keep calm, "take the high road," "don't let it get to you," and refuse to "internalize" the put-downs were all responses that built on personal strength and resisted letting racist encounters diminish one's physiological well-being and quality of life.

Rylan explained that when he was younger he would get angry, and conflict would escalate. So he took anger management training to learn how to negotiate living as a Black man in Vancouver more effectively:

> RYLAN: That helped me to sit back, assess the situation, don't jump to conclusions, and, you know, don't make things worse. That was one thing that helped me at that point.

He learned the importance of carefully assessing a situation before responding, a useful strategy in almost any encounter in a public space.

To some extent gendered discourses around Black men and women made it potentially more dangerous for African-Canadian men to respond directly to a racist encounter, and more important that they shrug it off and walk away. As noted previously, discourses around Black masculinity can instil both fear and unprovoked aggression in other men. African-Canadian women were less often perceived as threatening in the same way. Some of the women who participated in this research did challenge strangers without fear that it would escalate into violence. Challenging racialized discourses was another strategy some research participants employed, but it is important to recognize that it was not always safe to do so. It was essential to assess the situation before directly challenging racist encounters.

Male participants also provided specific advice for dealing with racialized encounters with the police, situations that, as previously discussed, most had experienced. Terrence explained how he handled problematic interactions with the police, a strategy that resonates with the stories of other participants who found themselves in similar situations:

> TERRENCE: I always try and stay calm. Basically, you just don't give them a reason to end up locked up, right? And the funny part about that is, when you do that, police officers don't like that. And when you try to be civil and sensible. And when you know your rights, it's always like, "why do you know your rights?" So, yeah, I've had bad experiences. So I always just try and stay calm and let them know that I do know my rights. Most of the time they get annoyed, then most of the time they back off.

The dual strategy of remaining calm while asserting one's rights in situations of unwarranted police harassment requires great self-discipline. It also challenges the discourse of aggressive Black men and can be an effective strategy of de-escalation. On one occasion, Terrence recalled, "I've had a cop apologize to me ... If I had exploded, that wouldn't have happened." Whether in response to problematic interactions with the police or racial micro-aggressions from strangers or co-workers, remaining calm is a strategy that can defuse a tense situation. As such it both relies on and helps to develop a high level of personal discipline.

Other participants chose to ignore the racial micro-aggressions that accompany living "under a microscope" and not let them outweigh all the positive things in their lives. For example, Kweku said that, although he recognized that racism occurs, "it's not anything that I think about." Similarly Forlan explained, "I just forget about that and try to move forward." Lamar thought that getting upset about things like name-calling was "childish" because "it's just words at the end of the day." And John argued that focusing on racism holds people back who instead need to "learn how to move on with life." Indeed, choosing to emphasize positive relationships, keeping focused, developing self-discipline, seizing opportunities as they emerged, and developing goals for the future were all elements of strength and resilience demonstrated by the second-generation African- Canadians who participated in this research. Their resilience did not eliminate White privilege or instances of anti-Black racism, but it did help them navigate public spaces in a context where they were living "under a microscope" as a small and hypervisible minority.

Chapter Eight

"People still ask me where I'm from": Belonging and Identity

"People still ask me where I'm from even though I grew up here"

– Shukre

The query "where are you from?" has different meanings depending on whether it is part of a conversation among intimates or a question asked by a stranger, and whether one is at home or away at the time. Strangers seldom question White Canadians about their origin unless visible markers, such as a different language, accent, or lack of familiarity with local conventions, suggest they are from somewhere else. In contrast, this question is commonly directed at people of colour in Canada. In the absence of a context where heritage might be a welcome conversation, queries about origins signal that some people are not perceived to be at home in Canada even when they are.

For African-Canadians born in or largely raised in Canada, routine queries about where they are from signalled that, although their bodies conveyed many local attributes, they nevertheless were seen as out of place, and were called to account for their presence by narrating origins from somewhere else. In a recent article on shifting discourses of racism in Canada, Fleras (2016, 7) includes "where are you really from?" as one example of a common racial micro-aggression. He argues that what the recipient of this question experiences is a pejorative statement: "you are a perpetual alien because of appearance" (7). In this chapter, I explore how the query "where are you from?" is central to processes of racialization in Canada and the complex ways these encounters mediate the second generation's sense of belonging and negotiation of identities as Canadian, as African, and as Black.

The First Generation and "Foreign" Origins

As we saw in Chapter 2, the first generation of adult migrants from sub-Saharan Africa experienced processes of racialization that cast them as perpetual "foreigners" in their new home, and shaped how they engaged with new identities as Canadian, as African, and as Black. They described being subjected to routine questions of "where are you from?" that underlined how their bodies were out of place and excluded from the imagined Canadian nation (Creese 2010, 2011; Creese and Wiebe 2012). For example, Wetu explained that, even though he saw himself as Canadian in most respects, people often made it clear to him that, because he is Black, he is not Canadian:

> WETU: Even though I change that, I will be Canadian, but somebody I pass, by my colour, he'll ask me, "where are you from?" ... Because you can be a citizen here for many years, you have been here for twenty, thirty years, but you still feel that there are some areas which the colour is playing a part ... Just the colour is [the reason] that we don't see you as a Canadian. (Creese 2011, 200)

Similarly Tungu explained that she could not be Canadian because she and her Canadian-raised children were routinely interrogated about their origins:

> TUNGU: I cannot say I am Canadian when they don't support I am Canadian ... Here you are Black. If you are twenty [years], you [were] born here, nothing. They will say, "where are you from?" They will still ask you. "I am Canadian." "No, where are you from? You born here?" "Yes." "Where are your parents from?" (Creese 2011, 199)

Tungu reflected on how interlocutors drilled down until the question of origin led to an acceptable answer that emphasized foreignness – even if you were born here, your parents could not be from here – leading Tungu to reject the very idea of Canadianness for herself or her children. Marked by racialized bodies and African-English accents that signified an origin from somewhere else, attempts by the first generation to claim local origins, even after many years of residence, typically were rebuffed. For example, Laziati held a Canadian graduate degree and was raising two Canadian-born children. She explained what happened when she tried to claim she was from

Surrey, a suburb of metro Vancouver where her family had lived for nearly a decade:

> LAZIATI: "I am from Surrey." They say, "no, I mean where are you from?" And I say, "well, I am from Surrey." But they say, "no, you are not from Surrey. I mean originally where are you from?" That's what they usually ask you. Yet when they ask other people "where are you from?" and someone says "I am from Surrey," when they are White, yeah, then you are from Surrey. (Creese 2011, 201)

Like Wetu and Tungu, Laziati noted that people were not content until she identified her origins in Africa, specifically Swaziland, where she grew up and attained her first university degree. The intrusiveness and pervasiveness of these queries about origins reaffirmed the salience of Blackness in Canada, and signalled that other residents could not conceive of people from Africa as Canadian, regardless of citizenship or the passage of time.

For adult migrants, some clues to origin from somewhere else usually persisted for a lifetime. For example, adults might have been in Canada for many decades but still spoke with an African-English accent that marked them as having a "foreign" origin. But did members of the second generation share this common experience of being treated as a perpetual "foreigner"? Or did the latter's literal embodiment of the local mean the second generation was recognized as people who were at home? Recall that, in Chapter 3, immigrants among the research participants said that part of their experience of migrating to Canada included initial difficulties making themselves understood, and the disparagement of their accents by other people. For a few who migrated as older teenagers, an African English accent could remain a telltale sign of having originally come from somewhere else. However, participants who were born in Canada or arrived as children all spoke with a local Canadian English accent. Most of this chapter draws on twenty-seven interviews with this group, in order to assess how embodying the local affected questions about origins.

Second-generation African-Canadians embodied the local through their Canadian English accent, locally attained education, work experience, and cultural capital. As a White woman with a local Canadian English accent, my immigrant background is invisible, and I am almost never asked where I came from. People assume that the place I grew up and the place I live are synonymous with where I come from. How does local cultural capital translate into recognition of being "from here" when bodies are Black? As I explore in this chapter, second-generation

African-Canadians might embody the usual markings of local accent, place-based knowledge, and cultural capital, but this did not mean they were perceived to be from Canada. Everyday interactions with others made it plain that having a Black body was enough to be seen as out of place and not at home. No markers of actually having come from somewhere else needed to be present. Queries about origin reaffirmed the racialized dimensions of belonging in local spaces, and affected the way second-generation African-Canadians negotiated their own identities, with some rejecting a Canadian identity altogether and others insisting that their Canadian heritage must be acknowledged.

Research participants were asked two questions about their identity: "what terms do you use to describe your identity today?" and "how do you think other Canadians see you?" These questions generated reflections about identity that were most often discussed with explicit reference to other residents' asking that they explain their "foreign" origin. The interviews illustrate three general ways of negotiating identity: 1) identifying only as African and not as Canadian; 2) identifying as African and also as Canadian; and 3) identifying only as Canadian. Identity is multifaceted, fluid, and situational (Hall 2000; Okeke-Iherjirika and Spitzer 2005), so boundaries between these three ways of framing identity are permeable and flexible, rather than fixed and static.

I begin by examining why African-Canadians who embodied the local were still routinely interrogated about "where are you from?" and how these queries constituted part of racialization processes in Canada. Following that, I draw on excerpts from interviews with second-generation participants to illustrate how frequent queries of "where are you from?" generated ambiguities about belonging in Canada and affected identity in complex ways.

Racialization and Identity

As we saw in Chapter 2, racialization processes in Canada mark people who are perceived as non-White as "others" who are located outside the "imagined community" of Canadians (Anderson 1991). Distinctions between strangers and locals (Ahmed 2000; Brah 1996) are embedded in historical processes, including settler colonialism, marginalization of Indigenous peoples, and centuries of preference for European immigrants and discrimination against people from Africa and Asia. Since the 1970s Canada has witnessed diverse immigration and the adoption of multiculturalism as public policy and its wide acceptance as an element of national identity. Alongside all this change, however, Whiteness continues to be at the centre of the "imagined community" of Canadians (Abu-Laban and Gabriel 2002; Barrett 2015; Day 2000; Mackey 2002; Walcott 2003). Racialized minorities are generally presumed to be recent immigrants even when their presence extends over many generations. Historical amnesia about Black Canadian history, in particular, helps to mark Black bodies as strange and new even though their Canadian lineage goes back centuries. Walcott (2003, 136) calls this amnesia "the absented presence of blackness in Canada."

African-Canadians navigate discourses of Blackness embedded in racist assumptions about inferiority, violence, and criminality that have a long history in Canada and that are reproduced in contemporary, mostly American, popular culture (Dei 2013). In this context, the common question "where are you from?" should be understood as central to processes of racialization that mark boundaries between "real" Canadians and "others." These verbal assaults are forms of racial micro-aggression, discursive forms of everyday racism "used to keep those at the racial margins in their place" (Huber and Solorzano 2015, 298). As Paul Barrett (2015) writes, these interactions are so common that novelists in the Canadian Black diaspora, including Tessa McWatt and Austin Clarke, employ characters musing about their responses to "where are you from?" as a means to explore the dissonance between the multicultural rhetoric of equality and the lived reality of racism in Canada.

Lack of familiarity with centuries of African-Canadian history and the prevalence of negative discourses of Blackness combine to render African and Black bodies as out of place even when they are at home. For the first generation, as noted above, language and accent are visible markers of difference that signalled an origin from somewhere else. Deeply rooted in the history of colonial domination, linguistic discrimination remains widespread against those who speak English with an accent from the Global South (Creese 2010, 2011; Amin and Dei 2006; Lippi-Green 1997). Although the second generation embodied a local Canadian English accent, their origins were still queried regularly, suggesting that signs of recent migrant history are not required to read Black bodies as originating from somewhere else. Indeed Whiteness is such a "defining feature of 'Canadian identity'" that non-White English language teachers in Toronto experience challenges as appropriate teachers of English as a second language (Ramjattan 2017, 4).

Identity is formed in the context of these processes of external labelling as well as subjective feelings of affiliation with groups, cultural practices, and landscapes (Gans 2017). Recent scholarship on identity formation in the African diaspora suggests that place, discourses around migration, racism, and economic opportunities all help to shape identity. For example, Onoso Imoagene (2012) argues that second-generation Nigerians in the United States display stronger belonging, in comparison to those in the United Kingdom, due to the United States' more favourable national identity myths ("a country of immigrants" versus migration as "invasion") and affirmative action policies to redress racism. In the Canadian context, a study of Ghanaian and Somali communities also finds that identity is "materially grounded" in place, economic circumstances, and racism (Mensah and Williams 2015, 52). The authors conclude that those less likely to identify as "just Canadian" and more likely to identify as "mainly ethnic" are more often recent migrants, perceive higher levels of racism, have lower incomes, and live in Vancouver rather than in Toronto.

Scholars have also examined how immigrants and the second generation in Canada differentiate themselves from the much larger Black and African-American community in the United States. Research suggests that first-generation immigrants stress their African origin to differentiate themselves from African Americans, although debate remains about whether this constitutes a "positive shield" against anti-Black racism (Adjepong 2018; Showers 2015). Msia Clark (2008, 2009) finds that the vast majority of the first generation identify as African and so do almost half of the second generation, who "all have, to varying degrees, been 'African Americanized'" (Clark 2008, 173). Anima Adjepong (2018) shows that African identity can be leveraged for specific purposes. Illustrating the intersections of race, class, and sexuality, Adjepong argues that middle-class, second-generation Ghanaians in Houston "engage in Afropolitan projects that claims [sic] blackness as an African identity, re-narrates [sic] Africa as a modern cosmopolitan, cultured, heterosexual space, and asserts [sic] belonging as middle-class citizens of the United States" (2018, 260). Janet Awokoya (2012) explores how second-generation Nigerians in the United States negotiate competing influences and demands to be "authentic" emanating from family, school, and peer groups by adopting multiple and shifting identities as African, Nigerian, African American, and Black. In a similar way, in his research on second-generation Ethiopian-American professionals, Kassahun Kebede (2017) argues that their complex navigation of race, ethnicity, and class leads them to recreate a unique transnational "twice-hyphenated" identity as "Ethiopian-African-American." Working with middle-class, second-generation Haitians, Clerge (2014) also emphasizes how shifting identities are linked to shoring up race, ethnic, and class boundaries: "being black in racially integrated schools, Haitian in predominantly black settings, and middle class in their [ethnic] neighbourhoods" (972). This scholarship points to the complex, situational, hybrid, and strategic nature of identity claims as the second generation navigates life as American, as Black, and as African (or in one case, Haitian) in the United States.

In Canada, the first generation "never knew they were black until they came to Canada" and encountered processes of racialization that made the new category of Blackness meaningful in their lives (Okeke-Ihejirika and Spitzer 2005, 221; see also Ibrahim 1999). In contrast, from a very young age the second generation was fully embedded in discourses of Blackness through immersion in school and popular culture, and navigated multiple African, Black, and Canadian identities. Several studies of second-generation African-Canadians focus on how teenagers learn to become Black through immersion in American popular culture, particularly hip hop (Creese 2015; Forman 2001; Ibrahim 1999, 2003; Kelly 2004). As Jennifer Kelly argues, discourses of Blackness in Canada emanate largely from the United States, so that it "comes to represent a sense of blackness within the lives of students" (2004, 148). As we saw in Chapter 4, the second generation in Vancouver navigated a world dominated by discourses of Blackness that spoke to the specificity of the African-American experience, which in turn framed their negotiation of identities during adolescence.

This chapter focuses on identities among second-generation adults, rather than adolescents. They were raised in metro Vancouver, where only 1 per cent of the population is of African descent,[1] and embody local attributes in substantive ways, and yet they were still frequently asked, "where are you from?" These experiences shaped their sense of belonging and expressions of identity. Some identified only as African, at least partly in resistance to other people's refusal to acknowledge their Canadianness. Others embraced an African identify while simultaneously claiming their Canadian heritage. And a few participants resisted answering the question, identifying only as Canadian and refusing to name an African origin. Many also adopted a Black identity, and almost everyone believed that other people saw them as "just Black." These expressions are strategic responses to racialization and discourses about Blackness, as much as they are articulations of complex, hybrid, and multiple cultural identities as the participants navigated across and between cultures.

---

1 Most previous studies of African-Canadian adolescents' identities have looked at Edmonton (Okeke-Iherjirika and Spitzer 2005; Kelly 2004), Toronto, and southern Ontario more broadly (Forman 2001; Ibrahim 1999, 2003). My own research (Creese 2015) is the only study to address adolescent identities in Vancouver.

"Growing up here, I've always been asked that question"

Shukre is a Canadian citizen who was an infant when her family came to Canada from Somalia. She grew up with a strong Somali culture at home, living in the suburb of Surrey, where, for years, "we were the only Black folks living in a community that was mostly entirely White." Shukre felt so alienated by the frequency with which she was still asked "where are you from?" that she identified herself only as Somali. She refused any identity as Canadian or Somali-Canadian, except as necessary when travelling on a Canadian passport:

> SHUKRE: I think that the assumption [is] that when you're Canadian you are White. And people still ask me where I'm from even though I grew up here.
> INTERVIEWER: Even after they have heard you and can tell you are local?
> SHUKRE: As long as I keep getting asked where I'm from, I'm not from here, you know? As that question is the first thing people ask me, I'm not from here. Like, there's this idea that the first [thing] folks notice is my difference and being like, "where are you from? I mean where are your ancestors from?"
> INTERVIEWER: And they don't mean Surrey?
> SHUKRE: Exactly. Then this isn't the place I'm from. I think that's actually the simplest way to put it.

Shukre's strong identification with Somalia was rooted in cultural and family heritage – "that's where I was born; that's the culture I understand" – and overdetermined by strangers' ongoing rejection of her Canadianness, "as that question is the first thing people ask me." Canadianness might be embodied in the quotidian activities of life, her work in Vancouver, her Canadian education, her cultural capital, her long-term residence (more than twenty-four years), and her locally accented and colloquial English, but her Canadianness was rendered unintelligible by her racialized body.

In response to the question, "how do you think other Canadians see you?" Shukre was blunt: "[I'm] seen as Black." Being seen as Black erased her Canadianness because, as a Black woman, she was presumed to be from somewhere else. It also rendered her Somaliness invisible, since Blackness is a category that highlights difference from Whiteness while ignoring diversity among people of African descent. As Shukre poignantly observed, "I grew up Somali and the entire world saw me as Black ... [and] I know people's perception of me as Black made them think of me as less." In Shukre's narrative of growing up in Vancouver, the persistent denial of her localness led to her rejecting Canadian identity, while the erasure of her Somali heritage through discourses of Blackness made Somaliness an even more critical touchstone of her identity.

Maxwell, a twenty-eight-year-old Canadian citizen, was born in Uganda but had lived in Vancouver since he was seven. He recalled that, as a teenager, he thought of himself as African-Canadian, but in adulthood he firmly rejected a Canadian identity. Maxwell explained, "I have come to the realization that this is not my country." At the time of the interview, he had never been back to Uganda to visit, but Maxwell strongly identified as both Ugandan and African. In our conversation, he used the terms Ugandan and African almost interchangeably to frame his identity, grounded in the location of his birth as much as in his family's cultural heritage:

> MAXWELL: I would say African, that's where I'm from. That's where my roots are. This is not my country … I've just come to the realization that this is not my country. That's just it. It's pretty simple.
> INTERVIEWER: And yet you've lived here most of your life?
> MAXWELL: I've lived here most of my life.
> INTERVIEWER: Does that mean you don't plan to continue living here?
> MAXWELL: Oh no, I plan to go on living here, yes, but my roots, where I was formed, [are in] Africa.

Although Maxwell's life would continue to play out in the Canadian landscape, he noted that place of birth mattered: "if I was born here, then I can say, 'yeah, I am Canadian.'" Not being born here, Maxwell identified his country as Uganda, where, "if I were deported I have somewhere that I can go and be safe there." As he was a Canadian citizen since childhood, there was no real likelihood of deportation,[2] so we need to interpret this insecurity through the prism of discourses about his (lack of) Canadianness.

Maxwell noted that he was treated differently from other Canadians, not really because of his place of birth, which his local accent and cultural capital rendered invisible, but because his racialized body signalled not belonging in Vancouver, regardless of birthplace. Needing to work harder and be better to get the same opportunities as White

---

2 This interview took place before the Harper government changed the Canadian Citizenship Act, making it possible to deport dual citizens under specific circumstances.

Canadians reinforced his belief that, for people like him, "this is not your country":

> MAXWELL: Being an African-Canadian, you need to work twice as hard [as] the next person because this is not your country. You're not expected to be on par with whoever is in front of you, or whoever is in line with you.

Unlike most research participants, Maxwell suggested that other people did not often ask him, "where are you from?" Instead people "just assume" he was from "the islands, from Trinidad, Dominican [Republic], things like that." Questions about origin took the form of assertions about where his non-Canadian ones might be, leaving Maxwell to correct misconceptions by indicating he was actually from Africa, or specifically Uganda.

Luke was twenty at the time of the interview, a Canadian citizen who had lived in metro Vancouver since he was an infant. He reacted to questions about where he was from by identifying his origins as Ugandan and both affirming and denying a Canadian identity:

> LUKE: I would say I'm Ugandan. I won't say I'm Canadian. I won't say that … Some people say, "where are you from?" "I'm from Uganda." And I'll be like, "I was born in Uganda but I grew up here, but I go back to Uganda almost every summer."
> INTERVIEWER: You've been here since you were five months old?
> LUKE: Yeah.
> INTERVIEWER: So if you say, "I'm from Surrey"?
> LUKE: No, I just wouldn't say it. I would say I'm from Uganda. A lot of people ask where I'm from, as in background, and then I'll say Uganda. And when they say, "where do you live?" Then I'll say Surrey or I'll say Vancouver.

Luke's response to questions about where he was from led him to claim Ugandan identity while still emphasizing his local roots, making it clear to interlocutors that "I grew up here." Luke believed his ongoing ties to Uganda, maintained through periodic visits, were as important for asserting his Uganda identity as were his birthplace and his family's cultural background. In contrast, although he was quick to identify himself as locally raised, hence challenging the assumption that he was from somewhere else, he refused to claim he was *from* metro Vancouver, acknowledging instead that this was the place he *lived* – indeed, except for several months when he was twelve years old,[3] the only place he has ever lived – but not the place he was *from*.

Like many participants, Luke expressed ambivalence about his Canadianness. He acknowledged that, "if they say, 'are you Canadian?' then I'll be like, 'I have Canadian citizenship.'" But he did not feel like a "full" Canadian, something he would feel only "if I was born in Canada." When asked how he though other Canadians saw him, it is clear from his response that Luke's racialized body mediated his refusal of Canadian identity:

> LUKE: I think they see me as Black. They don't know I'm from Africa or Jamaica, or Caribbean or Haiti, they just come up to me like, "there's a Black guy."

Luke's response to homogenizing discourses of Blackness as not Canadian was largely to reject a Canadian identity, while emphasizing both his Ugandan heritage and his local upbringing.

Ashley was twenty-one and had been in Canada since she was five months old. She too resisted defining herself as Canadian, even though she acknowledged that, in many ways, the term made sense because she was raised in Canada:

> ASHLEY: Probably the best term is African-Canadian, but I don't like that term. I would rather call myself African, but I guess, really, I mean I was raised here, so technically I am African-Canadian ... but my roots are in Ghana ... If people ask me where I am from, I would say I'm Ghanaian. I would never use Canadian, ever, ever, ever. I'm a Ghanaian ... because it's in my blood. It's my family history. I was raised that way, you know? I was taught the language.

Ashley's claim to African and Ghanaian identity was based on her deep connection to her family's cultural background and her continuing links with extended family in Ghana. She acknowledged that, when she was growing up in Vancouver, she wanted to be seen as Canadian, and "there were times when I wished I was White." As an adult, however, she had a very strong Ghanaian identity, and no longer called herself Canadian. When asked how other Canadians saw her, Ashley said, "they see me as the Black girl who sings," a homogenizing discourse that rendered both her Ghanaian heritage and her local upbringing invisible.

---

3 Luke attended school in Uganda for one term when he was twelve years old.

Denise had lived in Vancouver for twenty-one years, since she was five years old, and identified herself as both Black and African. "I've spent more of my life in Canada than I have in Africa but my roots are in Africa, so I am an African." She believed that most people saw her as "Black American." Denise did not identify as Canadian because people were always asking her where she was from – "because people look at me and they know I'm not from here." She used to say, "well, I was born in Uganda but I've lived here most of my life." She believed, however, that other people were only interested in identifying her foreign origins, and "they didn't care about the Canada part." So now Denise challenged people who dared to ask where she was from:

> DENISE: Nowadays if someone asks me, you know, "where you from?" because I'm so fed up with it, I'll just say "why you asking?" And I'm so rude about it, and I guess that kind of throws people back a little bit – "whoa, I'm just asking you a question." But then I ask them – sometimes, not all the time, – but if it's a White person who was asking me, I'm like, "if I was White would you be asking me where I am from?" … A lot of people [say], "oh, I didn't mean to insult you in any way, please don't get me wrong. I just wanted to make conversation." I'm like, "no, you didn't want to make conversation. You saw a Black person, and talked to her to find out [where she comes from]."

Although Denise refused to adopt a Canadian identity, her challenge to those who questioned her origins was also a bid to be recognized as local, as another Canadian who was "at home" in Vancouver.

Some participants among the second generation did adopt an unambiguous Canadian identity, although few escaped the pressure to identify another origin as well. Jessica, a twenty-two-year-old who was born in Canada to Ghanaian parents, said, "I thought of myself as Canadian" when she went to university in the United States. Unlike most other participants, she also believed that other Canadians "mostly see me as Canadian" because she embodied a local accent. Like other participants, however, she remained haunted by frequent questions about where she was from, which suggested that her local upbringing was not always so visible. Jessica learned to respond by telling people where her parents were from, even though she felt no connection to Ghana:

> JESSICA: It's weird saying it because, for example, even when people come up to me and like, "oh, where are you from?" and I'm like, "well, my parents are from Ghana." And I think it's part of that, that I don't feel like I have a connection to Ghana myself. I don't speak the language, I don't

know people there, I don't really eat the food. It's like I recognize I am from there but don't have the connections.

Tellingly, Jessica did not say "I am from Canada" when asked where she was from. Like other participants, she recognized that such an answer likely would not end the interrogation. She also noted that such queries occasionally came from people who were also Black, seeking to place her as they themselves were placed – outside local origin. She had learned that her own legibility required asserting an origin to which she felt little connection, even as she claimed an unambiguous Canadian identity.

Like Jessica, Jane was born in Canada and had also lived in the United States for a few years, an experience she credited with changing her identity. Jane identified as "just Canadian ... because it's not African American." Her resistance to having to explain her parents' origin was tied to the even greater importance of race she experienced in the United States compared to living in Vancouver:

JANE: I actually kind of hate race. As a whole, I don't really feel the need to differentiate myself based on where my parents come from. I mean, I appreciate it, don't get me wrong, and I love different cultures. But I hate the [racial stereotyping].

While not wishing to identify with her parents' ethnic background, she also added, "I'm definitely Black, I can't ignore that." As the child of a White Canadian mother and a Ghanaian father, her Black identity was tied both to her cultural heritage on her father's side and to recognition that other people in Canada and the United States saw her as Black, not as White. At the same time, she recognized that she was not always fully accepted as Black "because I am biracial, I feel like I am not, not a hundred per cent accepted by them either."

Claudia, another woman of mixed parentage, with a White Canadian mother and a father from South Africa, identified as African-Canadian, stressing the merger of her parents' backgrounds. At the same time, others did not recognize her dual heritage:

CLAUDIA: I very quickly realized that the Black part of my heritage actually spoke first, that I could not be White, that I had a White parent but that White society will never see me as White.

Identifying as Black and African-Canadian was partly due to her inability to claim Whiteness, and also deeply embedded in strong connections to her extended South African family, to her African partners, and to her own children, who were racialized as Black.[4] At the same time, as a light-skinned Black woman, Claudia was sometimes challenged by others of African descent who suggested, "you are not Black enough." For Claudia this only reaffirmed her African-Canadian identity and her determination to add her voice to the larger Black community in Vancouver: "I feel like my experience and my voice is extremely important in terms of going forward and creating community and Black community in Vancouver."

One other participant had a mixed heritage. Hobbes had a White Canadian mother and an African father from Togo, and, like Jane, identified as just Canadian. When people ask where he is from, Hobbes said, "my mom is from Alberta and my dad is from Togo." Hobbes identified himself as "half Black," rather than as African-Canadian. He recognized that in Canada other people perceived him as Black, but he pointed out that in Togo people called him "the Whitest Black person I've ever seen."

Rylan, a twenty-three-year-old Canadian-born man, first claimed his identity was "just African." He later explained that he knew little about his Ghanaian heritage and was trying to "get in touch with ... [my] African side" by learning more about the language, music, culture, and history of Ghana. At the same time, he recognized that he shared little in common with other Ghanaians, and acknowledged that his identity was really African-Canadian:

> RYLAN: For the most part, [I'm] still just African-Canadian, because if I'm talking to an African person, I don't know how to speak the language. Someone from my country that's speaking the language to me, I have no clue what they're saying, so I still kind of have to react [as] just ... "African-Canadian Rylan," because I really wouldn't know how to speak the language, things like that.

Rylan embraced a hybrid and hyphenated identity that linked his dual African and Canadian heritages. Yet in the eyes of other Canadians, his local attributes did not necessarily suggest Canadianness. Instead Rylan noted that other people typically assumed he was African American:

> RYLAN: Probably [other people] see me as some kind of African American ... People would say like, "oh, you sound like an African

---

4 Claudia had had two husbands, both of whom were adult migrants from two different African countries. She was raising children from both marriages.

American but you have this weird kind of tone to your voice like an accent." I'm like, "oh, it's probably because I speak French fluently."

Rylan was not alone in being mistaken for an African American. When faced with the combination of the "strange" Black body out of place in Vancouver and the embodiment of colloquial Canadian English, other residents often cast their gaze south of the border in search of a foreign origin that could explain this dissonance of the familiar and the "strange." For Rylan both the desire to strengthen his African and Ghanaian identities and his preference for a hyphenated African-Canadian identity were strategic moves away from being misrecognized as African American. Deepening his connections to Ghana moved Rylan further away from stereotypes of African Americans emanating from American popular culture, while also potentially distancing him further from the "imagined community" of Canadians that centres White bodies and European cultures.

The most common identity among research participants was hyphenated African-Canadian. Danielle, who was born in Canada, explained that she identified as African-Canadian because "it means having both cultures present in your family and in you." Joy, who came from Kenya at age eleven, also identified as African-Canadian because "me being Canadian, I feel very passionate about that," and at the same time "I still have my roots in Kenya." Canadian-born Ayad described herself as "first-generation Canadian or Ethiopian-Canadian." Terrence, who was nine years old when he came from Liberia, also identified as African-Canadian:

TERRENCE: I am African-Canadian, I guess. But more, now I look at myself, to be Canadian to be honest. I obviously do have my African-Liberian background. That's where I was born, but like I said, I grew up here.

Peter, who was ten years old when he came, called himself Liberian-Canadian "because I wasn't born here and I'm not going to say I'm Canadian. I'm Liberian-Canadian." Tina remembered calling herself African-Canadian when she was younger, but as she got older her Kenyan identity had become more important. Now she had adopted a dual identity: "I identify as a Canadian who is also very much Kenyan." Michael, who came to Canada when he was eight, reversed the order of the hyphenated identity and called himself "Canadian-Nigerian, not Nigerian-Canadian":

MICHAEL: I would say I am Canadian first because that's just how I think. If I were to go to Nigeria, they [would] see me as an outsider because they don't see me as one of them. They accept that I was born there, that I know the language, that I know the history. But ... I am Canadian when I go there.

Whether reversing the order of the hyphenation to put Canadian first, as Michael did, or, more commonly, to modify Canadian by preceding it with an African heritage, adopting a hyphenated identity simultaneously claimed a local origin and provided their other lineage that interlocutors frequently sought.

Some research participants might have embraced a hyphenated identity and still refused to communicate it to strangers or acquaintances who asked, "where are you from?" Emily was born in Ethiopia and had come to Canada twenty-seven years ago at the age of six. She believed her local accent might lead people to assume she was "Black Canadian" whose family might have been here for generations, except when other people heard her name. As a consequence, "I still get asked where I am from":

EMILY: I tell them Vancouver. I used to say Ethiopia to make you feel, or anyone who asked me, to make them feel comfortable. But now I say Vancouver, and they'll say, "oh, but like, where? Like where are your parents from?" And I'm like, "does that matter?" And I get that a lot actually, and at work too ... I don't like that question.

Emily tried to disrupt the dismissal of her Canadian upbringing by asserting her local origin and refusing to identify her Ethiopian heritage when people persistently asked about her parents' origins. Her own identity was as "Ethiopian-Canadian" – never one alone, always combined, "because I've known Canada so well, and being back in Ethiopia, I don't really fit there either." At one time, Emily recalled, she used to call herself African-Canadian, but no longer did because too many Canadians seemed to "think Africa is one country, and I hate that." Specifying an Ethiopian identity resisted the homogenization of Africa, while a hyphenated identity spoke to hybridity across and between two cultural milieus by claiming both origins simultaneously.

When asked how she thought other Canadians saw her, Emily responded: "I think people see me as Black because I don't have the [African immigrant] accent." Not perceived as an immigrant, given her local speech, but evidently not perceived as Canadian either, the discourse of Blackness undermined both elements of her heritage as Ethiopian and as Canadian. This made it all the more important for Emily to embrace a hyphenated identity that signalled the unique confluence of her joint Ethiopian and Canadian lineages.

As Betty explained, how she answered questions about where she was from was connected to the context and to who was asking her:

> BETTY: I think from them asking you, "where you're from?" I still have this "oh, I'm from Ethiopia," right? … It depends on who's asking, because that question is always asked. Like, growing up here, I've always been asked that question … So I think, right away, it depends on who is asking. If you're just no one, I don't know you, I'll say, "I'm from here." But let's say we are in school, and we are classmates or whatever, because it grounds me, like you know who I am. I'll be like, "oh, I'm from Ethiopia but I grew up here."

Betty, who had lived in Canada for twenty-four years, since she was seven, resented the fact that people routinely asked where she was from. If she knew the person asking well enough to develop a personal connection, she would express her Ethiopian identity, all the while emphasizing her local upbringing. However, she was more likely to refuse to respond with anything except a local origin if a stranger asked, thereby refusing to provide the origin narrative that the interlocutor demanded.

Betty illustrated the way her racialized body disrupted acknowledgement of her local origin by contrasting different responses to hearing her voice over the telephone and seeing her in person. Clients who heard her voice on the phone did not question Betty's Canadianness; but there was often confusion when the same person saw her body for the first time:

> BETTY: Other people get confused because let's say you're over the phone, they would be like, "oh, you're Canadian" right? You know, your accent. Then they come into the office or something, "oh, you're Black, you're African?" They don't get it right away, obviously. But I think, too, I will connect and say to answer that question, "I'm Ethiopian." But for just someone I don't really know, I just say, "I'm from here." Like, "I'm from Vancouver, downtown" or whatever.

To diffuse this confusion among clients Betty asserted an Ethiopian identity, while also making it clear that she really sought acknowledgement that she was at home.

Keenly aware of how her body mediated perceptions about her local accent and cultural capital, Betty navigated complex claims around her Ethiopian and Canadian identities. On the one hand she asserted, much like Luke, "I tend to say I'm Ethiopian and I live in Canada," downplaying her inclination to claim a Canadian identity. Yet she also mused about rejecting a hyphenated Canadian identity in favour of asserting her unmodified Canadianness:

> BETTY: I've never really felt like I'm Ethiopian-Canadian. Never said it, I don't think. I guess people could say that about me, but I would just say I'm Canadian.

Betty's complex meditations on identity reflected spaces of hybridity linked both to navigating life across cultures and to being keenly aware that other Canadians read her body as out of place in her own home.

Kweku, a nineteen-year-old man born in Canada to parents from Ghana, largely shifted between identities as Black and as Ghanaian. He asserted, "I don't say I'm a Canadian, no, I'd never use that." He later modified this comment to clarify that he never said he was Canadian when he was at home in Vancouver. He noted that his sense of identity was situational, and his Canadianness only emerged when he was not in Canada:

> KWEKU: If I was with a White [person], I'd say I'm Black, or the only time Ghanaian comes up is when I'm talking to another Black person ... When I go [to Ghana], then I'd be Canadian. You know what I mean? My identity is my difference from the environment I'm in. So, if I go there, I'm Canadian and that would be my identity because I'm really different from most people there.

What was it about being home in Canada that gave rise to a Black and Ghanaian identity, but only a Canadian identity when he was not at home? Partly it was what Kweku saw as differentiating himself from others around him. At home in Vancouver his difference was defined through Blackness and a Ghanaian heritage that he sought to dissociate from images of African Americans. At the same time, identity at home was shaped by clear messages about how he was perceived by others.

When asked how he thought other Canadians saw him, Kweku was clear: "Oh, you know, the Black guy. No way, never a Ghanaian-Canadian, even if I told them I'm from Ghana. It's all Black to them." These homogenizing discourses of Blackness were refracted through American popular culture, erasing the specificity of diverse African cultures as well as his Canadian heritage. Most research participants simultaneously acknowledged and resisted discourses of Blackness that signalled African American by reaffirming their African heritage and/or their Canadian identity. A few, like Kweku, made themselves legible by employing the dominant discourses of Blackness, identifying as Black when talking to White Canadians, as Ghanaian when talking to others of African descent, and as Canadian only when in Ghana.

Navigating Multiple Identities

Almost all second-generation African-Canadians in this research linked thinking about their identities to the way strangers and casual acquaintances frequently asked them, "where are you from?" The examples above are all drawn from interviews with participants who embodied local cultural capital, including expressions of the local Canadian English accent. And still these queries persisted. Participants experienced "where are you from?" as a form of racial micro-aggression that indicated Black bodies were perceived as outside the boundaries of the imagined community of Canada. Not surprisingly, these experiences shaped identities in diverse and complex ways.

Second-generation identities were negotiated at least partly as strategic responses to these discursive micro-aggressions. The three types of responses that emerged engaged in different ways with the frequent demand to identify a non-Canadian origin: 1) identifying only as African, or as from a specific African nation, and rejecting a Canadian identity; 2) identifying as African, or as from a specific African nation, and simultaneously claiming a Canadian identity; and 3) identifying only as Canadian or local, and refusing to name an African origin. These were permeable and fluid, rather than fixed and static categories. Discourses of Blackness animated identity formation, in most cases deepening the salience of specific national or pan-African identities in resistance to the homogenization of Blackness and its negative connotations in American popular culture. This strategic articulation of African identities to redefine and resist homogenizing discourses of Blackness, and Americanization, has resonance with the findings of Adjepong (2017), Awokoya (2012), Clark (2008, 2009), and Kebede (2017) in the United States. For most participants in this study, hybrid identities included both Canadian and African, although usually with considerable ambiguity about belonging in Canada.

Similar variations in identities were found among those who arrived as teenagers, even though their identity firmly linked to their original home culture and country was forged well before coming to Canada.

Depending on how long they had lived in Vancouver, this group was more likely to embody signs of having come from somewhere else (such as having an African English accent), and might experience even more frequent queries about "where are you from?" At the time of the interviews, a few participants had not been in Canada long enough for Canadian citizenship. Of the eight who had migrated to Canada between the ages of fourteen and seventeen, half (Markor, Charlotte, Ayinke, and John) identified only as African or as having a particular national origin, and half (Stella, Ali, Jack, and Forlan) identified as African-Canadian or just Canadian.

John and Markor identified themselves by their national homeland (Sierra Leone and Ghana, respectively), Charlotte considered herself African, and Ayinke embraced both a national and continental identity: "I'm still a Nigerian, still African." None of them identified themselves as Canadian. Markor, who came from Ghana when she was sixteen, suggested that teenage migrants face particular issues around identity:

> MARKOR: For the second generation I think their main focus is on identity. I think that is where most of us have a problem because we came here in our teenage years. And once you come here in your teenage years, you don't really know who you are. And so we watch a lot of TV. I fear that the media is influencing how we identify ourselves.

On the other hand, Ali identified as African-Canadian because "I have both qualities of the African and Canadian." Stella said her main identity was Nigerian-Canadian, but how she identified also depended on whom she was talking to, and sometimes it was "just Canadian":

> STELLA: Most of the time I would say I am Nigerian-Canadian. It usually depends on who you are talking to, too. Sometimes you just say a Canadian, sometimes you say a Nigerian, sometimes you say, yeah, Nigerian-Canadian.

Jack identified as African-Canadian, but would provide his home country of Liberia when pressed to do so. "I'm African-Canadian, but if someone asks me where are you from, I'll be like, I'm from Africa, I'm from this country." In contrast Forlan resisted the question by insisting on his local identity: "if they ask me where are you from, I'll just say Burnaby," a suburb of metro Vancouver. Among those who came to Canada as teenagers, almost all of those who adopted some form of Canadian identity had been in Canada several years longer than those who rejected a Canadian identity, suggesting that length of residence in Canada has a significant impact on the identities of teenage migrants.[5]

Second-generation identities were also affected by perceptions of racism in metro Vancouver, a finding consistent with research by Imoagene (2012) and Mensah and Williams (2015). Research participants who perceived higher levels of racism were either more likely to reject a Canadian identity altogether (like Shukre, Maxwell, Ashley, and Denise) or to emphasize their Canadianness and refuse to name another origin when strangers asked (like Emily, Betty, and Forlan). These different strategies were not linked to place of birth. A few participants identified birthplace as one reason they were not Canadian (for example, Shukre and Luke, even though both were infants when they came to Canada); others who came as young children (for example, Emily, Betty, and Joy) or as teenagers (Stella, Ali, Jack, and Forlan) insisted on their Canadianness. Most Canadian-born participants identified as Canadian (Jessica, Jane, and Hobbes) or, more often, hyphenated African-Canadian (Rylan, Danielle, Ayad, and Claudia), but a few did not. For example, Kweku defined himself as Black (to White Canadians) and as Ghanaian (to Black Canadians), and only identified as Canadian when he was in Ghana. Bob, who was also born in Canada, identified as Black and as Ethiopian, although as a teenager he identified as African-Canadian.

As we saw in Chapter 4, African-Canadian adolescents, especially boys, were much more likely to adopt an identity as Black, express strong affiliations with African Americans, and see themselves through hip hop and other forms of American popular culture (see also Forman 2001; Ibrahim 1999, 2003; Kelly 2004). When participants in this research reflected on their identities during high school, most men recalled performing the popular "cool black guy" of hip hop, while women recalled being more aware of their "difference" and their marginalization because popular culture does not provide Black teenage girls with the same avenues of acceptance. Although many men said they identified as African-Canadian as teenagers, in most cases the emphasis was on race and representations of Black masculinity in popular culture,

---

5 Forlan, Stella, and Ali had been in Canada for between eight and fourteen years, in contrast to three to six years for the group that identified only as African. Jack, however, had been in Canada for six years, and he also identified as African-Canadian.

with little appreciation of their heritage culture. Women were more cognizant of African cultural expectations during adolescence, so their sense of difference was mediated both by gendered family dynamics and by representations in popular culture.

As adults, however, gender did not constitute a discernable difference in the identities research participants expressed. Adult identities were complex, multidimensional, sometimes situational, and often fluid. Moreover, identities were much more attuned to the hybridity of living across and between cultures, and more deeply connected to their specific African heritage. For most women and men, maturing as young adults led to a stronger identification with their African heritage and the increased importance of transnational connections with extended family.

Some participants had extended family members living nearby in metro Vancouver and/or elsewhere in North America. For the majority, however, most extended family remained in Africa, and transnational connections were maintained largely by their parents through phone, text, Skype, and social media. Trips to visit family required more financial resources, and for most participants did not occur very frequently. For some who were Canadian-born or arrived so young they had little recollection of living anywhere else, trips to visit extended family as they got older served as turning points in their appreciation of their heritage. For example, Michael credited a trip to Nigeria when he was fifteen as "eye-opening" and transformative:

MICHAEL: Basically I was Westernized at that point, but my trip to Africa had given me new perspectives where I didn't want to assimilate fully. I was actually proud to be a Nigerian and be this different person in a sea of all these cultures, when honestly there's not that many Nigerians. I was the only Nigerian in that entire school.

Not only did his trip to Nigeria build a strong identification with his family and culture; it also made him appreciate the advantages he had in Canada. It "made me hard-working ... you know, not waste my opportunities." Similarly Luke recalled an extended trip to Uganda when he was twelve that included attending a local school for one term. He learned to appreciate the beauty of the country and the strength of cultural bonds, and developed a new understanding of both his Ugandan identity and how "I was blessed living in Canada." Luke credited the trip with providing him a new sense of identity and resilience. For Devon, trips to Ethiopia when he was in elementary school did little to change his identity as

Canadian, but travelling there recently as an adult had been like coming home, and he now identified as Ethiopian-Canadian:

> DEVON: I have been travelling around the world extensively, and I don't know what it was this time, I just wanted to go back [to Ethiopia] and it felt so good. Here I am always like a chocolate chip in a pile of popcorn, you know? When I was there, I just felt good. It was just, everyone was like me, and it felt so good. It was just like this is where I am meant to be. I just felt so at ease, you know?

Devon's new appreciation of his Ethiopian heritage extended to plans to return to Ethiopia and work there for the next few years, joining a large expatriate community of young Ethiopians who had been raised and educated in the West and possessed Canadian, American, or European passports – the cosmopolitan "Afropolitans" who figure in recent debates (Eze 2014; Selasi 2005).

Most of the second generation in this research had developed strong national or continental African identities, although very few had much connection to events or organizations that constitute part of the larger African community in metro Vancouver. Several of the young men who were interviewed took part in the annual African soccer tournament, and some men and women attended annual Independence Day celebrations and the Caribbean Days Festival held in North Vancouver every summer. In addition, some people, again mostly men, said they still attended occasional African parties. As we saw previously, most had developed a network of friends that included other first- and second-generation African-Canadians. None, however, noted any involvement in local national or continental African organizations.[6] For the most part, organizations created in the local African community have been built by and for the first generation, focusing on the interests and needs of adult immigrants, rather than addressing the issues facing the second generation. As such, the second generation feels little affinity with these groups and is not becoming involved with them. However, this might change: as we saw in Chapter 6, the types of careers some participants wanted to develop involved working with African immigrant youth and addressing the kinds of adaptation issues they themselves experienced when they were younger. In addition, some participants, particularly women, had

---

6 As we saw in Chapter 2, the first generation has created a wide range of local organizations, some of which are oriented towards African homelands and others are focused on connections among the local population in metro Vancouver (Creese 2011).

joined university and college organizations that focus on Africa, and both men and women had formed friendships with first-generation immigrants their own age they met as international students in local colleges and universities.

With one exception, participants did not identify African-focused organizations created by members of the second generation. The exception is a group of Ethiopian women who had organized a mentorship program for teenagers of Ethiopian descent. The program pairs young people in the community with Ethiopian professionals who act as mentors and can provide advice about education and careers and serve as role models. Betty and Ayad, who had helped to organize the program, noted that it is run almost entirely by women, and that they had difficulty recruiting male mentors even though they believed young boys in the community might need a mentor even more than girls.

Racial micro-aggressions, like the frequent query, "where are you from?" constitute important elements of the process of racialization in Canada. These exchanges signal that other people believe second-generation African-Canadians do not belong in this space and cannot be at home and from here. This in turn challenged research participants' feelings of belonging as Canadians and helped to strengthen most participants' African identities. Sometimes developing a stronger national or continental African identity occurred in opposition to a Canadian identity, rejecting an affiliation with those who had symbolically excluded them from the imagined community of Canadians. At other times a strong African identity occurred alongside the simultaneous assertion of Canadianness, embracing the hybridity of living across, between, and within two cultures.

In almost all cases, attachment to their African heritage deepened as the second generation become adults. This movement suggests that, although the second generation is quite distinct from its parents and much more fully "Canadianized" and "Westernized," by and large second-generation participants had not rejected their diverse African heritages. Discourses of Blackness remained culturally pervasive, but identifying with African Americans seemed to peak in adolescence, when it was stronger among teenage boys than girls. Embracing African and Canadian identities as young adults was part of their differentiating themselves from homogenizing discourses of Blackness that are rooted in African-American popular culture.

It is true that the second generation is not often visible within local organizations created by the first generation in the process of building an African community in metro Vancouver. This might be one reason parents worried so much that their children had abandoned their African culture and identity (Creese 2011). The second-generation participants in this research, however, were redefining, rather than abandoning, their African identities in the diaspora, and most expressed a deep sense of connection to and appreciation for their African heritage.

Chapter Nine

Growing Up African-Canadian in Vancouver: Race, Gender, Sexuality, and Place

Metro Vancouver is a diverse metropolis where four in ten people have been born somewhere else, and where half the population identifies as members of visible minorities or as people of colour (Statistics Canada 2016a, 2016b). Growing up in this environment, the experiences of the second-generation African-Canadian participants in this research were in many respects similar to those of other recent immigrant communities. The children of immigrants routinely negotiate across and between their parents' cultural expectations and the norms and values embedded in Canadian schools and other social institutions, and many experience tensions when these expectations collide. They also navigate local processes of racialization that shape who is and is not perceived to be part of the imagined community of Canadians. Most develop complex, fluid, and often situational hybrid identities drawing on both their parents' cultural heritage and their Canadian upbringing (Handa 2003; Hirji 2010; Kobayashi and Preston 2014; Nagra 2017; Pratt 2004, 2008; Wilson-Forsberg 2012).

Children of immigrants in Canada attain higher levels of post-secondary education than do children of Canadian-born parents (Abada, Hou, and Ram 2008, 2009; Abada and Tenkorang 2009a, 2009b), in part because their parents are more highly educated and communicate these expectations to their children. Armed with Canadian education, local work experience, and locally accented English – or French in Quebec – the second generation does not face the same disadvantages in the labour market as did their parents. At the same time, research suggests that names and other markers of "difference" affect access to jobs, even for those with Canadian education, and an income gap linked to race and ethnicity persists into the second generation (Oreo-poulos 2011; Pendakur and Pendakur 2011).

Although the second-generation African-Canadian participants shared some similarities across diverse origins, their experiences of growing up in metro Vancouver were also unique. Vancouver is diverse, but very few residents (1.3 per cent of the population) come from countries in Africa and fewer still (1.2 per cent) are racialized as Black (Statistics Canada 2016a, 2016b). As discussed in Chapter 2, the local Black population is composed largely of recent migrants from diverse countries in sub-Saharan Africa and their Canadian-raised children (Statistics Canada 2011a). In the context of small numbers and hypervisibility in a place dominated by people of European and Asian descent, a self-defined African community has emerged that links together Black residents with recent connections to countries in sub-Saharan Africa (Creese 2011). Vancouver's African community is still very small, and as such does not have access to the financial resources, dense networks of social capital, and cultural presence that larger migrant communities can provide their offspring.

Second-generation African-Canadians are both hypervisible and invisible at the same time. They grow up in neighbourhoods where they are usually the only Black and African children in their classrooms, and traverse multiple sets of cultural expectations without benefit of a large community presence locally. At the same time, they grow up in an environment where pervasive discourses about Blackness, with no meaningful connection to their families' cultural background, help to make their diverse African heritages invisible. All groups of colour in Canada are marginalized by legacies of settler colonialism and White privilege that are deeply embedded in the history of Canadian nation-building (Bannerji 2000; Mackey 2002; Walcott 2003). In addition, however, African-Canadians also have to contend with ubiquitous racist discourses in contemporary popular culture. Discourses about Blackness are homogenizing, masking the diversity of cultures, ethnicities, and national origins, and reinscribing evaluative judgments linked to beliefs about the lesser social, intellectual, and moral worth of people of African descent (Dei 2013, 2017; Deliovsky and Kitossa 2013). Entrenched Black/White divisions in the United States, our closest neighbour and the dominant force in global popular culture, shape these discourses in Canada, leading many Canadians to believe that anti-Black racism is only a problem south of the border. Instead, as we have seen, the narratives of African-Canadians growing up in Vancouver show that dominant representations of Blackness animate local anti-Black racism, and affect everyday experiences in both public and private spaces.

Members of the second generation who migrated when they were old enough to remember life before coming to Canada, navigate new discourses of Blackness as part and parcel of adapting to life in Canada. Children who arrive in elementary school, for example, quickly develop the local accent, and learn the official and hidden curriculum tied to liberal values and Eurocentrism as they try to fit in with their peers. Those who are born in Canada or arrive so young that their memories of childhood are all centred in Canada, are largely unaware of their "difference" from other children until they start school. As we saw in Chapter 3, many research participants recalled instances of peers in elementary school making fun of their African accent, name, the food they ate, their hair, and the colour of their skin, and some also recalled teachers making ill-informed comments about Africa. For the second generation in Vancouver, as in other parts of Canada, school is a critical institution, where negative discourses of Blackness are first encountered in interactions with teachers and other children, including harmful assumptions about African countries and stereotypes associated with being Black (Brathwaite and James 1996; Codjoe 2001; Dei et al. 1997; Ibrahim and Abdi 2016a, 2016b; James 2012; Maynard 2017; Shizha 2016).

Narratives of migration and growing up African-Canadian in Vancouver also highlight the importance of family support for navigating school while negotiating across parents' and Canadian norms, values, and cultural expectations. Although different expectations sometimes create family tensions, especially during adolescence, research participants focused more on the importance of parental support and guidance for promoting resilience. From their perspectives as young adults, participants appreciated the advice of parents, and sometimes of older siblings – and the models of discipline they presented – which helped keep them focused on school and the opportunities available to them in Canada. In the context of migration, families are central to transmitting cultural knowledge and heritage to their offspring (Costigan and So 2018; Kebede 2017). African families are also a critical source of positive counterdiscourses about the pride of being African and Black, with a wealth of experience available to help offspring navigate the racial micro-aggressions and more blatant forms of racism they encounter.

Processes of racialization are clearly central to the narratives of second-generation African-Canadians growing up in Vancouver. As this study shows, these processes, and discourses about Blackness, are profoundly gendered. Brothers and sisters might grow up in the same family, live in the same neighbourhood, and attend the same school, but their experiences growing up are significantly different. These differences are evident as early as elementary school, where half the women interviewed faced prolonged periods of isolation, sometimes spanning several years, when they were unable to make friends at school. In contrast, almost all the men interviewed remembered easily forming friendships with other boys, most often through playing sports together. These patterns are linked to gender differences in the way children form friendships, with boys bonding through activities while girls tend to make connections though more intimate conversations that rely on shared cultural understandings (Devine and Kelly 2006; Morrow 2006).

By high school, gender differences in relations with peers are connected to the gendered nature of discourses about Blackness. Most women participants recalled developing a small circle of girlfriends in high school, usually from other immigrant backgrounds. African-Canadian adolescent girls remain on the fringes of social circles in high school, partly due to stricter parental controls that limit interaction outside school, and also because of the lack of Black female role models in popular culture whom they can emulate. As a result, their peers express little interest in African-Canadian teenage girls. In contrast, the dominant narrative among African-Canadian men is about their great popularity and athletic achievements in high school. During adolescence African-Canadian boys can play the "cool Black guy" from hip hop and celebrity sports culture. Their scarcity in Vancouver high schools, combined with the high status of hip hop in youth culture, produces adulation among their peers, although popularity is superficial, short lived, and can impede their focus on academic achievement that would ensure a more promising future (James 2016).

Gender differences are even more pronounced among adults in the second generation. As they got older, both African-Canadian men and women participants developed more diverse friendship networks, including more people from the African diaspora. Patterns of heterosexual romantic relationships, however, are quite different. North American beauty norms and discourses of Black masculinity and femininity position African-Canadian men and women differently in the local heterosexual market. In short, African-Canadian men in Vancouver have a wide range of potential romantic partners, while their sisters are considered less desirable and are more likely to remain single. As we saw in Chapter 5, most men who participated in this research (56 per cent) had a current partner, while most women (74 per cent) were single. Only two men (12 per cent) but one-third of the women had no history of dating. Over 70 per cent of men's current and former partners were women who were not of African descent, all but two of whom were White. In contrast, 70 per cent of women's current and former partners were men of African descent, all but two of whom grew up in Africa and were adults when they came to Canada. Men raised in Africa possess Afrocentric beauty norms, but are also more likely to hold more traditional views about gender relations that can be a source of conflict.

Participants in this research all graduated from high school and pursued some form of post-secondary education, ranging from a few courses to a master's degree, but it is clear that this pattern is not necessarily representative of the second generation. As discussed in Chapter 6, research participants pointed out that, overall, second-generation women were doing very well in higher education while men were lagging behind. As we saw in Chapter 4, a majority of women encountered various obstacles to success in high school that were rooted in teachers' underestimating their capabilities. Women recalled that these experiences pushed them to work harder in order to prove themselves. Men who participated in this research did not recount similar narratives, but other research has documented similar experiences among African-Canadian men that results in a pattern of disengaging from school (Conroy 2013; Dei et al. 1997; Ibrahim and Abdi 2016; James 2012). Participant self-selection[7] limited the ability to examine the first-hand experiences of men who faced significant barriers in high school in Vancouver, although research participants provided examples of brothers and male friends who had not graduated or gone on to post-secondary education. As other scholars have shown, the stereotype of the "cool Black guy" that enhances Black male teenage popularity is associated with more negative assumptions in the broader society, including being unintelligent and prone to criminality and violence, assumptions that contribute to low teachers' expectations, alienation, and higher dropout (or "pushout") rates in high school (Conroy 2013; Dei et al. 1997).

As we saw in Chapter 2, second-generation African-Canadians in this research came from families with highly educated parents who placed great value on their children's education. Their family's material class position in Canada rarely matched the class privileges enjoyed in their home country, so that parents' financial support for their children's post-secondary education might have been limited, but they still passed on middle-class cultural capital that stresses education. This study does not provide a window into class differences among the second generation, but it does highlight the complexities of class relations

---

7 As discussed in Chapters 2 and 6, I was unable to recruit any participants who did not complete high school and did not pursue any further education. Several participants passed on information about the project to brothers and male friends who had not completed high school, but none agreed to be interviewed. This self-selection bias is a limitation of this research.

in the context of migration, where the first generation undergoes significant downward class mobility, putting additional pressure on the second generation to be ambitious in its educational goals. Given the hardships most parents experienced in migrating to Canada, a common theme in the interviews was the participants' drive to succeed and not waste the opportunities available to them.

As discussed in Chapter 6, at the time of the interviews, most participants were enrolled in a post-secondary program that would lead to a university degree; others had already completed a university degree or more specialized post-secondary occupational program. Career goals were diverse, ranging from professional occupations such as nurse, planner, teacher, college instructor, accountant, social worker, lawyer, and dentist, to skilled trades, technicians, and care workers. Some participants wanted to work with new immigrants and refugees in some capacity, and others planned to address social issues in their parents' homeland. It is noteworthy that those already working in jobs related to their career goals expressed satisfaction with how their careers were progressing and, like participants still working towards future career goals, were optimistic about the future and the opportunities they believed are available to them in Canada.

If we gauge how the second generation was doing based on educational attainment, careers, and optimism about the future for the older participants, and educational trajectories and career aspirations for the younger ones, we can conclude that these second-generation African-Canadians were fulfilling their parents' dreams of enjoying greater opportunities in Canada. With local post-secondary educational qualifications and the social and cultural capital associated with growing up in Canada, the second generation did not face the kinds of barriers in the labour market that their parents confronted. Moreover, the experiences of migration, including their own personal struggles to adjust and their witnessing the hardships their parents had endured, fuelled the second generation's motivation, hard work, focus, and drive to succeed. At the same time, however, the experiences of the second generation fell far short of their parents' dreams of equality in Canada. As we saw in Chapters 7 and 8, second-generation African-Canadians continued to face racial micro-aggressions and more blatant forms of racism at work and in other public spaces. These experiences illustrate the depth and persistence of racialized inequality in Canada.

A central theme in the interviews was the need to challenge discourses about Black men and women as less capable, competent, and responsible workers. As discussed in Chapter 7, participants explained how they had to overachieve and work "twice as hard" as others in order to be recognized as doing their job. Basic competence was questioned in subtle and overt ways, from co-workers expressing surprise at educational qualifications or accomplishments, to clients or patients refusing to be treated by African-Canadians or telling them to "go back to Africa." Subtle forms of racial micro-aggressions might have been the most common at work, but participants who worked in the service and health care industries also encountered troubling examples of blatant racist behaviour.

Racial micro-aggressions were even more common in public spaces. The analogy of living "under a microscope" highlights the heightened visibility of African-Canadians, who form a small minority in metro Vancouver but navigated expectations about their character drawn from popular discourses about Black masculinity and femininity. As a result, men had to be particularly careful about how they dressed as they moved through public spaces in order to distance themselves from images of Black men as gangsters and thugs. Both men and women recalled instances of being followed by security guards and sometimes being falsely accused of shoplifting. In addition, strangers sometimes harassed one participant who wears a headscarf because she is identifiable as Muslim. Almost all men who participated in this research had stories about being randomly stopped by the police while walking home at night, driving a car, or being with a group of Black men in a public place. Several recalled instances of being detained, searched, handcuffed, and in one case charged, for no clear reason. Women recalled similar instances involving their brothers and, less often, their fathers. One woman explained she felt "dehumanized" after a police officer stopped her and asked if she was a prostitute. In a city where the Black population is so small that it cannot possibly constitute a significant element in local crime, racialized discourses about Black criminality still resulted in heightened surveillance of African-Canadians, particularly men. In this context, always being conscious of the image they present, avoiding negative interactions with strangers, and keeping calm, affirming their rights, and de-escalating interactions with police were important strategies for living "under a microscope" in metro Vancouver.

As discussed in Chapter 8, the query "where are you from?" was one of many racial micro-aggressions that participants encountered with some regularity. To be asked frequently "where are you from?" when one was at home affected the identities of second-generation African-Canadians and contributed to a precarious sense of their belonging as Canadians. Although half the African-Canadians who participated in this research were born in Canada or came so young they had no memories of ever living anywhere else, skin colour nevertheless marked them as outside the imagined community of Canadians. Other residents routinely assumed that second-generation African-Canadians must belong somewhere else. Embodiment of a local Canadian English accent, dress, and cultural capital seemed invisible to strangers and acquaintances alike who sought a foreign origin to explain the presence of second-generation African-Canadians in their own home town.

At least partly as resistance to other residents' failure to acknowledge their local roots, some participants refused a Canadian identity while proclaiming a national African or pan-African heritage. Others insisted on their Canadian identity and refused to name any other origin. A majority of participants embraced fluid hybrid identities that acknowledged both their ancestral African heritage and their Canadian upbringing, articulating versions of African-Canadian identities, though often with considerable ambiguity about fully belonging in either place. Discourses of Blackness also animated the identities of the second generation, in most cases deepening the salience of national or pan-African identities in resistance to homogenizing notions of Blackness, and emphasizing Canadianness as a counterpoint to being mistaken as African American. Deeper connections with their African heritage were also a product of maturity. Many men, in particular, recalled little interest in their African roots when they were adolescents. As young adults, however, almost all research participants had developed more connections with others their age in the local African diaspora, including the majority of women's romantic partners. Second-generation participants expressed strong appreciation of parents' culture and values and a desire to foster transnational connections linking their own children with extended family in Africa. It seems, therefore, that, although second-generation participants were more likely to embody hybrid identities, they had not lost their identities as Africans as the first generation feared (Creese 2011).

Processes of racialization, gender, sexuality, and place all shaped trajectories of migration, settlement, and prospects for the second generation. Discourses of Blackness constitute a central element of racialization processes in Canada, so it is not surprising that they had a significant effect on shaping the lives of second-generation African-Canadians. In line with the findings of other Canadian studies, most research participants developed hybrid and situational identities that bridged connections between their parents' homeland and their Canadian identities. This study also suggests, however, that several dimensions of racialization processes require more attention to better understand the diversity of experiences across the country.

We also need to recognize that discourses about Blackness are profoundly gendered, and affect girls and boys and women and men differently. Key gender differences can be discerned beginning in childhood, and continue right through to adulthood, shaping interactions in public spaces, the formation of friendships, and romantic relationships. It is also clear that assumptions around Blackness are sexualized and, as a result, Blackness is navigated in complex ways across public spaces and private lives. African-Canadian women and men were located differently in public spaces, where Black men are more likely to be feared and surveilled, and in normative White hierarchies of heterosexual desirability, where Black women are more marginalized.

Place also matters for understanding how processes of racialization play out in particular contexts. Discourses of Blackness embedded in contemporary popular culture might be even more powerful in a place like metro Vancouver, where the local African and Black community is so small that it is hard to provide strong counternarratives of what it is to be African and Black. Small numbers also intersect with gender, sexuality, and popular culture, enhancing the desirability of African-Canadian men, while further marginalizing their sisters.

A unique aspect of this study is its focus on second-generation African-Canadians' experiences of childhood, adolescence, and young adulthood. Thus, the study allows us to consider how responses to racialization and identities change over time. In particular, it illustrates how adolescence is associated more strongly with influences in popular culture, and how maturity leads to reconnecting with parents' cultural influences. This puts previous research on teenagers in a somewhat different light, emphasizing adolescent flirtations with identities associated with African-American popular culture. Reclaiming stronger African and African-Canadian identities as young adults, including the desire to maintain transnational connections for their own families, is part of larger "Afropolitan" projects that are also documented among the second generation in the United States.

Finally, the sense of optimism and resilience among research participants should not be overlooked. Second-generation men and women developed strategies that helped them cope with living "under a microscope" as a hypervisible Black minority – indeed, to thrive. Anti-Black racism and White privilege persisted, but strategies of resilience were critical to moving forward in positive directions. Parental support was critical for developing resilience in offspring, pushing them to take advantage of educational and other opportunities and carve out a promising future. More research with those who do not pursue post-secondary education is required, but it seems clear that racialization in metro Vancouver schools poses barriers for many second-generation African-Canadians. The development of a more inclusive and anti-racist curriculum in British Columbia, including attention to Black Canadian history, an Afrocentric approach to the study of Africa, and anti-racist pedagogies, could help members of the second generation engage more positively with the academic side of school. Changes of this kind would help facilitate African-Canadian engagement, rather than disengagement, with school curriculum – and not just engagement with peers as the "cool Black guy" – and further foster the type of motivation, resilience, and optimism demonstrated by the men and women who participated in this research.

References

Abada, Teresa, Feng Hou, and Bali Ram. 2008. "Group Differences in Educational Attainment Among the Children of Immigrants." Analytical Studies Branch Research Paper. Cat. no. 11F0019M—No. 308. Ottawa: Statistics Canada.

Abada, Teresa, Feng Hou, and Bali Ram. 2009. "Ethnic Differences in Educational Attainment Among the Children of Canadian Immigrants." *Canadian Journal of Sociology* 34 (1): 1–28.

Abada, Teresa, and Eric Tenkorang. 2009a. "Gender Differences in Educational Attainment Among the Children of Canadian Immigrants." *International Sociology* 24 (4): 580–608.

Abada, Teresa, and Eric Tenkorang. 2009b. "Pursuit of University Education Among the Children of Immigrants in Canada: The Roles of Parental Human Capital and Social Capital." *Journal of Youth Studies* 12 (2): 185–207.

Abdel-Shehid, Gamal. 2005. *Who Da Man? Black Masculinities and Sporting Cultures*. Toronto: Canadian Scholars Press.

Abu-Laban, Yasmeen, and Christina Gabriel. 2002. *Selling Diversity: Immigration, Multiculturalism, Employment Equity, and Globalization*. Peterborough, ON: Broadview Press.

Adjei, Paul Banahene, Delores Mullings, Michael Baffoe, Lloydetta Quaicoe, Latif Abdul-Rahman, Victoria Shears, and Shari Fitzgerald. 2017. "The 'Fragility of Goodness': Black Parents' Perspectives about Raising Children in Toronto, Winnipeg and St. John's of Canada." *Journal of Public Child Welfare* 12 (4): 461–91. doi:10.1080/15548732.2017.1401575.

Adjepong, Anima. 2018. "Afropolitan Projects: African Immigrant Identities and Solidarities in the United States." *Ethnic and Racial Studies* 41 (2): 248–66. doi:10.1080/01419870.2017.1281985.

Agnew, Vijay. 2003. *Where I Come From*. Waterloo, ON: Wilfrid Laurier University Press.

Ahmed, Sara. 2000. *Strange Encounters: Embodied Others in Post-Coloniality.* London: Routledge.

Alexander, Ken, and Avis Glaze. 1996. *Towards Freedom: The African-Canadian Experience.* Toronto: Umbrella Press.

Amin, Nuzhat. 2006. "Language, Race and the Politics of Anti-Racism: Concluding Thoughts." In *The Poetics of Anti-Racism,* ed. Nuzhat Amin and George Sefa Dei, 149–58. Halifax, NS: Fernwood.

Amin, Nuzhat, and George Sefa Dei, eds. 2006. *The Poetics of Anti-Racism.* Halifax, NS: Fernwood.

Anderson, Benedict. 1991. *Imagined Communities.* London: Verso.

Anisef, Paul, Robert Brown, Lelli Phythian, Robert Sweek, and David Walters. 2010. "Early School Leaving among Immigrants in Toronto Secondary Schools." *Canadian Review of Sociology* 47 (2): 103–28.

Arthur, Damien. 2006. "Hip Hop Consumption and Masculinity." *Gender and Consumer Behavior* 8: 105–16.

Arthur, John. 2010. *African Disapora Identities: Negotiating Culture in Transnational Migration.* Lanham, MD: Lexington Books.

Awokoya, Janet. 2012. "Identity Constructions and Negotiations among 1.5- and Second-Generation Nigerians: The Impact of Family, School, and Peer Contexts." *Harvard Educational Review* 82 (2): 255–81.

Aydemir, Abdurrahman, and Mikal Skuterud. 2004. "Explaining the Deteriorating Entry Earnings of Canada's Immigrant Cohorts: 1966–2000." Analytical Studies Branch Research Paper. Cat. no. 11F0019MIE, No. 225. Ottawa: Statistics Canada. May.

Back, Les, and John Solomos, eds. 2000. *Theories of Race and Racism: A Reader.* London: Routledge.

Bannerji, Himani. 2000. *The Dark Side of the Nation: Essays on Multiculturalism, Nationalism and Gender.* Toronto: Canadian Scholars Press.

Barman, Jean. 1991. *The West Beyond the West: A History of British Columbia.* Toronto: University of Toronto Press.

Barrett, Paul. 2015. *Blackening Canada: Diaspora, Race, Multiculturalism.* Toronto: University of Toronto Press.

Bauder, Harald. 2011. *Immigration Dialectic.* Toronto: University of Toronto Press.

Beiser, Morton, Nelly Zilber, Laura Simich, Rafael Youngmann, Ada Zohar, Busha Taa, and Feng Hou. 2011. "Regional Effects on the Mental Health of Immigrant Children: Results from the New Canadian Children and Youth Survey." *Health and Place* 17 (3): 822–9.

Benoit, Cecilia, Leah Shumka, Rachel Phillips, Mary Clare Kennedy, and Lynn Belle-Isle. 2015. *Issue Brief: Sexual Violence Against Women in Canada.* Ottawa: Status of Women Canada. December. Available online at https://cfc-swc.gc.ca/svawc-vcsfc/issue-brief-en.pdf, accessed 19 February 2018.

Berry, John, Jean Phinney, David Sam, and Paul Vedder, eds. 2006. *Immigrant Youth Cultural Transition: Acculturation, Identity, and Adaptation Across National Contexts*. London: Lawrence Erlbaum Associates.

Bourdieu, Pierre. 1977. "The Economics of Linguistic Exchanges." *Social Science Information* 16 (6): 645–68.

Bourdieu, Pierre. 1984. *Distinction: A Social Critique of the Judgment of Taste*. Cambridge, MA: Harvard University Press.

Bourdieu, Pierre. 1986. "The Forms of Capital." In *Handbook of Theory and Research for Sociology of Education*, ed. John Richardson, 241–58. New York: Greenwood Press.

Boyd, Monica. 2001. "Gender, Refugee Status, and Permanent Settlement." In *Immigrant Women*, ed. Rita James Simon, 103–23. London: Transaction Publishers.

Boyd, Monica. 2009. "Social Origins and the Educational and Occupational Achievements of the 1.5 and Second Generations." *Canadian Review of Sociology* 46 (4): 339–69.

Boyd, Monica, and Jessica Yiu. 2009. "Immigrant Women and Earnings Inequality in Canada." In *Racialized Migrant Women in Canada: Essays on Health, Violence, and Equity*, ed. Vijay Agnew, 208–32. Toronto: University of Toronto Press.

Brah, Avtar. 1996. *Cartographies of Diaspora: Contesting Identities*. London: Routledge.

Brathwaite, Keren, and Carl James, eds. 1996. *Educating African Canadians*. Toronto: James Lorimer.

Brubaker, Rogers. 2005. "The 'Diaspora' Diaspora." *Ethnic and Racial Studies* 28 (1): 1–19.

Brunson, Rod, and Jody Miller. 2006. "Gender, Race and Urban Policing: The Experience of African American Youth." *Gender & Society* 20 (4): 531–52.

Butler, Judith. 1990. *Gender Trouble: Feminism and the Subversion of Identity*. New York: Routledge.

Butler, Judith. 2004. *Undoing Gender*. New York: Routledge.

Calliste, Agnes. 1993/94. "Race, Gender and Canadian Immigration Policy: Blacks from the Caribbean, 1900–1932." *Journal of Canadian Studies* 28 (Winter): 131–48.

Childs, Erica Chito. 2005. "Looking Behind the Stereotype of the 'Angry Black Woman': An Exploration of Black Women's Responses to Interracial Relationships." *Gender & Society* 19 (4): 544–61.

Clark, Msia Kibona. 2008. "Identity among First and Second Generation African Immigrants in the United States." *African Identities* 6 (2): 169–81.

Clark, Msia Kibona. 2009. "Questions of Identity among African Immigrants in America." In *The New African Diaspora*, ed. Isidore Okpewho and Nkiru Nzegwu, 255–70. Bloomington: Indiana University Press.

Clerge, Orly. 2014. "Balancing Stigma and Status: Racial and Class Identities among Middle-Class Haitian Youth." *Ethnic and Racial Studies* 37 (6): 958–77.

Clifford, James. 1994. "Diasporas." *Cultural Anthropology* 9 (3): 302–38.

Codjoe, Henry. 2001. "Fighting a 'Public Enemy' of Black Academic Achievement: The Persistence of Racism and the Schooling Experiences of Black Students in Canada." *Race, Ethnicity and Education* 4 (4): 343–75.

Collins, Patricia Hill. 1986. "Learning from the Outsider Within: The Sociological Significance of Black Feminist Thought." *Social Problems* 33 (6): 14–32.

Collins, Patricia Hill. 1990. *Black Feminist Thought: Knowledge, Consciousness, and the Politics of Empowerment.* New York: Routledge.

Collins, Patricia Hill. 2005. *Black Sexual Politics: African Americans, Gender, and the New Racism.* New York: Routledge.

Collins, Patricia Hill. 2006. *From Black Power to Hip Hop: Racism, Nationalism, and Feminism.* Philadelphia: Temple University Press.

Compton, Wayde. 2010. *After Canaan: Essays on Race, Writing and Region.* Vancouver: Arsenal Pulp Press.

Connell, R.W. 1995. *Masculinities.* Berkeley: University of California Press.

Conroy, Kathleen. 2013. "Black Males and Exclusionary Schooling Practices: 'Common-Sense' Racism and the Need for a Critical Anti-Racist Approach." In *Contemporary Issues in the Sociology of Race and Ethnicity: A Critical Reader,* ed. George Sefa Dei and Meredith Lordan, 169–81. New York: Peter Lang.

Corak, Miles. 2012. "Age at Immigration and the Education Outcomes of Children." In *Realizing the Potential of Immigrant Youth,* ed. Ann Masten, Karmela Liebkind, and Donald Hernandez, 90–114. Cambridge: Cambridge University Press.

Costigan, Catherine, and Vivien So. 2018. "The Role of the Family in Supporting the Development of Youth with Immigrant Backgrounds." In *Immigrant Youth in Canada: Theoretical Approaches, Practical Issues, and Professional Perspectives,* ed, Stacey Wilson-Forsberg and Andrew Robinson, 84–104. Don Mills, ON: Oxford University Press.

Craig, Maxine Leeds. 2003. "Beauty." In *Encyclopedia of Race and Ethnic Studies,* ed. Ellis Cashmore, 50–2. London: Routledge.

Creative Cultural Collaboration Society. 2014. "Black Strathcona: One Community, Six Decades, Ten Stories." Available online at http://rabble. ca/podcasts/shows/needs-no-introduction/2014/03/black-strathcona-one-community-six-decades-ten-stories, accessed 20 July 2017.

Creese, Gillian. 2010. "Erasing English Language Competency: African Migrants in Vancouver, Canada." *Journal of International Migration and Integration* 11 (3): 295–313.

Creese, Gillian. 2011. *The New African Diaspora in Vancouver: Migration, Exclusion and Belonging.* Toronto: University of Toronto Press.

Creese, Gillian. 2013. "Gender, Generation and Identities in Vancouver's African Diaspora." *African Disapora* 6 (2): 155–78.

Creese, Gillian. 2015. "Growing Up Where 'No One Looked Like Me': Gender, Race, Hip Hop and Identity in Vancouver." *Gender Issues* 32 (3): 201–19.

Creese, Gillian. 2019. "'Where Are You From?' Racialization, Belonging and Identity among Second-Generation African Canadians." *Ethnic and Racial Studies* 42 (9): 1476–94. https://doi.org/10.1080/01419870.2018.1484503.

Creese, Gillian, Isabel Dyck, and Arlene Tigar McLaren. 2008. "The 'Flexible' Immigrant? Human Capital Discourses, the Family and Labour Market Strategies." *Journal of International Migration and Integration* 9 (3): 269–88.

Creese, Gillian, Edith Ngene Kambere, and Mambo Masinda. 2013. "Voices of African Immigrant and Refugee Youth: Negotiating Migration and Schooling in Canada." In *African-born Educators and Students in Transnational America: Reprocessing Race, Language and Ability*, ed. Immaculee Harushimana, Chinwe Ikpeze, and Shirley Mthethwa-Sommers, 169–84. New York: Peter Lang.

Creese, Gillian, and Brandy Wiebe. 2012. "'Survival Employment': Gender and Deskilling among African Immigrants in Canada." *International Migration* 50 (5): 56–76.

Curran, Sue, Steven Shafer, Katharine Donato, and Filiz Garip. 2006. "Mapping Gender and Migration in Sociological Scholarship: Is It Segregation or Integration?" *International Migration Review* 40 (1): 199–223.

Currie, Dawn, Deirdre Kelly, and Shauna Pomerantz. 2009. *'Girl Power': Girls Reinventing Girlhood*. New York: Peter Lang.

Dabiri, Emma. 2016. "Why I Am (Still) Not an Afropolitan." *Journal of African Cultural Studies* 28 (1): 104–8.

Davis, Angela. 1982. *Women, Race and Class*. London: Women's Press.

Day, Richard. 2000. *Multiculturalism and the History of Canadian Diversity*. Toronto: University of Toronto Press.

Dei, George Sefa. 2005. "Racism in Canadian Contexts: Exploring Public and Private Issues in the Educational System." In *The African Diaspora in Canada: Negotiating Identity and Belonging*, ed. Wisdom Tettey and Korbla Puplampu, 93–110. Calgary: University of Calgary Press.

Dei, George Sefa. 2006. "Language, Race and Anti-racism: Making Important Connections." In *The Poetics of Anti-Racism*, ed. Nuzhat Amin and George Sefa Dei, 24–30. Halifax: Fernwood.

Dei, George Sefa. 2013. "Reframing Critical Anti-Racist Theory (CART) for Contemporary Times." In *Contemporary Issues in the Sociology of Race and Ethnicity: A Critical Reader*, ed. George Sefa Dei and Meredith Lorber, 1–14. New York: Peter Lang.

Dei, George Sefa. 2017. *Reframing Blackness and Black Solidarities through Anti-Colonial and Decolonial Prisms*. New York: Springer International Publishing.

Dei, George Sefa, Josephine Mazzuca, Elizabeth McIsaac, and Jasmine Zine. 1997. *Reconstructing 'Drop-out': A Critical Ethnography of the Dynamics of Black Students' Disengagement from School*. Toronto: University of Toronto Press.

Deliovsky, Katerina, and Tamari Kitossa. 2013. "Beyond Black and White: When Going Beyond May Take Us Out of Bounds." *Journal of Black Studies* 44 (2): 158–81.

Derwing, Tracey, Marian Rossiter, and Murray Munro. 2002. "Teaching Native Speakers to Listen to Foreign-Accented Speech." *Journal of Multilingual and Multicultural Development* 23 (4): 245–59.

Devine, Dympna, and Mary Kelly. 2006. "'I Just Don't Want to Get Picked on by Anybody': Dynamics of Inclusion and Exclusion in a Newly Multi-Ethnic Irish Primary School." *Children and Society* 20 (2): 128–39.

Devine, Dympna, Mairin Kenny, and Eileen Macneela. 2008. "Naming the 'Other': Children's Construction and Experience of Racisms in Irish Primary Schools." *Race, Ethnicity and Education* 11 (4): 369–85.

Donato, Katharine, Donna Gabaccia, Jennifer Holdaway, Martin Manalansan, and Patricia Pessar. 2006. "A Glass Half Full? Gender in Migration Studies." *International Migration Review* 40 (1): 3–26.

Dossa, Parin. 2004. *Politics and Poetics of Migration: Narratives of Iranian Women from the Diaspora*. Toronto: Canadian Scholars Press.

Elabor-Idemudia, Patience. 2000. "Challenges Confronting African Immigrant Women in the Canadian Workforce." In *Anti-Racist Feminism*, ed. Agnes Calliste and George Sefa Dei, 91–110. Halifax, NS: Fernwood.

Emerson, Rana. 2002. "'Where My Girls At?' Negotiating Black Womanhood in Music Videos." *Gender & Society* 16 (1): 115–35.

Essed, Philomena. 1991. *Understanding Everyday Racism: An Interdisciplinary Theory*. Newbury Park, CA: Sage.

Essed, Philomena, and David Theo Goldberg, eds. 2002. *Race Critical Theories*. Oxford: Blackwell.

Eze, Chielozona. 2014. "Rethinking African Culture and Identity: The Afropolitan Model." *Journal of African Cultural Studies* 26 (2): 234–47.

Fanon, Frantz. [1957] 2000. "The Fact of Blackness." In *Theories of Race and Racism: A Reader*, ed. Les Black and John Solomos, 257–66. London: Routledge.

Farley, Reynolds, and Richard Alba. 2002. "The New Second Generation in the United States." *International Migration Review* 36 (3): 669–701.

Fleras, Augie. 2015. *Immigration Canada: Evolving Realities and Emerging Challenges in a Postnational World*. Vancouver: UBC Press.

Fleras, Augie. 2016. "Theorizing Micro-Aggressions as Racism 3.0: Shifting the Discourse." *Canadian Ethnic Studies* 48 (2): 1–19.

Forman, Murray. 2001. "'Straight Outta Mogadishu': Prescribed Identities and Performative Practices among Somali Youth in North American High Schools." *Topia* 5: 33–60.

Francis, Jenny. 2010. "Missing Links: Youth Programs, Social Services, and African Youth in Metro Vancouver." Working Paper Series 10–07. Vancouver: Metropolis British Columbia, Centre of Excellence for Research on Immigration and Diversity. July.

Francis, Jenny, and Miu-Chung Yan. 2016. "Bridging the Gaps: Access to Formal Support Services among Young African Immigrants and Refugees in Metro Vancouver." *Canadian Ethnic Studies* 48 (1): 77–100.

Frenette, Marc, and Rene Morissette. 2005. "Will They Ever Converge? Earnings of Immigrant and Canadian-Born Workers over the Last Two Decades." *International Migration Review* 39 (1): 228–58.

Fumanti, Mattia, and Pnina Werbner. 2010. "The Moral Economy of the African Diaspora: Citizenship, Networking and Permeable Ethnicity." *African Diaspora* 3: 3–12.

Galabuzi, Grace-Edward. 2006. *Canada's Economic Apartheid: The Social Exclusion of Racialized Groups in the New Century.* Toronto: Canadian Scholars Press.

Gans, Herbert. 2017. "Racialization and Racialization Research." *Ethnic and Racial Studies* 40 (3): 341–52.

Goldring, Luin. 2001. "The Gender and Geography of Citizenship in Mexico-U.S. Transnational Spaces." *Identities: Global Studies in Culture and Power* 7 (4): 501–37.

Gregoire, Nicole. 2010. "Identity Politics, Social Movement and the State: 'Pan-African' Associations and the Making of an 'African Community' in Belgium." *African Diaspora* 3: 160–82.

Hall, Stuart. 2000. "Old and New Identities, Old and New Ethnicities." In *Theories of Race and Racism: A Reader*, ed. Les Black and John Solomos, 144–53. London: Routledge.

Halli, Shiva, and Vedanand. 2007. "The Problem of Second-Generation Decline: Perspectives on Integration in Canada." *International Migration and Integration* 8 (3): 277–87.

Handa, Amita. 2003. *Of Silk Saris and Mini-Skirts: South Asian Girls Walk the Tightrope of Culture.* Toronto: Women's Press.

Haraway, Donna. 1991. *Simians, Cyborgs, and Women.* New York: Routledge.

Hawkins, Freida. 1991. *Critical Years in Immigration: Canada and Australia Compared.* Montreal: McGill-Queen's University Press.

Henderson, Carol, ed. 2010. *Imagining the Black Female Body: Reconciling Image in Print and Visual Culture.* New York: Palgrave Macmillan.

Henry, Frances. 1999. "Two Studies of Racial Discrimination in Employment." In *Social Inequality in Canada.* 3rd ed., ed. James Curtis, Ed Grab, and Neil Guppy, 226–35. Scarborough, ON: Prentice Hall Allyn and Bacon Canada.

Henry, Frances, and Carol Tator. 2009. *The Colour of Democracy: Racism in Canadian Society*, 4th ed. Toronto: Nelson Education.

Hirji, Faiza. 2010. *Dreaming in Canadian: South Asian Youth, Bollywood, and Belonging.* Vancouver: UBC Press.

Huber, Lindsay Perez, and Daniel Solorzano. 2015. "Racial Microaggressions as a Tool for Critical Race Research." *Race Ethnicity and Education* 18 (3): 297–320.

Ibrahim, Awad. 1999. "Becoming Black: Rap and Hip-Hop, Race, Gender, Identity, and the Politics of ESL Learning." *TESOL Quarterly* 33 (3): 349–69.

Ibrahim, Awad. 2003. "Marking the Unmarked: Hip-Hop, the Gaze, and the African Body in North America." *Critical Arts: South-North Cultural and Media Studies* 17 (1–2): 52–70.

Ibrahim, Awad. 2006. "Rethinking Displacement, Language and Culture Shock: Towards a Pedagogy of Cultural Translation and Negotiation." In *The Poetics of Anti-Racism,* ed. Nuzhat Amin and George Sefa Dei, 43–58. Halifax, NS: Fernwood.

Ibrahim, Awad, and Ali Abdi, eds. 2016a. *The Education of African Canadian Children: Critical Perspectives.* Montreal: McGill-Queen's University Press.

Ibrahim, Awad, and Ali Abdi. 2016b. "The Education of African Canadian Children: An Introduction." In *The Education of African Canadian Children: Critical Perspectives,* ed. Awad Ibrahim and Ali Abdi, 3–18. Montreal: McGill-Queen's University Press.

Imoagene, Onoso. 2012. "Being British vs Being American: Identification among Second-Generation Adults of Nigerian Descent in the US and UK." *Ethnic and Racial Studies* 35 (12): 2153–73.

Jacobson, Matthew Frye. 1999. *Whiteness of a Different Colour: European Immigrants and the Alchemy of Race.* Cambridge, MA: Harvard University Press.

James, Carl. 2012. "Students 'at Risk': Stereotypes and the Schooling of Black Boys." *Urban Education* 47 (2): 464–94.

James, Carl. 2016. "The Alchemy of Sport and the Role of Media in the Education of Black Youth." In *The Education of African Canadian Children: Critical Perspectives,* ed. Awad Ibrahim and Ali Abdi, 164–86. Montreal: McGill-Queen's University Press.

James, Carl. 2018. "Race, Racialization, and Canadian Children of Immigrant Parents." In *Immigrant Youth in Canada: Theoretical Approaches, Practical Issues, and Professional Perspectives,* ed. Stacey Wilson-Forsberg and Andrew Robinson, 33–48. Don Mills, ON: Oxford University Press.

Jeffries, Michael. 2011. *Thug Life: Race, Gender, and the Meaning of Hip-hop.* Chicago: University of Chicago Press.

Kanu, Yatta. 2008. "Educational Needs and Barriers for African Refugee Students in Manitoba." *Canadian Journal of Education* 31 (4): 915–40.

Kaufman, Michael. 1987. "The Construction of Masculinity and the Triad of Men's Violence." In *Beyond Patriarchy: Essays by Men on Pleasure, Power and Change,* ed. Michael Kaufman, 1–29. Toronto: Oxford University Press.

Kebede, Kassahun. 2017. "Twice-Hyphenated: Transnational Identity among Second-Generation Ethiopian-American Professionals in the Washington DC Metropolitan Area." *African and Black Diaspora: An International Journal* 10 (3): 252–68.

Kelly, Jennifer. 1998. *Under the Gaze: Learning to Be Black in White Society*. Halifax, NS: Fernwood.

Kelly, Jennifer. 2004. *Borrowed Identities*. New York: Peter Lang.

Kilian, Crawford. 2008. *Go Do Some Great Thing: The Black Pioneers of British Columbia*. Burnaby, BC: Commodore Books.

Kobayashi, Audrey, and Valerie Preston. 2014. "Being CBC: The Ambivalent Identities and Belonging of Canadian-Born Children of Immigrants." *Annals of the Association of American Geographers* 104 (2): 234–42.

Krahn, Harvey. 2017. "Choose Your Parents Carefully: Social Class, Post-Secondary Education, and Occupational Outcomes." In *Social Inequality in Canada: Dimensions of Disadvantage*, ed. Edward Grabb, Jeffrey Reitz, and Monica Hwang, 90–103. Don Mills, ON: Oxford University Press.

Kusow, Abdi. 2006. "Migration and Racial Formations Among Somali Immigrants in North America." *Journal of Ethnic and Migration Studies* 32 (3): 533–51.

Laryea, Samuel, and John Hayfron. 2005. "African Immigrants and the Labour Market: Exploring Career Opportunities, Earning Differentials, and Job Satisfaction." In *The African Diaspora in Canada: Negotiating Identity and Belonging*, ed. Wisdom Tettey and Korbla Puplampu, 113–31. Calgary: University of Calgary Press.

Li, Peter. 2003. *Destination Canada: Immigration Debates and Issues*. Don Mills, ON: Oxford University Press.

Lippi-Green, Rosina. 1997. *English with an Accent: Language, Ideology and Discrimination in the United States*. New York: Routledge.

Livingstone, Anne-Marie, and Morton Weinfeld. 2015. "Black Families and Socio-Economic Inequality in Canada." *Canadian Ethnic Studies* 47 (3): 1–23.

Lutz, Helma. 2010. "Gender in the Migratory Process." *Journal of Ethnic and Migration Studies* 36 (10): 1647–63.

Mackey, Eva. 2002. *The House of Difference: Cultural Politics and National Identity in Canada*. Toronto: University of Toronto Press.

Mahler, Sara, and Patricia Pessar. 2006. "Gender Matters: Ethnographers Bring Gender from the Periphery toward the Core of Migration Studies." *International Migration Review* 40 (1): 27–63.

Manuh, Takyiwaa. 2003. "'Efie' or the Meanings of 'Home' among Female and Male Ghanaian Migrants in Toronto, Canada and Returned Migrants to Ghana." In *New African Diasporas*, ed. Khalid Koser, 140–59. London: Routledge.

Matsuoka, Atsuko, and John Sorenson. 2001. *Ghosts and Shadows: Construction of Identity and Community in an African Diaspora*. Toronto: University of Toronto Press.

Maynard, Robyn. 2017. *Policing Black Lives: State Violence in Canada from Slavery to the Present*. Winnipeg: Fernwood Press.

McIntosh, Peggy. 1995. "White Privilege and Male Privilege." In *Race, Class and Gender: An Anthology*, 2nd ed., ed. Margaret Anderson and Patricia Hill Collins, 76–87. Belmont, CA: Wadsworth.

Mensah, Joseph. 2002. *Black Canadians: History, Experiences, Social Conditions*. Halifax, NS: Fernwood.

Mensah, Joseph, and Christopher Williams. 2015. "Seeing/Being Double: How African Immigrants in Canada Balance Their Ethno-Racial and National Identities." *African and Black Diaspora: An International Journal* 8 (1): 39–54.

Mercer, Kobena. 1987. "Black Hair/Style Politics." *New Formations* 3 (Winter): 33–54.

Mianda, Gertrude. 2004. "Sisterhood versus Discrimination: Being a Black African Francophone Immigrant Woman in Montreal and Toronto." In *Sisters or Strangers? Immigrant, Ethnic, and Racialized Women in Canadian History*, ed. Marlene Epp, Franca Iacovetta, and Frances Swyripa, 266–84. Toronto: University of Toronto Press.

Milan, Anne, Helene Maheux, and Tina Chu. 2010. "A Portrait of Couples in Mixed Unions." *Canadian Social Trends* 89: 70–80.

Miles, Robert. 1989. *Racism*. London: Routledge.

Mondain, Nathalie, and Solene Lardoux. 2013. "Transitions to Adulthood among First Generation Sub-Saharan African Immigrant Adolescents in Canada: Evidence from a Qualitative Study in Montreal." *Journal of International Migration and Integration* 14 (2): 307–26.

Morrow, Virginia. 2006. "Understanding Gender Differences in Context: Implications for Young Children's Everyday Lives." *Children and Society* 20 (2): 92–104.

Munro, Murray. 2003. "A Primer on Accent Discrimination in the Canadian Context." *TESL Canada Journal* 20 (2): 38–51.

Myers, Kristen. 2012. "Exotica: The Deployment of Intersecting Binaries." *Journal of Contemporary Ethnography* 41 (1): 7–33.

Nagra, Baljit. 2017. *Securitized Citizens: Canadian Muslims' Experiences of Race Relations and Identity Formation Post-9/11*. Toronto: University of Toronto Press.

Naples, Nancy. 2003. *Feminism and Method: Ethnography, Discourse Analysis, and Activist Research*. New York: Routledge.

Ng, Roxana. 1990. "Immigrant Women: The Construction of a Labour Market Category." *Canadian Journal of Women and the Law* 4 (1): 96–112.

Nunes, Fernando. 2018. "The Education of First-and Second-Generation Immigrant Youth in Canada." In *Immigrant Youth in Canada: Theoretical Approaches, Practical Issues, and Professional Perspectives,* ed. Stacey Wilson-Forsberg and Andrew Robinson, 151–71. Don Mills, ON: Oxford University Press.

Okeke-Ihejirika, Philomina, and Denise Spitzer. 2005. "In Search of Identity: Intergenerational Experiences of African Youth in a Canadian Context." In *The African Diaspora in Canada: Negotiating Identity and Belonging,* ed. Wisdom Tettey and Korbla Puplampu, 205–24. Calgary: University of Calgary Press.

Oreopoulos, Philip. 2011. "Why Do Skilled Immigrants Struggle in the Labor Market? A Field Experiment with Thirteen Thousand Resumes." *American Economic Journal: Economic Policy* 3 (4): 148–71.

Oware, Matthew. 2011. "Brotherly Love: Homosociality and Black Masculinity in Gangsta Rap Music." *Journal of African American Studies* 15: 22–39.

Pendakur, Krishna, and Ravi Pendakur. 2011. "Color by Numbers: Minority Earnings in Canada 1995–2005." *Journal of International Migration and Integration* 12 (3): 305–29.

Pessar, Patricia. 2003. "Engendering Migration Studies: The Case of New Immigrants in the United States." In *Gender and US Immigration: Contemporary Trends,* ed. Pierrette Hondagneu-Sotelo, 20–42. Berkeley: University of California Press.

Petchauer, Emery. 2009. "Framing and Reviewing Hip-Hop Educational Research." *Review of Educational Research* 79 (2): 946–78.

Phillips, Layli, Kerri Reddick-Morgan, and Dionne Stephens. 2005. "Oppositional Consciousness Within an Oppositional Realm: The Case of Feminism and Womanism in Rap and Hip Hop, 1976–2004." *Journal of African American History* 90 (3): 253–77.

Picot, Garnett, and Feng Hou. 2003. "The Rise on Low-Income Rates among Immigrants in Canada." Analytical Studies Branch Research Paper. Cat. no. 11F0019MIE, No. 198. Ottawa: Statistics Canada. June.

Picot, Garnett, and Arthur Sweetman. 2005. "The Deteriorating Economic Welfare of Immigrants and Possible Causes: Update 2005." Analytical Studies Branch Research Paper. Cat. no. 11F0019MIE, No. 262. Ottawa: Statistics Canada. June.

Portes, Alejandro, and Min Zhou. 1993. "The New Second Generation: Segmented Assimilation and Its Variants." *Annals of the American Academy of Political and Social Science* 530: 74–96.

Potts, Karen, and Leslie Brown. 2015. "Becoming an Anti-Oppressive Researcher." In *Research as Resistance: Revisiting Critical, Indigenous, and Anti-Oppressive Approaches,* 2nd ed., ed. Susan Strega and Leslie Brown, 17–41. Toronto: Canadian Scholars Press and Women's Press.

Pratt, Geraldine. 2004. *Working Feminism*. Philadelphia: Temple University Press.

Pratt, Geraldine, and the Philippine Women Centre of BC. 2008. "Deskilling across the Generations: Reunification among Transnational Filipino Families in Vancouver." Working Paper Series 08–06. Vancouver: Metropolis British Columbia. September.

Puplampu, Korbla, and Wisdom Tettey. 2005. "Ethnicity and the Identity of African-Canadians: A Theoretical and Political Analysis." In *The African Diaspora in Canada: Negotiating Identity and Belonging*, ed. Wisdom Tettey and Korbla Puplampu, 25–48. Calgary: University of Calgary Press.

Queeley, Andrea. 2003. "Hip Hop and the Aesthetics of Criminalization." *Souls* 5 (1): 1–15.

Ramazanoglu, Caroline. 2002. *Feminist Methodology: Challenges and Choices*. London: Sage.

Ramjattan, Vijay. 2017. "Racist Nativist Microaggressions and the Professional Resistance of Racialized English Language Teachers in Toronto." *Race Ethnicity and Education* 22 (3): 374–90. doi:10.1080/13613324.2017.1377171.

Ray, Rashawn, and Jason Rosow. 2012. "The Two Different Worlds of Black and White Fraternity Men: Visibility and Accountability as Mechanisms of Privilege." *Journal of Contemporary Ethnography* 41 (1): 66–94.

Reichert, Tom, and Jacqueline Lambiase, eds. 2006. *Sex in Consumer Culture: The Erotic Content of Media and Marketing*. Mahwah, NJ: Lawrence Erlbaum Associates.

Reitz, Jeffrey, Josh Curtis, and Jennifer Elrick. 2014. "Immigrant Skill Utilization: Trends and Policy Issues." *Journal of International Migration and Integration* 15 (1): 1–26.

Reitz, Jeffrey, and Ye Zhang. 2011. "National and Urban Contexts for the Integration of the Second Generation in the United States and Canada." In *The Next Generation: Immigrant Youth in Comparative Perspective*, ed. Richard Alba and Mary Waters, 207–28. New York: New York University Press.

Rice, Carla. 2013. "Exacting Beauty: Exploring Women's Body Projects and Problems in the 21st Century." In *Gender and Women's Studies in Canada: Critical Terrain*, ed. Margaret Hobbs and Carla Rice, 390–410. Toronto: Women's Press.

Richardson, Elaine, and Gwendolyn Pough. 2016. "Hiphop Literacies and the Globalization of Black Popular Culture." *Social Identities* 22 (2): 129–32.

Roberts-Fiati, Gloria. 1996. "Effects of Early Marginalization on African Canadian Children." In *Educating African Canadians*, ed. Keren Braithwaite and Carl James, 69–80. Toronto: James Lorimer.

Rose, Tricia. 2008. *The Hip Hop Wars*. New York: Basic Books.

Rumbaut, Ruben. 2004. "Ages, Life Stages, and Generational Cohorts: Decomposing the Immigrant First and Second Generations in the United States." *International Migration Review* 38 (3): 1160–205.

Rumbaut, Ruben. 2012. "Generation 1.5, Educational Experiences of." In *Encyclopedia of Diversity in Education*, ed. James Banks, 982–83. Thousand Oaks, CA: Sage.

Scholtz, Jennifer, and Robbie Gilligan. 2017. "Encountering Difference: Young Girls' Perspectives on Separateness and Friendship in Culturally Diverse Schools in Dublin." *Childhood* 24 (2): 168–82.

Selasi, Taiye. 2005. "Bye-Bye Babar." *The LIP*, 3 March. Available online at http://thelip.robertsharp.co.uk, accessed 20 April 2018.

Shakya, Yogendra, Sepali Guruge, Michaela Hynie, Arzo Akbari, Mohamed Malik, Sheila Htoo, Azza Khogali, et al. 2010. "Aspirations for Higher Education among Newcomer Refugee Youth in Toronto: Expectations, Challenges, and Strategies." *Refuge* 27 (2): 65–78.

Shizha, Edward. 2016. "Marginalization of African Canadian Students in Mainstream Schools: Are Afrocentric Schools the Answer?" In *The Education of African Canadian Children: Critical Perspectives*, ed. Awad Ibrahim and Ali Abdi, 187–206. Montreal: McGill-Queen's University Press.

Showers, Fumilayo. 2015. "Being Black, Foreign and Woman: African Immigrant Identities in the United States." *Ethnic and Racial Studies* 38 (10): 1815–30.

Simmons, Alan. 2010. *Immigration and Canada: Global and Transnational Perspectives*. Toronto: Canadian Scholars Press.

Smith, Dorothy. 1987. *The Everyday World as Problematic*. Toronto: University of Toronto Press.

Statistics Canada. 2011a. "National Household Survey: Data Table, Vancouver CMA, Visible Minority, Immigrant Status and Period of Immigration." Available online at http://www12.statcan.gc.ca, accessed 14 July 2017.

Statistics Canada. 2011b. "National Household Survey Profile, Vancouver CMA, Immigration and Citizenship." Available online at http://www12.statcan.gc.ca, accessed 13 July 2017.

Statistics Canada. 2013. *Immigration and Ethnocultural Diversity in Canada, National Household Survey, 2011*. Cat. no. 99-010-X2011001. Ottawa: Statistics Canada.

Statistics Canada. 2016a. "Census Profile, 2016 Census. Vancouver Census Metropolitan Area, Visible Minority." Available online at http://www12.statcan.gc.ca, accessed 2 May 2018.

Statistic Canada. 2016b. "Census Profile, 2016 Census. Vancouver Census Metropolitan Area, Immigration and Citizenship." Available online at http://www12.statcan.gc.ca, accessed 2 May 2018.

Statistics Canada. 2016c. "Census Profile, 2016 Census. Vancouver Census Metropolitan Area, Ethnic Origin." Available online at http://www12.statcan.gc.ca, accessed 2 May 2018.

Statistics Canada. 2016d. "Census Profile, 2016 Census. Canada, Visible Minority." Available online at http://www12.statcan.gc.ca, accessed 30 May 2018.

Statistics Canada. 2016e. "Census Profile, 2016 Census. Toronto Census Metropolitan Area, Visible Minority." Available online at http://www12. statcan.gc.ca, accessed 26 June 2018.

Stephens, Dionne, and April Few. 2007a. "The Effects of Images of African American Women in Hip-Hop on Early Adolescents' Attitudes toward Physical Attractiveness and Interpersonal Relationships." *Sex Roles* 56: 251–64.

Stephens, Dionne, and April Few. 2007b. "Hip Hop Honey or Video Ho: African American Preadolescents' Understanding of Female Sexual Scripts in Hip Hop Culture." *Sexuality and Culture* 11 (3–4): 48–69.

Stepick, Alex, and Carol Dutton Stepick. 2010. "The Complexities and Confusions of Segmented Assimilation." *Ethnic and Racial Studies* 33 (7): 1149–67.

Sterling, Cheryl. 2015. "Race Matters: Cosmopolitanism, Afropolitanism, and Pan-Africanism via Edward Wilmot Blyden." *Journal of Pan African Studies* 8 (1): 119–45.

Thobani, Sunera. 2007. *Exalted Subjects: Studies in the Making of Race and Nation in Canada*. Toronto: University of Toronto Press.

Trapp, Erin. 2005. "The Push and Pull of Hip-Hop: A Social Movement Analysis." *American Behavioral Scientist* 48 (1): 1482–95.

Turcotte, Martin. 2011. "Intergenerational Education Mobility: University Completion in Relation to Parents' Education Level." *Canadian Social Trends* (August): 37–43.

Vancouver Sun. 2018. "Racial profiling cited as groups demand probe into Vancouver Police carding." 14 June.

Walcott, Rinaldo. 2003. *Black Like Who? Writing Black Canada*. 2nd ed. Toronto: Insomniac Press.

Wane, Njoki Nathani, Katherina Deliovsky, and Erica Lawson, eds. 2002. *Back to the Drawing Board: African-Canadian Feminisms*. Toronto: Sumach Press.

Wasik, Adrienne. 2006. "Economic Insecurity and Isolation: Post-Migration Traumas among Black African Refugee Women in the Greater Vancouver Area." Working Paper 06–17. Vancouver: Centre of Excellence Research on Immigration and Integration in the Metropolis.

Waters, Mary, Van Tran, Philip Kasinitz, and John Mollenkopf. 2010. "Segmented Assimilation Revisited: Types of Acculturation and Socioeconomic Mobility in Young Adulthood." *Ethnic and Racial Studies* 33 (7): 1168–93.

Werbner, Pnina. 2010. "Many Gateways to the Gateway City: Elites, Class and Policy Networking in the London African diaspora." *African Diaspora* 3: 132–59.

West, Candace, and Don Zimmerman. 1987. "Doing Gender." *Gender & Society* 1 (2): 125–51.

Wilkins, Amy. 2012a. "Becoming Black Women: Intimate Stories and Intersectional Identities." *Social Psychology Quarterly* 75 (2): 173–96.

Wilkins, Amy. 2012b. "Not Out to Start a Revolution: Race, Gender, and Emotional Restraint Among Black University Men." *Journal of Contemporary Ethnography* 41 (1): 34–65.

Wilkins, Amy. 2012c. "Stigma and Status: Interracial Intimacy and Intersectional Identities across Black College Men." *Gender & Society* 26 (2): 165–89.

Wilkinson, Lori. 2008. "Labour Market Transitions of Immigrant-Born, Refugee-Born, and Canadian-Born Youth." *Canadian Review of Sociology* 45 (2): 151–76.

Wilkinson, Lori, Aiu Chung Yan, A. Ka Tat Tsang, Rich Sin, and Sean Lauer. 2012. "The School-to-Work Transitions of Newcomer Youth in Canada." *Canadian Ethnic Studies* 44 (3): 29–44.

Willinsky, John. 1998. *Learning to Divide the World: Education at Empire's End.* Minneapolis: University of Minnesota Press.

Wilson-Forsberg, Stacey. 2012. *Getting Used to the Quiet: Immigrant Adolescents' Journey to Belonging in New Brunswick, Canada.* Montreal: McGill-Queen's University Press.

Wilson-Forsberg, Stacey. 2018. "Just Trying to Fit In: The Importance of Friendship for Immigrant Youth." In *Immigrant Youth in Canada: Theoretical Approaches, Practical Issues, and Professional Perspectives,* ed. Stacey Wilson-Forsberg and Andrew Robinson, 121–37. Don Mills, ON: Oxford University Press.

Wingfield, Aida Harvey. 2008. "Bringing Minority Men Back in: Comments on Anderson." *Gender & Society* 22 (1): 88–92.

Yesufu, Adenike. 2005. "The Gender Dimensions of the Immigrant Experience: The Case of African-Canadian Women in Edmonton." In *The African Diaspora in Canada: Negotiating Identity and Belonging,* ed. Wisdom Tettey and Korbla Puplampu, 133–46. Calgary: University of Calgary Press.

Zaami, Mariama. 2015. "I Fit the Description: Experiences of Social and Spatial Exclusion among Ghanaian Immigrant Youth in the Jane and Finch Neighbourhood of Toronto." *Canadian Ethnic Studies* 47 (3): 69–89.

Zeleza, Paul Tiyambe. 2008. "The Challenges of Studying the African Diasporas." *African Sociological Review* 12 (2): 4–21.

Index